The 6 Underlable Truths that Lead to
Professional and Personal Success

IT'S ALL

ABOUT

JUDGMENT

CDR Barry W. Hull, USNR (Retired)

Saranac Press

This publication is designed to provide accurate and authoritative information in regard to the subject matter covered. It is sold with the understanding that the publisher and author are not engaged in rendering legal, accounting, or other professional services. If legal advice or other expert assistance is required, the services of a competent professional should be sought.

Published by Saranac
Spartanburg, SC
AthenaQ.com
PilotJudgment.com
Copyright ©2017 Pilot Judgment, Inc.

Distributed by River Grove Books

Design and composition by Greenleaf Book Group
Cover design by Greenleaf Book Group
Author photograph by Clay Terrell Photography

Cataloging-in-Publication data is available.

Hardcover ISBN: 978-0-9990193-0-6

Paperback ISBN: 978-0-9990193-1-3

eBook ISBN: 978-0-9990193-2-0

Second Edition

To Beth

It is not by muscle, speed, or physical dexterity
that great things are achieved, but by reflection,
force of character, and judgment.

— Marcus Tullius Cicero, 106 B.C.–43 B.C.
(Roman lawyer, writer, scholar, orator, statesman)

CONTENTS

Part 2—Judgment Truths

Part 3—Judgment Assassins

PREFACE

A good friend of mine, Steve Greene, was at his desk, working. Steve was in the middle of his very successful career in the construction industry. A few doors down the hall from Steve, a coworker and friend of his, in the middle of his own successful career, suffered a heart attack, fell over, and died.

Steve took his friend's death hard and, over the next several months, Steve reevaluated his own life and priorities. One outcome of that reevaluation was an annual get-together of Steve's old high school buddies. I am fortunate to be one of them.

I've known Steve since we were kids. We were, in fact, college roommates until I transferred to another school. We had somewhat drifted apart over the past thirty years or so, with our own families and careers, but Steve made the phone calls and insisted, and suddenly there we were, together again. It was wonderful to see the old gang—hanging out, relaxing, pretending to be golfers, and laughing at the same old stupid stories.

This was a group I was proud to be associated with: a chemical and civil engineer, a pediatric surgeon, a Washington insider, a clandestine operative, a successful salesman, a talented artist, and several business owners, all scattered across the country now.

They were surprised at my life's path. I was a fighter pilot in the U.S. Navy, flying the F/A-18 Hornet. The Navy had taken me across the globe and back. I had experienced launching and trapping (landing) aboard the aircraft carrier, in combat, at night. My squadron mates were my brothers-in-arms, and our combat experiences together had formed lifelong bonds. At times the excitement was so thick we felt our hearts would explode. I witnessed firsthand the triumph of good decisions and the ultimate horror of bad ones, and throughout my Navy career, I learned.

By the time of our annual get-togethers I had left active duty in the Navy and joined the Navy Reserves. I was flying for American Airlines, and I had also become a retail business owner.

One year, while I was sharing a golf cart with Billy Wilson (people now call him Bill), whom I've known since the third grade, he described to me a new venture with which he was involved. Through his successful insurance brokerage firm, Billy had met and established a personal and working relationship with C. Stephen Byrum, PhD, the world's foremost authority on value and evaluative judgment. Billy explained the primary reason people do what we do: our judgment. He informed me that he had a statistically accurate way to measure the strength (or weakness) of our judgment.

I was intrigued. It was the level and kind of intrigue that wakes you up in the middle of the night, thinking about ideas and possibilities. It wasn't long before I flew to Chattanooga, Tennessee, to meet with Billy and Dr. Byrum.

A few months after that, I was participating in their joint venture as well.

Steve Byrum, now a good friend, had been a graduate student at the University of Tennessee in the early 1970s under the tutelage of Robert Hartman, PhD. Dr. Hartman had quite a life. Born in 1910 in Berlin, Germany, he was considered by many to be a genius. He was highly educated and fluent in many languages, having attended the German College of Political Science, the University of Paris (Sorbonne), the London School of Economics and Political Science, and the University of Berlin. Hartman believed in the infinite value of human life, and his speeches and articles during the 1930s brought him into direct confrontation with the

Nazi party. Ultimately he fled Germany, barely escaping with his life. In 1941, Hartman, with his wife and son, immigrated to the United States.

Hartman was a teacher of philosophy at the College of Wooster and at Ohio State University, and a visiting professor at Massachusetts Institute of Technology and Yale. He held more than fifty lectureships all across the United States, Canada, Latin America, and Europe. He was a research professor at the National University of Mexico and the University of Tennessee. His reputation was worldwide.

In the late 1960s and early 1970s, Hartman devised an instrument to measure judgment. His work on promoting self-understanding was so groundbreaking that it was nominated for a Nobel Prize.

Unfortunately, Dr. Hartman died suddenly in 1973. Fortunately, Dr. Byrum went on to continue Hartman's work, further developing and enhancing it, and adding his own statistically valid interpretations to Hartman's original assessment.

Over the past ten years I have added to those interpretations as well.

Dr. Byrum, another partner, and I formed Athena Assessment, a consulting firm that helps corporations identify potential employees with particular kinds of judgment. We also help corporations improve the judgment of their current workforce.

I would go on to found Pilot Judgment, a consulting service designed to help individuals better understand, improve, and strengthen their evaluative judgment and, ultimately, achieve success.

Since their founding, Athena Assessment and Pilot Judgment have assessed hundreds of thousands of people, collected millions of data points, conducted thousands of interviews, and completed over one hundred best/worst performer studies. The amount of data we have amassed is enormous. The study and analysis of that data provide the basis for this book, which shares with you, the reader, what we have learned.

PROLOGUE

On February 1, 2008, just before sunset at 5:01 p.m., a forty-five-
year-old pilot and her ten-year-old son were driving to the local airport
in the beautiful and tranquil town of Augusta, Maine. The two had spent
the week in Maine, and the plan was that within an hour or so they would
be flying back to their home in Steamboat Springs, Colorado, in her
plane, an immaculate and well-kept Cessna Citation Jet CJ1. She was
talking to Flight Service on her cell phone as she drove.

Flight Service is an FAA (Federal Aviation Administration) air traffic facility that provides information and services to pilots. She was fil-
ing her flight plan and receiving a weather report: ice, fog, mist, sleet,
freezing rain, snow, and turbulence. In other words, terrible and only
getting worse. There was already over a quarter inch of ice on the cars,
the planes—*her* plane—the entire parking lot, the airport, everything. It
was a mess.

The family twosome arrived at the airport about 5:15 p.m. She
loaded her luggage into her plane, returned the rental car, and paid for
the fuel. The employees at the airport remember that she commented
that the weather was "just cruddy"—and it was. They asked if she would
like them to de-ice her airplane. She declined. She said she was in a hurry.

Her son asked if he could go to the bathroom. She told him to be
quick because they had to get going.

By 5:30 p.m., she and her son were in the plane. It was now dark outside. She closed the doors, cranked up the engines, and called Air Traffic Control (ATC) to initiate the clearance she had previously filed with Flight Service. She received it and, soon after, announced on the local airport frequency that she was taxiing to the runway.

She taxied to the wrong runway, twice. At smaller airports that do not have an operating control tower (such as the one in Augusta), pilots can turn on the runway and taxiway lights themselves by clicking the transmitter button on their microphone a specified number of times. This is a very common practice, and all pilots who fly in and out of small airports know this. But on this night, she failed to turn on the lights.

Moreover, there was so much snow and ice on the ground that the taxiway border lights were barely visible; only the very tops of them poked up through the snow. It was impossible to determine the edge of the taxiways—that point where the pavement ended and the grass began. At one point, she taxied off the pavement and into a ditch. Her jet broke through the ice and sank into the mud. The airport employees heard her throttle up her jet, powering it back onto the pavement. When the workers realized what was happening—that it was now dark outside and the taxiway lights were off—they turned the lights on for her.

At 5:41 p.m., after her roundabout taxi, she finally made it to the correct runway, and advised ATC that she was ready for departure. ATC released her for departure and instructed her to climb to ten thousand feet. *Climb and maintain ten thousand* is a very common departure instruction.

At 5:44 p.m., she checked in with ATC departure control, advising that she was airborne and climbing to ten thousand feet.

One minute later, at 5:45 pm, ATC instructed her to *Ident*. She leaned forward and pressed the Ident button on the plane's transponder, a piece of equipment on the control panel. This sent a signal to the controller so that he could positively identify her plane on his radar screen. Asking pilots to Ident is a very common and normal request after departure.

Shortly afterwards, the controller replied that he had established her in "radar contact." Her plane was now positively identified on his radar screen.

One minute after that, at 5:46 pm, she declared an emergency.

Thirty-eight seconds later, she and her son were dead.

They crashed and died that stormy night just outside the beautiful and tranquil town of Augusta, Maine.

PART 1

JUDGMENT MATTERS

YOUR JUDGMENT JOURNEY

The Navy Calls It *Headwork*

The only item graded on every single flight in the entire U.S. Navy flight-training syllabus is *headwork*. Not even *basic air work* or *emergency procedures* (which, together with headwork, comprise what the Navy calls the *Big Three*) is graded on every single flight.

Many student naval aviators wash out of the flight program because they lack headwork. Imagine the disappointment of being kicked out of Navy flight school, your dream of becoming a military pilot shattered, all because you lack headwork?

As you can imagine, to a naval aviator, headwork is a very big deal. Actually, no matter what we do, or who we are, or where we go, headwork is a very big deal.

But what do we know about it? Where does it come from? What are its origins? Can we define it? Can we identify it? Can we improve it? Can we measure it? If we lose it, can we get it back? Just what exactly *is* headwork?

When I ask my corporate clients these questions, I receive all sorts of answers—sometimes a blank stare, a chin scratch, or just a faraway look.

The term itself, if we stop and think about it—*headwork*—seems a bit unusual, as it suggests "work performed by your head." Ponder that concept for a moment: *work performed by your head.*

Webster's New World Dictionary, Third College Edition, defines *headwork* as "mental effort; thought."

The U.S. Navy (not to be outdone) defines it as follows:

The ability to understand and grasp the meaning of instructions, demonstrations, and explanations; the facility of remembering instructions from day to day, the ability to plan a series or sequence of maneuvers or actions, the ability to foresee and avoid possible difficulties, and the ability to remain alert and spatially oriented.

The Navy didn't arrive at this definition overnight. They spent a great deal of effort in their attempt to define *headwork*, because in the military we know what a very big deal headwork is. However, in all likelihood, unless you are a U.S. Navy pilot, you probably rarely, if ever, use the word *headwork*. You probably use another word: *judgment.*

Webster's defines *judgment* as "the ability to come to opinions about things; power of comparing and deciding; understanding; good sense." And that is such a big deal, and so incredibly important, because if we "get it right"—and learn to better understand and improve our judgment, our good sense—we can improve upon, strengthen, and reinvigorate all areas of our life, both professionally and personally. Furthermore, we can do so no matter how wonderful our lives are already.

Simply put, judgment is the primary key to our success.

In the work we do at my two consulting firms, Athena Assessment and Pilot Judgment, many of our clients tell us that good judgment is absolutely vital to their company and its success. They say that when hiring, if forced to choose between two candidates—one with good judgment and the other with job skills—they would choose the candidate with good judgment. If our clients could be sure that they were obtaining superior judgment, they would often be willing to skimp a bit on skill-set competency. Of course, we want both: judgment and skills. Nevertheless, the point is that in many situations, good judgment is as important, or possibly even more important, than skill.

This brings us to the heart of our work, which is the study, measurement, and improvement of judgment. Our goal is to help individuals improve their decisions, choices, and actions, to assist them on their path toward further success and happiness—what I call a *judgment journey.* You have already taken a first step: the furthering of your understanding of the personal value structure, which you will explore in this book.

Whether you are a homemaker, a doctor, a pilot, a carpenter, a teacher, a coach, a military veteran, a college kid, a retail salesperson, an engineer, a ditch digger, unemployed, or *whatever*, I am going to share with you the six irrefutable truths of success, gleaned from over ten million statistically predictive data points, as well as many thousands of judgment assessments, interviews, and studies. Do not underestimate the power of these truths. Follow them. They lead to higher levels of professional and personal success.

Your World Lens

Think back to your first consciousness or awareness of life . . .

For most of us, our earliest memories are a bit fuzzy or blurry, absent of detail and specificity. Back then we lacked any sort of comprehensive awareness of our surroundings or ourselves. Nevertheless, even though we had only a rudimentary grasp of our surroundings, we learned (and quickly!) to react to our surroundings. Some particular stimulus would enter our world—and we would react. Something would scare us, and we would cry. Then Mom would show up, and we would be happy and giggle.

Later, as we became more conscious and more aware, something amazing happened: We learned to incorporate deliberation, consideration, and assessment of our surroundings and ourselves. We learned to move beyond the simple process of *reaction*, to that of *evaluation*.

This ability to evaluate is the underlying structure of human consciousness. Evaluation occurs constantly throughout our lives. It is real, extremely complex, decisive in influence, and unique to each of us.

What that last bit means is that your particular underlying structure is the lens through which *you* see the world. Your world lens helps you assign value, guides you to your decisions and actions, and in great part makes you the person you are today. So whether a decision is solely reactionary, includes the higher-order activity of evaluation, or involves some combination of each approach, your world lens is what leads you to your choices, decisions, and behavior.

Our values make us who we are. Our underlying structure is specifically a *value structure*, and it is based primarily on our individual, personal values. It provides for us the ability to engage in evaluation— the process of assigning value—which goes far beyond mere thinking. True, evaluation involves thinking, *but* evaluation is a much higher-order activity, and much more complex.

The primary manifestation of our evaluation process is into our judgment, which is the primary driver of our decisions and behavior, from our first initial consciousness of something to the moment we make our final decision on it.

Evaluation and judgment—or *evaluative judgment*—set us apart both as a human race and individually. Evaluative judgment is the ability, when presented with an issue, problem, or situation, to observe and understand the dynamics of the situation; to determine what actions will make the situation better; and to act ultimately to improve the situation.

Continuously, incessantly, throughout every day, our value structure guides us through a process of evaluations, judgments, and decisions. The process has a far-reaching range, from small and inconsequential decisions ("Should I take the car or ride the train to work today?") to the occasional enormously life-altering decisions ("Do I quit my job to fulfill my lifelong dream of traveling around the world?"). The process is based on our very own, very specific, very personal, one-of-a-kind, unique value structure. Our value structure influences every decision and choice that we make.

Even individuals with similar education, similar backgrounds, similar experiences, and similar lives often will see the same exact situation in two completely different lights because of differences in their value structures. This happens whether we are workmates, siblings, friends, or squadronmates. Our values are as varied as the humans on this planet.

Whether we are buying a car, making a marriage proposal, studying for an exam, asking the boss for a pay raise, mowing the lawn, shopping for groceries, flying a plane, fighting in combat, or arguing a case in a court of law, our unique value structure is with us, helping shape and guide our decisions and choices.

This important point cannot be overemphasized. The concept that our values manifest into our underlying value structure—which manifests into our evaluations, which manifest into our judgments, which manifest into our decisions and choices, which more than anything else determine who we are as an individual—is a *very big deal.*

Many factors—upbringing, training, education, experience, advice, trauma—coalesce to form our value structure, and this process never ends. Our value structure is dynamic and *always changing.* It will continue to develop over the course of our entire life. It grows as we grow.

People are always changing and always growing. As we encounter daily living, new experiences, more education and training, various adversities, and so forth, our value structure evolves and brings new understanding to the way we see and relate to people, work, places, and things. New problems and challenges may force us to mature and grow in ways we cannot always foresee. Nevertheless, at any given time, our value structure is operating within us, and it significantly determines how we process the world and how we react.

The Determining Factor

For over one hundred years, personnel assessments have been used to help gain various insights into individuals and/or organizations. Typically, individuals undergo assessments for the primary goal of personal improvement of some kind or another. Organizations employ such assessments to augment hiring and promotion decisions, and/or to facilitate the development and enhancement of the organization's current workforce. Furthermore, there are two main types of personnel assessments: skills-based and non-skills-based.

Skills-based assessments are usually pass/fail type exams—for example, the Private Pilot exam, the Automotive Service Excellence (ASE) technician test, the Certified Public Accountant (CPA) final exam, or the United States Medical Licensing Exam (USMLE). They test for competency and knowledge within a particular occupation or activity. Skills-based assessments are typically graded, with a minimum qualifying score required for the test-taker to receive a particular certification or qualify for a particular job. Skills testing is required in many occupations in fields such as surgery, engineering, accounting, aviation, and professional sports. Occupations such as these demand an extremely high level of precision and skill, and the assessments make sure that adequate skills are present in those who wish to work in a certain field.

However, merely passing the test and possessing necessary skills is not sufficient for long-term success. To achieve high levels of success, we need to wrap any skills and knowledge we possess in the blanket of good judgment. If we are to succeed at anything, there is a strong need for both skills and good judgment.

As for most *non-skills-based assessments*, they fall into one of three categories: (1) IQ tests, (2) personality profiles, and (3) psychiatric/emotional balance inventories. Though many organizations require the completion of one or more of these types of assessments as a prerequisite for employment, they have very little to do with, and are not predictive of, success.

First off, success is not about IQ. There are individuals with high IQs who are "book smart" and yet have little common sense, wisdom, or decision-making or problem-solving ability. They may struggle to achieve success and be lackluster performers within their chosen work. Rational intelligence alone is simply not a predictor of high performance or success. Make no mistake: Having superior rational intelligence can be, and often is, a wonderful advantage, and many highly intelligent people are extremely successful. However, many are not. Common sense, wisdom, and evaluative judgment are much more predictive of success.

Second of all, success is not about personality type. Many people are able to overcome very real, supposedly negative personality traits and characteristics, and to perform their work in an excellent fashion and achieve high levels of success. The overwhelming majority of personnel assessments used today are personality profiles. Some try to suggest that certain personality types will result in certain kinds of competencies (or a lack thereof). But depending on personality tests to predict success in a certain occupation or role is short-sighted. Simply, personality is *not* a valid predictor of success. Our work in the arena of value and judgment goes far beyond personality.

Thirdly, most people who experience social or emotional breakdowns, or who show extreme lapses in judgment, do so because of the presence of overwhelming stress and a corresponding lack of the ability to cope. True, many suffer from a bona fide psychiatric disorder or dysfunction, and psychiatric tests aid in the detection and diagnosis of mental illness. Excluding that, the remedy for most emotional breakdowns is to get stress under control.

In this context, an "emotional breakdown" is the phenomenon of using extremely poor judgment when you actually know better: cussing out a coworker over a minor difference of opinion, making a completely irresponsible financial decision, engaging in out-of-character risky behavior, or even just feeling overwhelmed with life and letting that impact your choices. What individuals in these situations really need to do is to learn better coping skills. If they reduce the negative effects of stress, they will be able to regain control of, and feel better about, their life. A reduction in stress can promote feelings of comfort, confidence, peace, and control. Evaluative judgment plays a vital role in our ability to contend with stressors and adversity.

So, if IQ, personality, and emotional balance are not the determining factors in success, what is?

Without equivocation, the single most determining factor in personal or professional success is the all-important, all-critical dimension of *judgment*. It provides and presents our unique value perspective on life and work, and it is the primary driver of our choices, decisions, actions, and behavior.

Your Value Structure

Remember that our values are natural to us, because our values *are* us. The lens through which we view various situations, people, places, and things is the lens that defines who we are as individuals, and that influences, more than anything else, our decisions.

Yet we must make a great effort to objectively scrutinize and self-assess, to be unbiased as we examine our behavior and choices. It is important to base our examination of our value structure on the decisions and choices we *actually* make, not on those we *wish* we would make.

For many, accurate self-assessment is difficult. There is a common tendency to believe that the way we desire to be is the way that we are in reality. But that is not always the case. How many times have you heard people describe themselves very differently from how others describe them? It is as if they are talking about two different individuals. If you find that others describe you in ways that are strikingly different from how you view yourself, be open to the honest critique—especially if you receive it from associates or close friends who know you well and have your best interests at heart.

As we go about the business of making decisions and choices, we might overemphasize certain areas of value and ignore other areas. If someone points that out to us, we might disagree. The disagreement would be rooted in our differing personal value structures—each value structure a different and unique lens to the world.

So, be open to the world lens of others—and what their lens says about you. Consider that others may see things differently from you, and that their value structure may have more clarity than yours, allowing them to point out areas that you tend to disregard. If you incorporate their suggestions into your value structure and decision-making process, it may well lead you to higher levels of success.

Nevertheless, self-assessment is not just about what our friends, family, and peers are able to tell us about ourselves. If we truly want to examine and improve our value structure, we must do our best to study our behavior as it *is*, not as we *wish it to be*. And no matter the nature and character of your particular value structure—strong, weak, or in between—or whether your self-assessment is even accurate, *you will discover that a clearer understanding of the basis of judgment is a great aid to finding your success.*

So, place any ego and insecurity aside, and make a cold, hard, impartial examination of your decisions and behavior. It is not always easy to do, and an objective look in the mirror can be quite uncomfortable. But if you want to fully understand and develop your value structure and give yourself the best chances for reaching your success, it is a great first step.

The Values of Success

The measurement of judgment using our judgment assessment, followed by the improvement of judgment, is exactly the work that my colleagues and I perform at Athena Assessment and Pilot Judgment. Our judgment assessment is based on the original work of Robert Hartman, PhD, the Nobel Prize nominee I mentioned in the preface. Since Dr. Hartman's death, and for the past forty-five years, C. Stephen Byrum, PhD has furthered Dr. Hartman's work. And for the past ten years, I have added to it as well.

Our judgment assessment is accurate, valid, and statistically predictive, and provides the unvarnished truth regarding the nature and character of individuals' and teams' value structures. Our study of hundreds of thousands of judgment profiles comprises the data that allows us to unequivocally determine the structure of success—the specific underlying values that lead us to higher levels of achievement or to lower levels of achievement, even failure.

This analysis of personal value structure goes beyond statistical *reliability* to statistical *predictability*. The *predictive* quality is so important because it allows us to gauge a person's future performance on the job or with a corporation. That's why businesses across the nation seek Athena Assessment to help with hiring their workforce. *We know what leads to success.*

The distinction between those two terms—*reliable* and *predictable*—is important to understand. With an accurate scale and tape measure, we can *reliably* measure someone's weight and height. However, those reliable measurements do not necessarily allow us to make valid *predictions* about, for example, their degree of job performance. Our conclusions, drawn from years of detailed analysis, are not merely a collection of fanciful ideas that we believe are helpful—they are statistically *predictive* of success. The data drove the conclusions, and if you pay heed, your judgments will improve, as will your success.

Your strength within the values and judgments we've pinpointed determines just how successful you are in handling the matters, issues, and people before you. Thus, there is an actual value structure for success.

If there are any weaknesses within your value structure, you can improve upon them—with effort. And with that effort, your judgments and decision-making abilities will improve.

The value structure of success incorporates an integrated and coordinated set of guiding principles. A small sampling of those guiding principles includes, for example the ability to

- Relate to people
- Accomplish tasks
- Consider implications and consequences
- Be aware of your surroundings
- Make effective decisions while under stress
- Be open-minded to change

- ▸ Follow directions

- ▸ Maintain focus

These success-related evaluative judgments act as a helping hand, guiding us toward decisions and actions that are more likely to lead to success.

If we are lucky, our own unique value structure comports closely with the value structure of success. However, if it turns out that our value structure is far different from the structure of success, we have the ability, through effort and diligence, to change it.

Yes, we can alter our personal value structure so that it is akin to the structure of success.

How do we know if our value structure is the structure of success? Every day as we make decisions, we emphasize and prioritize certain values. But the reality is, we may not always be cognizant of them and how strong an influence they have on our evaluations and our actions. Therefore, it is important to be as open-minded and objective as we can be, to assess—*accurately*—the strengths and weaknesses of our value structure, and to understand how they are influencing our behavior. Only then can we truly understand our current value structure—and mold it into the value structure of success.

Before Us . . . and Beyond Us

In 1856, French archaeologist and Egyptologist Émile Prisse d'Avennes discovered in Thebes, Egypt, what has come to be known as the Prisse Papyrus. In 1906, English Egyptologist Battiscombe Gunn translated the papyrus document. Dating back to the twenty-sixth century B.C. (4,600 years ago!), it contains the last section of *The Instruction of Ke'Gemni* and the entirety of *The Maxims of Ptah-hotep*.

Ke'Gemni and Ptah-hotep were high-ranking public officials who held the title of vizier within the Egyptian government. Ptah-hotep, a very wise man, was a direct advisor to the pharaoh at that time,

Djedkare Isesi. On the papyrus, Ptah-hotep recorded for his son the wisdom he had gained over the course of his life and from his ancestors. His maxims exalted virtues such as kindness, justice, truthfulness, tradition, self-control, generosity, etiquette, morality, and honesty. And even though not all historians are in exact agreement with the details surrounding Ptah-hotep, undoubtedly the values and advice expressed in his maxims influenced the value structure and the evaluative judgments of his children, and their children, and their children, for many generations to come.

The point of introducing this bit of ancient history is that people's values, which define their value structure and lead to their evaluative judgments and behaviors, have been an ongoing *conversation* for thousands of years. To this day, the specific influence of Ptah-hotep and his maxims, written over 4,400 years ago, may be influencing the evaluative judgments of many people, and maybe even you—an interesting idea indeed.

A long list of influential documents, teachings, and philosophies have literally shaped the world. The powers of religious doctrine and political ideology, and their influence on the values of humanity, are immense and long-lasting.

The values taught in the Bible have been inspiring evaluative judgments and behaviors over much of the world for more than two thousand years. In force since 1789, the U.S. Constitution was inspired, in part, by the Magna Carta, issued in 1215 and one of the first attempts to limit the power of the king of England and establish the rule of law. Socrates, Plato, and Aristotle, who lived in Greece some 2,400 years ago, are credited for developing the foundations of Western philosophy, ethics, and logic.

Long-standing values influence us daily, from the Mayflower Compact, the Declaration of Independence, and the Federalist Papers of our own nation's founding in the late eighteenth century . . . to Confucius and Sun Tzu (author of *The Art of War*) in sixth-century B.C. China . . . to Greek slave Aesop and Cleisthenes, father of Athenian democracy, in the same century. Even more obscure or hard-to-pin-down concepts and events—such as Stoicism, a third-century B.C. philosophy that negativity results from errors in judgment, and Queen Elizabeth's *Proclamation to Forbid Preaching* (1558)—may be responsible for the values, traditions, and behaviors that guide some individuals or groups today.

What are the sources of your own values? Reflecting on the origins of your value structure may help guide you on your judgment journey, encouraging you to embrace certain positive influences—and enabling you to reject the negative ones.

Most people readily recognize that they are influenced by their parents, grandparents, teachers, coaches, siblings, friends, and so forth. Pause for a moment, however, to think about the fact that the values passed to you from your parents were likely passed to them from their parents, and so on, for generations.

I sometimes wonder just how far back my own values originated. I know that my grandfathers' value structures are a part of who I am today. But my father was by far my biggest influence. I remain curious about the specific events and experiences that shaped his values.

You may have already discovered that your value structure, and therefore your behavior, is taking on a similar structure to that of your parents. The reality is that our values survive on, for long after we have "gone on to glory" (as my father used to say).

Every time you befriend, give advice, counsel, coach, teach, or share a piece of wisdom, you are passing along a bit of your value structure—a tiny bit of yourself. So the next time you hear someone say, "I am becoming more and more like my father (or mother) as I get older," know that those are values that are carrying on. The wisdom you share will long outlast your time on this earth—so make it count, and make it worthwhile!

Hierarchy of Value

Inevitably, the question arises as to how our values manifest into our evaluative judgments. Well, our value structure is made up of particular values and combinations of values. To each person, place, situation, or endeavor with which or whom we engage, we assign value. Some of these values are positive, and some are negative.

As seen through the lens of your unique value structure, each endeavor will inspire within *you* a particular reaction, sensation, or emotion. Some situations might cause a very positive reaction, whereas others might elicit a very negative reaction. Some might inspire only a minor reaction from you—one neither overly positive nor overly negative. This is exactly what guides our evaluations: a hierarchy of value based on our value structure.

For example, if you are more *people*-oriented than *task*-oriented, you tend to emphasize and prioritize those decisions and situations more closely associated with people, placing them higher in your value structure.

Others might place equal emphasis on people and tasks or ideas. Their unique value structure determines that which they consider the "best," all the way down to that which they consider the "worst."

Each of us has our own value structure uniquely our own. No two structures are exactly alike. Yet if two people maintain a degree of consistency and uniformity within their own personal value structure, each can exhibit a high level of evaluative judgment and be likely to find his or her own way to success despite having individual structures that are different (and sometimes vastly so).

Training Your Judgment

Ironically, despite the fact that our evaluative judgment—more than anything else—influences our behaviors and thus our achievements, the topic of evaluative judgment is something that most of us rarely give a great deal of consideration. We continually make decisions, but we give little thought to the tangible process of evaluating, judging, and making those decisions, even though it is precisely the use of superior evaluative judgment that lies at the heart of success. Well, now is the time to learn to focus not only on the decision itself, but on the evaluative judgment used to arrive at the decision.

A word of caution here: Making improvements in your evaluative judgment, and thus improvements in your performance and success, is a lifelong endeavor. There is no "quick fix." True, some judgmental improvements, such as trainability, are rather easy; for most people, they come relatively quickly and do not require substantial effort. However, comprehensive improvements in evaluative judgment do not happen *immediately*. Maintaining strong evaluative judgments, and improving upon weak judgments, takes persistent, conscious, and long-term contemplation and consideration.

The results are worth it.

Just as you might choose physical exercise to improve the fitness of your body, so too might you choose to "exercise" and improve the "fitness" of your evaluative judgments. And just as with physical exercise, it's something you can and should do *for the rest of your life*.

Put forth a great effort toward understanding and improving your value structure. Guard and protect it. Be wary of any enemies to it—and always remain vigilant to keep it sound, strong, and fit.

A Snowball Effect

Keep this book handy—and refer to it often. Let it be a catalyst for self-reflection, self-awareness, and positive change. The way you see yourself, and the personal responses you make, will be a primary agent, and possibly *the* primary agent, for improvement. Never underestimate the power of self-awareness and an open mind.

Unfortunately, many find the process of self-reflection, and the acceptance of constructive self-criticism, neither easy nor particularly comfortable. This may be especially the case if you know that some areas of your judgment are weak. Try to be as open-minded as possible to both the analysis of your judgments and the subsequent interpretations, no matter what they indicate—even if they are quite negative.

Make a great effort to be as objective as you can about the strengths and weaknesses in your value structure. Be honest. If certain areas of judgment are not as strong as you would like, do not give up hope; those areas can be improved. Take care to focus your attention, closely studying those weaker areas. Do your best to assimilate the information, explanations, and suggestions. And pay close attention also to any areas in which you exhibit *exceedingly strong* judgment, as they may bring their own set of issues, such as conflict and frustration.

Over time, if you give ample consideration to not only your decisions but also *how you arrived at them*, you will notice an improvement in your decision-making and problem-solving abilities. Subsequently, you will experience improvements in many areas of your life, from success in the workplace to higher levels of satisfaction in your personal life and relationships. When your judgment begins to improve, a catalyst occurs and a positive snowball effect leads to further improvement.

What *Success* Means

When I refer to "success" in this book, I am referring to an ability to move into a work environment and perform at a high level—to be successful in a work environment.

Certainly it is possible to be successful at what you do and yet not be living a happy, fulfilling life. Yet some people equate being successful to being happy or being contented with their life. They believe that if you are not happy, you are not successful—and that is a valid point. For this book's discussion, however, we are going to draw a specific distinction between success and happiness. *Success* in this work implies professional or work-related success, not personal happiness.

Yes, happiness can be measured, improved, and mastered though analysis and conscious effort, just as success can. And we readily acknowledge that professional success and personal happiness are intertwined, as one often impacts the other. Nevertheless, *the structure of happiness* is a different conversation for another time. For the sake of this conversation, separate the two in your mind.

Success here refers specifically to an ability to perform to a high standard in a work environment—an ability to do good work.

Work itself has many expressions. For this discussion, *work* is considered to be whatever endeavor with which you are engaged. It might be the more classic definition of work—a job for which you receive a paycheck—or it might be the business that you own. It might be going to school, or homemaking, or a serious hobby or pastime. Essentially, *work* is whatever you consider to be "what you do."

So, for this conversation, being successful is being good at what you do.

Welcome!

Intuitively, you already know the majority of the ideas presented in this book. Even so, there will be ideas that you have not considered, or have considered only in passing. These ideas will help you further understand and improve your decisions, your behavior, and your success. I will share with you my own ideas as well as those I have learned from others, particularly my good friend, C. Stephen Byrum, PhD, the world's foremost authority on the structure of value, and my very own judgment mentor. Dr. Byrum has devoted forty-five years of his life to the study of evaluative judgment.

Examining your personal value structure is like viewing "an X-ray of your soul." The profound insights shared with you here are real, long-lasting, and life-changing. You will gain a better understanding of why you do the things you do, and why you are the way you are.

It is commonplace for someone to encompass the entire spectrum of strengths, with areas of his or her value structure ranging from very strong to very weak. The techniques for strengthening weak areas come in many forms—and, at times, these techniques are beyond the scope of the advice in any single book. Countless books, seminars, coaches, counselors, and mentors offer further personal improvement. Depending on your level of need and what works best for you, you may use the advice in this book as a springboard to seek out additional assistance and support.

For many, the guidance and advice provided here will prove sufficient. Others who have larger value structure inconsistencies might find additional ideas and resources helpful as they progress on their judgment journey. If, after reading this book and practicing the advice, you continue to have difficulty with, for example, relating to other people, accomplishing work tasks, crafting a workable plan, reducing clutter, managing stress, or any of the various other important areas of your judgment, consider pursuing outside professional help for specific areas of weakness.

Remember, no matter how weak certain areas of your evaluative judgment might be, do not despair. Should you so desire, you will learn how to improve your judgment, and you will become good—*really* good—at what you do.

It is my sincere hope that you will find inspiration and great personal benefit as you uncover the structure of your judgment. Consider this study and improvement to be a lifelong judgment journey that never ends, but keeps revealing for you new opportunities and possibilities, always furthering your life . . . and your success.

WHAT IS GOOD?

At the heart of success is the ability to answer one simple, funda-mental question: *What is good?* Successful people answer this question all the time—all day long, every day, over and over, continually. Most of them don't even realize it. They do it automatically and intuitively. But whether or not they realize it, they are answering this question routinely and effectively.

And as simple as it may seem, this question is actually quite complex.

Before you read any further, I want you to pause and think, and then answer for yourself: What is *good?* What comes into your mind when you think of *good?* Don't overthink it. Don't use the dictionary either, because the definition is entirely inadequate. Instead, think about it from your personal perspective. For you, in your own words, right now, what is *good?*

Don't think that this is a trivial question. It is not. Nor is this some sort of clever play on words. Being able to answer this question consistently and effectively is extremely important. In fact, it is the very foundation of your success.

After all, we don't just want a career; we want a *good* career. We don't just want things; we want *good* things. We don't just want relationships; we want *good* relationships. We don't just want to live a life; we want to live a *good* life. We don't just want to make decisions; we want to make *good* decisions. We don't just want to have judgment; we want to have *good* judgment.

As you can see, we can apply the notion of *good* to literally everything in our life. And in the context of our personal and professional lives, *poor* judgment is the most powerful detriment to success, and *good* judgment is the most powerful enhancement to success. Therefore we must fully understand and be able to answer that fundamental question: What is *good*?

What It *Should* Be

Well, for everything in our life, no matter how big or small, how important or trivial—every person, place, or thing; everything we want to do; every experience we have; every event and situation we face; every opportunity and crisis we tackle; every endeavor we engage in; every choice we make—we have an idea of what it "should be." Granted, sometimes our idea of what something *should be* is not always credible or well thought out. Nevertheless, we have an idea of what something *should be*.

Consider the examples in the list below. Create a mental image of each one. Think about what it would take for each item to be *good* according to *your* idea of good:

- ‣ A good pair of shoes
- ‣ A good car
- ‣ Good music
- ‣ Good food
- ‣ A good spouse or mate
- ‣ A good experience
- ‣ A good job or career
- ‣ A good life

- ▸ A good idea

- ▸ A good decision

- ▸ Good judgment

Notice that as you consider each item on the list, you naturally, almost instinctively project in your mind a concept of what it should be. This is something we do constantly throughout each day—we project our viewpoints and conceptions onto people, places, situations, ideas, things, *everything*.

During corporate presentations I make the point that we have inner conditions for what is *good*, with a few very simple examples. I present a list similar to the one above, slightly tailoring it to the particular audience. So, for example, I ask the audience to give me one characteristic of a good pair of shoes. Invariably someone holds up their hand and says, "Comfortable."

Many members of the audience nod their heads in approval. I nod my head in agreement too, and then look down at my shoes. "Of course!" I say out loud. "For how can a pair of shoes be considered a *good* pair of shoes if they are not comfortable? Can you imagine walking around all day in uncomfortable shoes?"

I let the audience ponder that for a few seconds.

Then I reach into a bag and pull out a pair of very expensive, very stylish, very sexy high-heeled shoes. I usually get a good laugh, because clearly this pair of shoes—these strappy, six-inch platforms—is *not* comfortable.

I observe that this style of shoe is very pricey, and has been worn by some of the most elegant, sophisticated, and successful women in the world. With a smile, I ask the person who said "comfortable" whether these are good shoes. Usually the person smiles back and acknowledges that even though comfort is a characteristic of good shoes, and even though six-inch platforms seem to be *not* very comfortable, he or she would consider them to be good shoes.

The wheels in the audience's brains start to turn. We have just come up against our first conundrum, albeit a silly, simple one. In order for a shoe to be a *good* shoe, it must be comfortable. Yet at the very same moment they agree that six-inch platforms, while uncomfortable, can be good shoes.

I move to another example: a good car. The audience will suggest *good* characteristics such as dependability, high fuel mileage, safety rating, and cargo capacity. Many people agree with these responses. Yet someone usually scoffs at those characteristics and says, "Who cares about fuel mileage and cargo capacity? It's all about horsepower! The only *good* car is a car that goes zero to sixty in under four seconds."

How about good music? As you can imagine, the opinions on what makes music *good* range from one end of the spectrum to the other.

What about a good spouse? This always provokes joking and laughter. The audience suggests characteristics such as *loving, caring, easygoing, agreeable, fun, romantic, a good listener, sexy, low-maintenance,* and *high-maintenance*. The most laughs come after people shout out *rich, silent,* and *absent*.

It quickly becomes obvious that we can apply this notion of *good* to literally everything. It also quickly becomes obvious that *different people have different ideas about what makes something good*. What someone considers good, someone else considers not good, even bad or horrific. The notion of *good* reaches far and wide, and encompasses the entire spectrum of possibilities. Yet it is vitally important that we understand the notion of good, because we want to be able to apply that notion to everything in our lives and everything that we do. Remember, good judgment is the foundation of our success.

So, getting back to the question *What is good?*—if each of us has our own ideas of what something should be, then we can pin it down this way: If whatever you are dealing with fulfills the concept of what you think it should be, then to you it is good.

Simply put: *Good* is concept fulfillment.

In order for you to consider something—anything—to be good, it must fulfill your concept of what it should be. If it does that for you, then you will consider it to be good.

Furthermore, for something to be *really* good, not only must the concept of it be rich, strong, and well thought out, but additionally there must be follow-through, execution, and implementation. In other words, there must be *fulfillment of the concept.*

Concept fulfillment may sound somewhat philosophical and esoteric. It is not. It is a tangible, simple test—a test of what should be, and thus of what is good—that you can (and must) use routinely, daily, in almost everything that you do.

The ability to employ concept fulfillment is important because it provides the foundational underpinnings of success. A few moments devoted to *understanding* a concept and then *fulfilling* it delivers an enormous boost to the pursuit of our most desired personal and professional goals.

Applying the *Good* Test

To be successful, we must be able to make consistently good choices—in other words, decisions and choices that fulfill the concept. First, we need to be able to understand the concept (which might be extremely complicated). Second, we need to be able to fulfill it (which might be extremely difficult). This is where our evaluative judgment comes to our aid, because strong evaluative judgment helps us do both: (1) understand the concept, and (2) fulfill the concept.

Never forget that it is *not* your brilliant, high-level genius IQ that enables you to make good decisions. Nor is it your magnificent, emotionally balanced psychology or your delightfully pleasing, radiant personality that provides you with that ability. Sure, at times those things help. But it is primarily and overwhelmingly your *evaluative judgment* that provides your decision-making ability and, thus, the structure of your success. And this is why strong evaluative judgment is so essential.

It allows you to

1. understand the concept, and

2. fulfill the concept.

It is worth repeating: *Our evaluative judgment is the primary factor of our success, because it allows us to make consistently good decisions*—in other words, decisions that fulfill the concept.

Remember, you don't just want to make decisions—you want to make *good* decisions. And a good decision is one that fulfills whatever it is you are trying to do. If your decision does not fulfill the concept and does not accomplish what you are trying to do, then it is not a good decision.

The examples are limitless (don't worry, I'll limit them):

- To be caring, you must fulfill the concept of caring.

- To be dependable, you must fulfill the concept of dependability.

- To be a good worker, you must fulfill the concept of a good worker.

- To be a safe pilot, you must fulfill the concept of a safe pilot.

- To be a good teacher, you must fulfill the concept of a good teacher.

- To be a good ax murderer, you must fulfill the concept of a good ax murderer—*and on and on and on.*

Let's dwell for a moment on the concept of a good spouse. If your spouse fulfills your concept of what you think a spouse should be—whatever that is—then you will consider your spouse to be a good spouse. Conversely, if you fulfill the concept of what your spouse thinks a spouse should be, then your spouse will consider you a good spouse.

This brings up another key point: *Our success depends in part on being acutely aware of other people's concepts.* So if we want to be perceived as a good employee, then we must fulfill *the boss's* concept of a good employee.

Now, your boss's concept may not be the same as yours, so if you desire success as their employee, you must do your best to

1. understand any differences between your concept and your boss's concept, and then

2. work hard to fulfill your boss's concept.

If you can do that, then your boss will consider you a good employee.

Another important point about the concept of *good* is that it evolves and matures as our evaluative judgment evolves and matures. What we consider to be good now, we may not consider to be good later.

What's more, *good* may apply to none, part, or all of a situation. So it is also crucial to distinguish the particular characteristic to which you are applying the *good* test.

Here is an example: A century ago, a motivated young European man was given the opportunity and responsibility to improve a railway system. He did so in spectacular fashion, working long and hard to make sure that the trains moved precisely on schedule. The railway system became a model of efficiency, able to move more passengers than ever before. The man received many accolades from his superiors—and so it could be said that he fulfilled the concept of a railway administrator.

As it turns out, this man was Adolf Eichmann, a German soldier of the Third Reich. His passengers were Jewish people on their way to Nazi death camps. Eichmann was, in part, responsible for the deaths of over five million Jews. Therefore, it could be said that he also fulfilled the concept of a criminal mass murderer.

So even though Eichmann was one of the most evil men in the history of humankind, and was hanged in 1962 for war crimes and crimes against humanity, it can be said that he had some *good* qualities. He was a *good* railway administrator and a *good* mass murderer, because he fulfilled the concept of both. Of course, in totality, he was the personification of evil, and not a good person. Eichmann's life story shows it is possible to be good . . . at being evil.

Understanding the nuance and subtlety of good is imperative. Good weaves its way throughout our lives daily, moving in and out of our decisions, choices, and interactions. Those who learn to apply it are much more successful. Those who fail to grasp it often fail, sometimes in spectacular fashion. If you learn to apply the *good* test to everyday situations, you will notice improved clarity in your decisions and your overall judgment.

Good According to Others

One day my son and I were watching *The Walking Dead*, a television show about zombies. Throughout the show, my son would throw up his hands in exasperation, exclaiming, "This is ridiculous. Zombies aren't like that!"

I asked him what was wrong.

"Zombies can't run," he explained, clearly annoyed. "Their Achilles tendon rots, so they can only plod along at a slow pace. Everybody knows that!"

He also told me that covering yourself in smelly zombie guts doesn't mean you can walk through a crowd of zombies undetected—another faulty and ridiculous scene in the show, according to him. The same goes for cutting off the arms and jaws of zombies (so they can't grab and bite you) and leading them around by chains. This does not cause other zombies to ignore you. "Ridiculous!" insisted my son.

Clearly, he has more zombie expertise than I have.

The point is that the show did not depict zombies correctly *according to my son*. The *Walking Dead* zombies did not fulfill his concept of zombies, and therefore they were not *good* zombies. We watched the show anyway—it was quite entertaining, and I had an interesting lesson in all things zombie.

Success requires that you not only grasp your own concepts, but understand the concepts of others. Individuals who are unable to move beyond their own concepts, and who fail to appreciate the values and the *good* concepts of others, are much less successful, both personally and professionally.

Here's another example: A sports fan went to a pawn shop to sell a piece of wood. As far as wood goes, it was entirely ordinary, practically worth nothing. However, this piece of wood also happened to be a hockey stick used by Hall of Fame hockey player Bobby Orr during Orr's rookie season. If you are not a hockey fan, the hockey stick likely fulfills the concept of nothing more than a simple piece of wood, and has little value to you. However, if you are a hockey fan, it fulfills the concept of a priceless heirloom. This man made quite a bit of money selling the hockey stick, all because he understood the value it held for other people.

Recently, my wife visited an automotive dealership. The knowledgeable salesman started by explaining to my wife about the child safety seat attachments, dependability, gas mileage, and overall safety rating. She interrupted him several times during his sales pitch, to let him know that those items did not matter to her. She explained she was more interested in ground clearance: "Could the truck pull a large horse trailer? And how many bags of feed could it hold?"

The two enjoyed a good laugh as he explained to her what he had been taught: that because she seemed to fit the profile of a thirty-to-forty-something married housewife, she would likely be interested in the items he discussed. Once he realized she didn't fit that profile, he finally stopped with his preprogrammed sales presentation and just asked her what *she* wanted to know.

The salesman's original presentation fulfilled what he thought was her concept of a vehicle. However, as it turns out, my wife's concept was very different. This salesman was smart enough to refocus on those items that mattered to my wife—and when he did, he achieved success. To make the sale, he showed my wife that the vehicle fit her concept of a vehicle. He used good judgment, asked good questions, and provided good answers—and my wife bought what was, to her, a good vehicle. The salesman excelled at job performance because he adjusted *his* concept of a vehicle to *her* concept.

The story doesn't always have a happy ending. Multibillion-dollar corporations have been brought to their knees because the decision-makers lacked either the evaluative judgment to *understand* the necessary concepts or the ability to *fulfill* the concepts. Two business executives may disagree on the concept of a company, or they may disagree on how to fulfill that concept via a work process or a way to take care of an angry client. It is also quite possible for them to agree on or share an *understanding* of the concept, but still disagree on how to *fulfill* the concept.

When you are working with a team or group that can't agree on what makes something good, how is the group supposed to agree on what makes a good decision? The answer lies, again, within evaluative judgment.

Each of us has a particular structure to our evaluative judgment. The better we understand that structure, and the better we strive to understand the structure others have and use, the better we are able to collaborate and collectively arrive at good decisions and choices. And when we get together and pool our good judgment, success can be even more far-reaching. Good corporations have individuals with good judgment. Great corporations have teams with collectively good judgment.

Either way, success always begins with good judgment.

THE PARTICULARS
OF JUDGMENT

Within our evaluative judgment, there are two components:
conceptualization and actualization.

Conceptualization

Before we decide, select, speak, move forward, or take action—in essence, before we do *anything*—we first need to "get things right" in our head so that we can do it as well as we can. We need to form in our minds a strong *conceptualization* (also referred to as *conceptual orientation*) about what it is we want to do—*before* we do it. This is a very important first step toward having and using good judgment.

When we conceptualize, we gain an understanding and awareness of the details and dynamics of the situation, problem, opportunity, or issue with which we are about to engage. This strength in orientation is the *conceptualization* component of judgment. If we lack this when we make a judgment or problem-solve, our actions may not get off to a good start. The results are often ineffective, chaotic, or misdirected.

Our individual conceptual orientation is critically important and has a great deal to do with our day-to-day integration with people, situations, and work, and with the capabilities we show within the world at large. If our conceptualization is not strong, our outcomes in a situation might turn out to be good—but it is just as probable that outcomes will turn out to be bad.

Here is a simple practical example of just how useful a strong conceptualization is: Imagine that you are invited over to a friend's house for a barbecue. At some point after your arrival, your friend points to a large grill and says, "Be careful around that grill. It is very hot." That one nonchalant comment about the hot grill sets your conceptual orientation in motion and facilitates your acclimation to this particular environment. For the remainder of the party, no one needs to tell you not to lean on or put your hand on the grill. No one needs to lecture you about the risks of throwing a football in proximity to the grill.

When you have a strong conceptual orientation to your environment (in this case, the backyard), you likely use better judgment, and so you make better decisions about what to do when you're there. Your conceptual orientation to the backyard targets safer areas for horseplay or games, and bolsters your "backyard judgment."

Within the realm of our work environment, it is highly desirable to have a strong conceptual orientation. The need for strong, healthy conceptual orientation applies to all kinds of decisions: critical and noncritical; emergency and nonemergency; big and small; routine and atypical. It is much easier to make good and even superior decisions when we understand the dynamics of the situation and the environment through having things "right" in our heads first.

Strong conceptual orientation also helps deliver that hidden extra boost of judgment toward high-quality decisions for those times when you might find yourself plopped in the middle of a seemingly out-of-control crisis or emergency scenario. Even better, a formidable conceptual orientation might help you entirely avoid such a crisis. There is a need for strong conceptual orientation in the legal, medical, sports, education, aviation, political, and engineering fields, and so forth—though emergencies can occur within most occupations.

If you should ever overhear someone describe how they resolved a seemingly unresolvable situation or emergency, pay close attention. As you contemplate the person's words, you should come to realize, without exception, the existence of their strong conceptual orientation to their environment. Their orientation offers a partial answer to the oft-asked question: "How did they think of that?"

Without a strong conceptual orientation, our judgment is more limited, incomplete, and inadequate. Imagine how inferior would be our ability to handle difficult or emergency-type scenarios if we lacked conceptual orientation. A hot grill would be only the beginning of our worries.

Fortunately, if our conceptual orientation is weak, it can be strengthened—as we shall see later in this book.

Actualization

In order for some situation, decision, or opportunity to turn out exceptionally good, not only must its concept be rich, strong, meaningful, and well-conceived, but also there must be follow-through, execution, implementation, and accomplishment. In other words, we need *fulfillment* of the concept. We want to be able to apply and integrate our orientation in concrete ways in our everyday world. We need to be able to *act on* what we are *conceptualizing*—so that we might fulfill that concept.

Fulfillment suggests action, achievement, and accomplishment. However, for some, *fulfillment* also implies a state of mind such as contentment or satisfaction; it does not necessarily infer something *to do*. Therefore, in the context of evaluative judgment, we are going to refer to this ability to fulfill our concept as *actualization*.

Actualization is vitally important in everything we do, in every decision we make. For a decision to be a good decision, it must achieve the desired outcome. Therefore, it is essential that we develop our ability to actualize.

Actualization is more concerned with what we *do* rather than what we *think*. The actualization component of our judgment helps guide our behavior to specific actions and choices. Using the previous example: For you to be a good guest at your friend's barbecue, not only must you have an understanding of the backyard (your conceptual orienta-tion), but you also must use that understanding to make *and enact* your backyard decisions. You must *fulfill the concept* of a backyard guest—and actually keep your hands (and the football) off that grill. Only when you actualize the concept of a backyard guest are you a *good* backyard guest.

Ideally, the actualization component of your judgment will be as strong as, or stronger than, the corresponding conceptualization com-ponent. For example, take your people judgment. If your actualization in this area is stronger than your conceptualization, you are likely to be capable not only of understanding a relational or personal problem but of *resolving* the problem. That is, you not only talk the talk, but also walk the walk.

Conversely, if the conceptualization component of your judgment is stronger than your actualization, you are apt to think more about a problem rather than deal with it directly. You have a good understanding of the issue or person—but you struggle with follow-through. You tend to be, as they say, "all talk, no action" (or if you hail from Texas, "all hat, no cattle").

If you turn out to be conceptually dominant—your ability to concep-tualize is stronger than your ability to actualize those concepts—you can, with effort, become more action oriented. It is not always easy to do, but it can be done. We'll discuss how in the pages that follow.

WORK-SIDE JUDGMENT

Our very survival depends on how we interact with our circum-stances and environments—how we perform both with them and in them—to meet our basic human needs. Of course, we hope to do more than just meet our basic human needs. We hope to thrive and to achieve success. And we are much more likely to achieve success if we have and use good judgment.

Before we reach an understanding of what primes us for success, let's pause for a moment and consider an overarching judgment principle.

Within the study of judgment, we speak of two "sides":

1. *Work-side* judgment

2. *Self-side* judgment

Work-side judgment is also known as *external* or *outward-looking* judgment—the judgment of what we do—whereas self-side judgment is also known as *personal* or *inward-looking* judgment, or the judgment of who we are.

Work-side judgments are those that we use to interact with people, places, things, situations, ideas, events, problems, opportunities, and so forth. They help us make our way in the world at large, and are extremely important to achieving success.

Self-side judgments are those that we use to interact with ourselves. They determine how we deal with, view, and feel about ourselves. Self-side judgments help us on a deeply personal level and are extremely important to our happiness, self-esteem, self-confidence, and overall satisfaction with life.

Just as success and happiness are intertwined (see page 18), so are work-side and self-side judgments intertwined. However, for this book we draw a distinction between the two sides of judgment. And since work-side judgments are more predictive of our success, these are the primary focus of this book.

Remember that the simple word *work*, in the context of this book, is considered to be *whatever endeavor with which we are engaged* (see page 19). Think of work as "what you do." Indeed, work, in its many and varied representations, is the thing that we human beings spend most of our time doing.

To do what we, and others, consider *good* work, we must accept certain prerequisites. These include the abilities to

- perceive the details of the various circumstances and environments surrounding us;
- assess those details and circumstances and make sense out of them;
- connect any distinct and separate experiences into a larger whole; and
- develop the skills necessary for making the best use of our world and our talents.

Our proficiency at each and every one of these enables us to do good work in the world around us.

Yet our environment is never static. It is ever-changing as time marches on. We continually encounter unforeseen and unexpected situations, problems, and opportunities. Thus our ability to cope with, and excel at handling, current and upcoming decisions, situations, and issues remains a work in progress. We must continually build and advance the aforementioned abilities—to perceive, assess, and connect our experiences, and also to develop our specific skills and training. Ultimately this helps us better evaluate any forthcoming situations and circumstances, guiding us toward success.

As you can well imagine, our work-side judgments are highly important, and highly predictive of success. Work-side judgments provide the underpinning of our professional skills, and the springboard from which we can propel to our highest levels of accomplishment.

For the aviator, strong work-side judgment may be all that stands between a safe landing and disaster. For teachers, it is not only knowledge of the material, but strong work-side judgment that enables them to guide their students from poor behavior and academic failure to a place where they desire to learn and harness the benefits of a good education. For a CEO, manager, or consultant, effective work-side judgments and decisions may be the primary catalyst that helps reverse a negative, downward trend or leads a company to new levels of success.

Our work-side judgments consist of two key components:

1. Our ability to evaluate and improve the circumstances and situations within our work environment

2. The degree of importance we place on our work

The first component is facilitated through the strength and character of our evaluative judgment. Our ability to evaluate and improve a situation is primarily based on our value structure, and thus is unique and different for each of us. There are several specific areas of our evaluative judgment, each of which provides distinct abilities for certain individuals.

For example, some people notice things in incredible detail and are attuned to the intricacies and minutiae around them, the particularly subtle or underlying happenings and occurrences. They are well aware of the "trees" in the "forest."

Some people are very alert, responsive, and empathetic to the feelings of others.

Some individuals are very good at conceptualizing, and repeatedly come up with new ideas.

Some are excellent executors who move beyond conceptualizing to actualizing their work and ideas—they "get things done."

Some people are good at all of the above, whereas others excel in only certain areas of work-related judgments. Those individuals who are able to perform these and other judgment-dependent activities effectively—to comprehend important issues and ideas, complete tasks effectively and efficiently, work well with others, and ignore inconsequential distractions—are much more likely to reach their goals and achieve success.

The second key component of work-side judgment is rather simple and straightforward. It is *the degree of importance we place on our work.*

The level of importance that each of us places on work is highly personal. As such, it has a large impact on our attitude toward work, and thus on our ability to handle difficult work-related problems and to cope with work-related stress.

In general, the more importance we place on our work, the more we pay attention to our work. And the more we pay attention to our work, the better our overall work-related judgment is. We tend to notice more and to show more interest in our work. We spend more time devoted to resolving problems. We're less likely to give up or quit when our work holds a place of importance for us. We are more apt to overcome and resolve issues and problems, even in the face of intense adversity, when work holds a high level of importance for us.

On the flip side, it can be difficult to go that extra mile when work holds little importance for us.

We don't necessarily need to *like* our work to believe that our work is important, but our data indicates that in general, the more someone likes what they do, the more importance they place on their work. So while liking your work is not essential, it does provide a boost toward work-side judgments. After all, liking what you do is a judgment call in itself. You can choose to like it or not.

Without a doubt, the level of importance you place on your work has a tremendous influence on your work-related behaviors and your level of success.

· · ·

No one ever says, "I think I'll use bad judgment today and ruin my life." Yet people often make decisions that lead to their downfall, whether it's professional failure or even death—or perhaps simply to a life less well lived.

It doesn't have to be that way.

Poor judgment is not written in stone. Judgment can *always* be improved upon—and dreams and goals can be fulfilled.

It has always been, and forever will be, through the exercise of *good* judgment that we are able to fulfill our highest levels of potential and—with gusto—make steps toward the highest levels of professional and personal success. In the next section we are going to start taking those steps.

Simply put, my friend, your good judgment can help you live a satisfying, *good* life.

PART 2

JUDGMENT TRUTHS

THREE GLOBAL JUDGMENTS

So far in this book, we have established that successful people—
those who make *good* decisions—use their skills in evaluation and judgment to achieve their version of personal or professional success. In fact, their evaluative judgment is fundamental to their success, and within their work-side judgment, or how they interact with the world at large, is the chief predictor of that success.

Now we are ready to take our understanding one step further by exploring the three primary work-side judgments: *intrinsic, extrinsic,* and *systemic.* We refer to these three judgments as *global judgments* because they are basic, fundamental, and broad in scope.

The global judgments represent the first three of the six undeniable truths at the heart of success:

- **Truth #1:** *Intrinsic judgment* (the "human factor")

- **Truth #2:** *Extrinsic judgment* (work, tasks, processes, and tactics)

- **Truth #3:** *Systemic judgment* ("big picture" strategy)

Successful people include a component of each of these global judgments in their decisions, whether they realize it or not. Learn as much as you can about each of them—they are an essential factor in your success. Be consciously and acutely aware of them. Incorporate the words *intrinsic, extrinsic,* and *systemic* into your everyday vocabulary. Remember, success is all about using good judgment—and these are your three primary judgments.

The three global judgments are *not* mutually exclusive. So it is important to understand, develop, and then incorporate all three of these truths into your decision-making process. This is particularly true regarding any important and crucial decisions.

Contained within each global judgment, intrinsic, extrinsic, and systemic, are the previously discussed judgment components of *conceptualization* and *actualization.* (For a review of conceptualization and actualization, see pages 31 to 34.) These components manifest quite specifically into our value structure as

- ▸ Intrinsic Conceptualization—*tolerance*
- ▸ Intrinsic Actualization—*compassion*
- ▸ Extrinsic Conceptualization—*trainability*
- ▸ Extrinsic Actualization—*dependability*
- ▸ Systemic Conceptualization—*understanding strategies*
- ▸ Systemic Actualization—*using strategies*

The conceptualization and actualization components of each global judgment form a corresponding pair. For example, tolerance and compassion are a pair, with each measuring a component of intrinsic judgment. Tolerance has more to do with the conceptualization component, or what we *understand* intrinsically. Compassion has more to do with the actualization component, what we *do* intrinsically.

If your intrinsic actualization is stronger than your intrinsic conceptualization, you are likely to be good at not only *understanding* an intrinsic predicament but also *resolving* it.

If your intrinsic conceptualization is stronger than your actualization, you probably tend to *think* more about an intrinsic issue rather than *deal* with it directly.

Ideally, your actualization is *equal to* or *stronger than* your conceptualization. If that is the case, you move beyond the ideas and concepts of tolerance, to exhibit the actions of caring and compassion.

These characteristics also apply to the extrinsic and systemic.

Decisions of great consequence that exclude one or more of the global judgments are often the decisions that bring anguish and heartbreak. They are the decisions that bankrupt companies. They are the decisions that destroy careers. They are the decisions to blame for yet another fired employee, a washed-up athlete, an airplane crash, a ruined client relationship, an obliterated opportunity, or perhaps another life less well lived.

Conversely, decisions that include each of the global judgments will be your best decisions, and those that lead you more quickly to your success.

As you read through this book and recognize yourself in the discussion of judgment, you may discover that you have very strong or even exceptional abilities in certain of the three key areas of judgment. Or you may have to acknowledge that areas of your judgment are weak and undeveloped—a menace, ready to strike, often without warning. Fortunately, no matter how strong (or how weak) one or more of your three global judgment areas are, you can improve upon them.

If you have *weak* areas of judgment, this book will show you how to improve them.

If you have *strong* areas of your judgment, this book will show you how to best use and take advantage of that powerful judgment.

Some *moderately* developed areas of judgment have their own specific issues. If so, those chapters include a moderate description in order to explain any distinct manifestations of moderately developed judgment in that area. However, if the significance of moderate judgment strength is simply "in between" strong and weak, then a moderate section is not included. As such, not all chapters include a description of *moderate* strength of judgment.

If your judgment areas are *very strong*, or *exceptional*, we'll congratulate you . . . and tell you whether there is something you should still be cautious about, or something about that strength that has the potential to hurt you.

So study the following material closely—and with an open mind. Honesty about yourself, your abilities, and your values is key.

Then, carefully and thoughtfully go about honing and improving your judgments and decisions. Doing so will lead undeniably to your success.

Let's get started.

TRUTH #1: INTRINSIC JUDGMENT

The following is a portion of a floor speech by U.S. Representative Trey Gowdy of South Carolina's Fourth Congressional District (Trey and I grew up in the same neighborhood, so even though he is a politician, I have always considered him more of a neighbor):

We are surrounded by fame, Mr. Speaker, and it's easy to forget that while those people made contributions to our country, the country was built and is being built and will continue to be built by average ordinary woman and men who lead quiet lives of conviction and courage; average folks doing above average things, ordinary folks doing extraordinary things. That is the essence of who we are as a people, and while there may not be a monument or a portrait dedicated to those ordinary men and women, there is something even better, and it's called a legacy.

So in honor of those women and men, Mr. Speaker, who lead quiet lives of conviction, I want to honor a man who was just like them. Bruce Cash was a pharmacist [Representative Gowdy's voice trembled here, holding back tears] in my hometown of Spartanburg. He was buried last week—way too soon, in my opinion, but such are the ways of the Lord. He was a pharmacist, so we saw him when we were sick, and more importantly we saw him when our children were sick. And he was compassionate and he was kind, and he acted

Continued

like you were the only person that he was taking care of that day. He was active in his church, doing everything from driving a bus on choir tour to being chairman of the Board of Deacons to taking his vacation and time to chaperone other people's children while they went and sang to prisoners in prisons.

He was a devoted father and husband. He and his wife, Kitty, had six children, scores of grandchildren. And when you walked into his pharmacy, Mr. Speaker . . . you didn't see his business license and you didn't see his pharmacy license. You saw a picture of his children. He wanted to quietly signal to you that that was the most important thing in his life.

And I would tell you, Mr. Speaker, to look up Bruce Cash on the Internet, but you're not gonna find much. In fact, he never even bothered to change the name of his pharmacy. He left on his pharmacy the name [Gowdy's voice trembled again here] of the man who owned it before him.

Mr. Speaker, he had the quality that best defined the Lord Jesus that he believed in, which is humility. He didn't want to talk about himself. He wanted to talk about you. He didn't want to tell you his opinion. He wanted to ask you your opinion. He didn't want to talk about his illness. He wanted to talk about your illness. He didn't want to talk about how life had dealt him an unplayable hand of cards. He wanted to talk about grace and hope and things that last beyond our lifetime.

So, Mr. Speaker, in conclusion, Bruce was humble and he believed it was more important to live a sermon than to preach one. I want to thank you, Bruce, for setting an example of average ordinary people building this country, and the next time a child asks me who is the most famous person I have met is, I will tell them it's you.

Intrinsic judgment represents the first of the three global judgments. Often referred to as "global intrinsic," "global I," or "I-judgment," it measures the ability to understand and relate to people.

When someone refers to "people skills" or the ability to "read" people, that person is referring to intrinsic judgment.

The *conceptualization* and *actualization* components of intrinsic judgment (see pages 31 to 34) manifest as *tolerance* and *compassion*.

If you have strong intrinsic judgment, you size people up in a discerning manner. You are sharp and savvy about people and their behaviors; you have "street smarts" about others and their motivations. You are able to distinguish subtleties of people, too. If you are a good salesperson, you are able to determine quickly whether someone is a serious buyer or merely a casual looker. Your ability to do so resides within your intrinsic judgment.

Some experts in the study of judgment and valuation believe in a hierarchy of judgment, and are convinced that the intrinsic is the most important area of judgment. After all, intrinsic judgment is the foundation of our connections, relations, and interactions with other people, and provides the basis of our humanity, charity, and kindness. Rarely is any endeavor accomplished without some form of contact or collaboration with others, and it is our intrinsic judgment that provides the ability to work together with a wide range of people in a wide range of scenarios and situations.

A great deal of leadership ability resides within intrinsic judgment, making it one of the most important components of success. To be an effective leader, you must effectively use intrinsic judgment to understand, relate to, and interact with people. Intrinsic judgment is what provides that ability. Merely being "in control" or being "the boss" in no way infers true leadership. True leadership requires an ability to motivate, influence, and persuade. The ability to inspire others is associated with some form of a connection to others, and that ability to connect lies within intrinsic judgment.

Occurrences of poor intrinsic judgment lead to remarkably poor leadership, and are often deemed the primary catalyst for the downfall of many organizations, large and small. An uninspired, unmotivated, unenthusiastic workforce is not healthy for the long-term viability of any organization. Countless organizations have suffered under leaders who fostered a toxic culture within the company.

Conversely, positive leadership, precipitated and advanced through strong intrinsic judgment, has been the catalyst for bringing many organizations back from the brink of impending collapse. Difficult economic times come and go, and a leader who uses good intrinsic judgment rouses the workforce to persevere.

No matter your profession, even if your work seems more technical than people-oriented, never underestimate the power of the intrinsic. For example, many aviators might consider their job to be inherently mechanical or procedural, but they also should consider the many interactions they have with others. Aviators must communicate and collaborate with fellow pilots, controllers, briefers, gate agents, crew schedulers, plane captains, crew members, mechanics, passengers, and so on. Even the leader-like term *pilot in command* has a deeply intrinsic connotation. Without equivocation, a pilot's intrinsic judgment adds to his or her "in command" decision-making effectiveness. Intrinsic judgment is a valuable component of safe aviating and effective leadership, and applies to pilots as well as to individuals in every occupation.

As everyone knows, however, people are not always what they seem. Some individuals may be marginally unlike their public image; some are even entirely dissimilar from it. Occasionally, there are traits hidden within a person that deviate sharply from his or her public persona. Such individuals often create a particular public persona to deflect, mislead, and deceive, or to hide areas of weakness. Any revelation or expression of these traits may surprise us—for example, when a highly regarded individual is discovered to be disreputable, scandalous, or lacking in moral character. Your intrinsic judgment helps you see through others' subterfuges, cons, and scams, guiding you beyond any pretense and outward show.

Strong

With strong intrinsic judgment, you are people-wise, people-perceptive, savvy, and shrewd; you see through the façades of people who are phony.

You "read" people with clarity and are able to relate to others—even those who are dissimilar to you in many ways.

Others view you as possessing strong people skills. This does not imply that you are an extrovert necessarily, but rather that you possess confidence in social settings and in your dealings with other people. The reality is, whether you tend toward extroversion or introversion has no bearing on the level or strength of your intrinsic judgment. Furthermore, whether you tend to be either extroverted or introverted has no bearing on your *success*.

With strong intrinsic judgment, you are inherently tolerant and compassionate. Here, *tolerant* is not a code word for "anything goes." Instead it means that you are not arbitrarily intolerant of others just because they happen to be different from you. Nor does tolerance in any way imply that you lack a moral compass, are willing to put up with any type of behavior, or lack any sort of censorious opinion against those who contravene your sense of morality. Indeed, there may be specific behaviors that another individual exhibits to which you are very much opposed. Generally, however, if you have strong intrinsic judgment, you are tolerant of and compassionate toward others.

A well-developed ability to discern how others are feeling can be one of the most satisfying and fulfilling benefits of strong intrinsic judgment. A mere glance at a friend, colleague, or loved one—and sometimes even at a stranger—can alert you to their inner workings. With strong intrinsic judgment, you easily read body language and detect subtle, nonverbal cues about others' moods and attitudes. You sense the joy of others and often are able to revel in it yourself.

Strong intrinsic judgment also enables you to sense difficulty or hardship that others may be experiencing, which affords you the opportunity to help and assist them. For example, a doctor or nurse with strong intrinsic judgment may walk into a patient's hospital room and quickly "feel" the ambience or atmosphere. This allows the caregiver to size up the patient and determine whether he or she is getting better or getting worse before they even examine the patient's medical records and charts.

Strong intrinsic judgment usually is found in the physicians who exhibit a comforting bedside manner.

Rarely is there a situation of importance that does not include an intrinsic component. A successful resolution of the issue, whether maintaining workforce morale during corporate downsizing or dealing with an angry client, typically requires that you include an intrinsic component to your judgments and decisions.

Ignore the intrinsic at your peril, no matter your occupation.

Very Strong

Some words of caution apply here: When strong intrinsic judgment crosses over into *very* strong intrinsic judgment, it becomes possible to take advantage of others because you recognize and understand their motivations. Therefore, use strong intrinsic judgment wisely and carefully.

It is also possible that your intrinsic judgment is so well developed and exceptionally strong that you may find it difficult to render decisions that are hurtful to others, even when you know that those are unquestionably the best decisions in the long run. So reflect on your own level of intrinsic strength. This frame of mind—not wanting to hurt someone else—is rather common. Our data reveals that a substantial percentage of the population has exceptionally strong intrinsic judgment.

For example, a professor may recognize that a student who dreams of a career as a physician is intellectually incapable of handling the rigors of medical school. A check airman who observes a student pilot perform below standards on a check flight knows the student should not pass. A business owner may feel that he cannot bring himself to lay off employees even at the risk of bankrupting the company. Exceptionally strong intrinsic judgment may impede the professor, the check airman, or the business owner from making the proper, but demoralizing, decision.

If your strong intrinsic score dominates your other global judgments, consider that you might spend too much time and energy on *getting along* and not enough time and energy on *getting things done*. This is a very common issue for intrinsically dominant teams or groups.

Additionally, within strong intrinsic judgment there is an occasional tendency to justify, *incorrectly*, a poor decision. In other words, through an overemphasis on the intrinsic, you might factor too much hope, compassion, or empathy into your decision-making, causing you to make decisions that are—ironically—against your better judgment. The outcomes may be similar to those made by individuals with poor intrinsic judgment, but the underlying reasons are markedly dissimilar. If you have exceptionally strong intrinsic judgment, *you know better.*

Here's an example from my own experience working with someone whose exceptional intrinsic judgment worked against her.

Laurie is a former supervisor at a large retail chain location, whose duties included hiring and firing, training, scheduling, and disciplining cashiers. She was recently demoted.

To fill a position at this retail company, applicants must complete our judgment assessment, and then interviews are conducted. Laurie admitted after her demotion that during the hiring process, she would not consider our assessment at all. She would only consider how badly the applicant needed the job, and nothing else. She felt it was her obligation to society to give the best possible opportunities to the most desperate individuals—period.

Her situation caught my attention, as Laurie had received an unusually strong intrinsic score on our judgment assessment. Her I-judgment dominated her other judgments. Laurie was all about the intrinsic and not much else. Here's how that worked against her.

Prior to being demoted, Laurie had hired a new cashier—a single mother of four children with a spotty work history and long periods of unemployment. Laurie was determined to give this woman a job and make it work, despite the woman's erratic work history and lack of experience as a cashier.

Immediately, the cashier struggled with the necessary shift paperwork, which consisted of counting the money in the cash drawer at the beginning and end of each shift. As you can imagine, the company did not take any cash drawer mistakes lightly. Any such discrepancies required a supervisor to override and approve. Multiple discrepancies were subject to disciplinary action against the employee, up to and including termination.

The new cashier had far more mistakes than the typical trainee, and well after her training period, she continued to record cash totals incorrectly. Each time, Laurie would override the mistakes and correct them herself, never bringing them to anyone else's attention and never writing up the employee, which was the company protocol. In order to continue this practice, Laurie had to be certain to schedule this cashier for work only when her own schedule would permit her to directly supervise this person.

The other cashiers became aware of this and other problems with the new cashier, and became irritated that they were constantly subjected to extra duties due to the new employee's lack of attention in shift-change procedures and other tasks. While Laurie was out of work for a few days, another supervisor filling in for her noticed the problems with the newest cashier. The problems were reported, and the head office conducted an audit. They found a history of mistakenly reported cash totals followed by overrides, with not one single disciplinary action taken by the supervisor on duty (who had always been Laurie).

Whether the problems were due to theft, incompetence, or collusion between Laurie and the cashier, the problems had to stop. The new cashier was fired and Laurie was demoted. Laurie was offered the option to work at the cashier level again, with no authority over any other employee. Laurie took the lower-level job; her supervisory days were over.

I spoke with Laurie after her demotion, and I asked her why she did not follow company protocol in disciplining the employee. I also inquired as to why she had hired this cashier in the first place, when she had extremely weak judgment scores and a questionable work history. After all, there were other more qualified applicants.

Laurie revealed to me that yes, she suspected this employee was never going to work out. Training had gone poorly, and the new employee did not seem concerned about the cash totals or the accuracy of other tasks. However, Laurie felt that by adjusting the cash totals so no one else would know about the mistakes, she was simply doing a "nice thing" for another person who needed a helping hand.

In Laurie's mind, being nice and not making the new employee feel that she was incapable of doing the job was more important than following the company's rules. It was a concept that Laurie previously had not grasped as wrong and improper (and possibly illegal), because the impact on her had never been so severe. She had often done what she considered "nice things" for employees, such as baking and bringing in cupcakes for them. In her mind, bringing in cupcakes for someone's birthday and covering up financial discrepancies were one and the same; she was just being "nice."

Laurie and I talked for a while, until she started to see that her over-emphasis on her perception of someone else's possible hurt feelings were detrimental to everyone involved, and ended up hurting others (including herself). The new cashier had been in a job that she could not grasp and would not succeed in—and worse, had someone else not intervened, she might have been accused of a crime. Laurie had to break multiple company rules to cover up the cashier's ineptness. And other employees had to deal with the morale issues caused by working with someone who was not subject to the same rules and standards that they were.

Strong intrinsic judgment is necessary for success—but in Laurie's case, it was a runaway horse that entirely dominated and misled her decisions and negatively impacted her personal success.

Laurie told me she plans on committing whatever time it takes, at the lower pay and lesser job title, to work her way back up again. This outcome is entirely possible, given that Laurie has newfound clarity in her own decision-making process.

Laurie's case is a textbook example of someone who *knew better* but allowed her overly strong intrinsic judgment to overpower every other consideration and to work against her success. If you recognize that you occasionally fall prey to the same tendency as Laurie, consider seriously the following bits of advice to avoid finding yourself in a similar predicament.

Success Tip #1: Stop thinking about other people.

The words *Stop thinking about other people* may sound incredibly harsh, and to someone with very strong intrinsic sensibilities, they are. If I speak those words during a coaching session with someone who has exceptionally strong intrinsic judgment, it is quite common for him or her to gasp in disgust. The act of ignoring people may contradict your strongest core values. However, you need to calibrate your concern for people in relation to other factors and concerns.

Success Tip #2: Compartmentalize your intrinsic judgment.

Put away your intrinsic thinking cap for a moment, and consider non-intrinsic aspects before deciding on the matter at hand. An area of judgment loses its way when used improperly, and may diminish a person's overall judgment and decision-making. So when you are faced with a particularly difficult or high-level decision, take care to compartmentalize your intrinsic judgment. Set it aside briefly, and consider additional, non-intrinsic aspects of the situation before making your decision. Do not worry that you will somehow lose your intrinsic spirit and heart if you do this. You will not.

For example, if you are operating as pilot in command, consciously compartmentalize the intrinsic aspects of your flight, which might be the desires of your passengers or clients, or even your own intrinsic desires. Intrinsic aspects—a yearning to say yes to whatever is asked, even when that is counterintuitive to well-being and safety—often cause enormous intrinsic stress. Place any intrinsic demands and pressures on hold, and consider non-intrinsic judgments before deciding on the matter. You may find that various intrinsic pressures—such as an appeal to complete the flight, pass the student, agree to the mission, or say yes to anything asked of you—are in conflict with what you know is the right thing to do. The bottom line: make sure you are not allowing your exceptionally strong intrinsic judgment to override all other aspects of your judgment and decision-making.

Success Tip #3: Be conscious of frustration.

When collaborating with others, always be aware of frustration rearing its ugly head and hijacking your good judgment. Beware of turning to the "dark side" of very strong intrinsic judgment (see page 70).

Strong intrinsic judgment provides an extraordinary degree of comprehension and perception, particularly where it involves people. With strong intrinsic judgment, you are able to sense and detect the deep-seated intrinsic valuations of others—their likes, dislikes, dreams, wishes, desires, aspirations, goals, and so forth—and so you will have the power to use their valuations against them in cruel, vindictive ways. If you disagree with certain individuals, and you allow your frustration to take hold of your judgment when collaborating and interacting with them, and to overwhelm and negatively influence your intrinsic capabilities, you may deliver severe intrinsic harm.

This is not to suggest that you would do such a thing, but with exceptionally strong intrinsic judgment, you have that capability. Therefore, you must be very careful when you find yourself in the midst of clutter, chaos, confusion, stress, and angst.

The first, and very best, way to avoid intrinsic frustration is to always be conscious of the potential for it to appear. As the saying goes, an ounce of prevention is worth a pound of cure. If you allow very strong judgment to manifest into frustration, your frustration can quickly undermine your inherently strong judgment, and you will behave as someone with poor judgment behaves.

Once you've identified that rising sense of frustration, move to do whatever is necessary to reduce it. This can mean taking an action as extreme as changing your career or as simple as counting to ten as you calm down. Intrinsic frustration often relates to a lack of open and honest communication.

Finally, remember to always use intrinsic judgment as a force for good—to help people, not undermine them. Do not let frustration trigger an unwitting slide into condescension or mean-spirited behavior toward others.

. . .

Despite these cautionary notes, you should celebrate strong intrinsic judgment. If you have it, consider yourself fortunate. It is a *fantastic* tool. Should you know that your intrinsic judgment is exceptional, be excited and grateful, and do not fear its power. True, there are pitfalls to watch out for—but well-developed intrinsic judgment within your value structure can serve as an enormous strength, and greatly facilitates your potential for professional success.

Moderate

Moderately strong intrinsic judgment is less than desirable, as our culture tends to be intrinsically driven and motivated. Very little—indeed, almost nothing—is accomplished without some communication or collaboration with others. If you want to succeed at the work of your choice, it will be to your benefit to improve the strength of your intrinsic judgment.

The vast majority of people have been raised and nurtured with some understanding of the value of intrinsic judgment. Through education and work and life experiences, most people come to fully comprehend the need for solid intrinsic judgment. To increase your chances of success, review the advice on the pages that follow, for those with weak intrinsic judgment.

The relationship between intrinsic judgment and success is not difficult to understand; most people get it. They have observed the power of the positive relationship in action, and can readily equate intrinsic judgment and success. As a result, the majority of people, whatever their motivation—be it a desire to get along with workmates or to achieve success—have developed relatively solid intrinsic judgment. And the overwhelming majority of *successful* people have developed strong intrinsic judgment as described previously.

Weak

If you have weak intrinsic judgment, you struggle when faced with high-level intrinsic problems and situations. You lack a keen awareness of others and their motivations, and you have difficulty relating to other people.

If you lack the "human factor," you are less adept at reading people's moods. People may come across to you as mostly vague and nonspecific. If other people's motivations usually do not seem clear to you—unless they are extremely angry, frustrated, or otherwise emphatic—then consider that your intrinsic judgment might be weak. Put simply, your people skills are in short supply.

Individuals who are not "people savvy" and who generally have poor people judgment often feel they are in over their head when forced to make difficult decisions relating to, or in conjunction with, other people.

To figure out if these descriptions fit you, think about your likely responses to these scenarios:

▸ When confronted with "people" issues, do you often feel blindsided, as if you are the last to know? Do you frequently receive "Huh?" as a reaction when you converse with others?

▸ Are you are likely to miss any evidence of intrinsic conflict? For example, are you apt to remark, "I don't know what went wrong. He just blew up at me out of nowhere!"

▸ Do you often misunderstand others? Do others misunderstand you? Do you regularly irritate others while feeling misread? Do you often hear, or say, "But that's not what I meant!"?

> ‣ Are you ever disciplined, formally or informally, for issues that have nothing to do with your actual work, but instead for how you interact with others?

> ‣ Have you ever been accused of saying something thoughtless—an accusation that has nothing whatsoever to do with actual truthfulness or accuracy of the statement, but because of the manner or timing in which it was delivered?

Of course, it's true that different people engage in similar behaviors for a multiplicity of reasons. For example, someone might misread your meaning because he or she lacks self-confidence or is highly conflict avoidant. However, if you experience these scenarios—common manifestations of weak intrinsic judgment—with different individuals, you may lack the human factor.

Competence and ability alone are usually not enough for success. You must be able to

> ‣ relate to others,

> ‣ say the right (appropriate) things,

> ‣ get along with others, and

> ‣ know how and when to speak your mind to those around you.

Those with weak intrinsic judgment—people who place insufficient emphasis on intrinsic or relational priorities—find becoming successful a struggle because the intrinsic element is downplayed or entirely lacking in their decisions and actions. Good intrinsic decisions are possible for them, but only if the decisions to be made are simple and cut-and-dried. If the issue includes a sense of urgency, chaos, or relational complexity, making good intrinsic decisions is difficult for someone who lacks strong intrinsic judgment.

If you lack intrinsic judgment, it is not easy for you to find an appropriate balance between following the rules, completing the mission, setting policy, and extending empathetic consideration. Your decisions may seem overly harsh to others, and they lack relational or intrinsic consideration. In the eyes of others, this diminishes your perceived leadership qualities. In some vocations where leadership is considered a premium skill—such as an executive position or a team leader—this deficiency may undermine your current position and impede your path to greater professional success.

Do not despair: If you struggle to understand and relate to others, you *can* improve your weak intrinsic judgment. And you should do so, if you wish to attain higher levels of accomplishment.

Here is how to begin.

Success Tip #1: Think about the people involved.

Before you make high-level decisions, pause and think about any possible relational aspects. Have you given the people involved in the situation their due consideration? Have you treated them reasonably, honestly, and equitably?

Success Tip #2: Ask the "experts" for feedback about tolerance and compassion.

Take into account that your tolerance and compassion might be somewhat lacking, and assess this accurately by asking for input on your decisions from others who are perceived as good leaders.

Success Tip #3: Work with a mentor.

Choose and start working with a mentor who is empathetic by nature. Seek out someone you consider a "people person," and who relates well to others. You'll know they're empathetic by nature if they respond favorably to your request for mentoring. A large gregarious extroverted personality is not what matters here. Many introverts have very well-developed intrinsic judgment. The point is to find someone who is kind and compassionate.

. . .

Weak intrinsic judgment can lead others to believe (unjustly) that you are distant, cold, and uncaring. If you desire to achieve success, however, following this advice can improve your intrinsic valuations.

Within most occupations, the ability to connect with others is crucial. As a professor, an advertising executive, a salesperson, an instructor, or in any other role, you are at your most effective if you have a sense of tolerance and compassion, and are able to read and relate to others. You may even discover, after developing a new habit of intrinsic consideration *before* you act, that you really enjoy how others start reacting to you and your decisions.

Intrinsic Conceptualization—*Tolerance*

As mentioned earlier (page 44), the *conceptualization* component of intrinsic judgment manifests as *tolerance*. It determines the degree to which you orient yourself conceptually to others, and the degree to which you accept and relate to people who are not like you in some significant way.

Tolerance determines whether a person will be open-minded or closed-minded toward people who are different from him or her, and reveals how well a person is able to relate to others.

- ▸ If you have a strong ability to conceptualize intrinsically and orient yourself to others, you tend to be a tolerant person.

- ▸ If you do not have a strong conceptual orientation toward people, then often you are unaccepting and intolerant of others.

Differences among people include not only what many consider the usual disparities—age, gender, race—but also other departures, such as education, religion, politics, income, mannerisms, accent, height, hairstyle, hobbies, and so forth. Even the pace at which people work can set them apart. In essence, the differences include *anything* that makes someone different from someone else.

Tolerant people are better able to accept and even appreciate these differences, and thus are better able to interact with dissimilar people. They generally have a more agreeable disposition, as their experiences with differences in others do not naturally manifest into negativity.

People who are *intolerant* often are able to relate only to someone who is similar to them in appearance, likes and dislikes, background, and so forth. It is important to realize that associating and congregating with similar people who have similar ideas does not necessarily imply intolerance. Intolerance here is specifically associated with negativity and with illogical, indiscriminate, and arbitrary disapproval of other people who are different from you. Intolerance is an inability to orient yourself—conceptually or mentally—to others who are different.

Intolerance can prove detrimental to success, particularly as twenty-first-century workplaces—much more so than in the past—often employ a workforce that is varied in many ways. In today's world, it is likely that you will interact with people who are dissimilar to you in striking and conspicuous ways, so a strong intrinsic conceptual orientation is beneficial and can guide you toward better people judgments and decisions.

As discussed earlier (see page 51), it is very important not to confuse tolerance with a lack of moral clarity. In fact, you might well have very defined viewpoints about right and wrong, and you may be very opinionated about what you consider to be appropriate and inappropriate behaviors. Tolerance allows for that strength of opinion while also providing an ability to relate to, and understand, others' positions and behaviors that are markedly different from yours. You are intolerant if you have adopted an illogical arbitrariness to your intrinsic values and judgments, whereas you are tolerant if you are more reasoned in your intrinsic valuations. Intolerant people have trouble relating to someone who is dissimilar, without regard to how appropriate or inappropriate they consider that person's behavior to be.

I have worked with people who dismiss the importance of tolerance. After all, they ask, what difference could tolerance possibly make within the confines of a technical occupation—say, in the field of engineering, accounting, or aviation? The answer is *a lot*. Regardless of field or occupation, very little is done without interaction of people or teams of people.

Tolerance allows us to disregard irrelevant intrinsic differences that might otherwise distract us from important issues. It helps us infuse higher-quality intrinsic judgment into our decisions. Moreover, intolerant people are often distracted by frustration, stress, chaos, and inconsequentialities. Therefore, tolerant people tend to be much more successful within their workplaces.

Strong

If you have strong intrinsic conceptualization judgment, you are tolerant of people who are unlike you in some significant way: in age, gender, or race; in beliefs, education, and income; or even in pace or speed of work. You appreciate the individuality of other people. You respect, and may even embrace, the uniqueness of others. You see others as individuals first instead of considering them through the lens of gender, race, nationality, socioeconomic status, and so forth.

Strong judgment here indicates a movement toward respect and away from caricature, stereotype, bigotry, and prejudice. You possess the ability to enthusiastically embrace the differences in people and reflect openness to others, including to those who are notably different from you. If you have difficulty interacting with someone, it is not because of an arbitrary intolerance on your part. You reflect the same agreeable disposition to everyone.

Strong intrinsic conceptualization means you likely take pleasure in exploring new cultures. You derive excitement from, and are stimulated by, individuals from differing backgrounds, geographic regions, nationalities, and occupations.

Your tolerance of others should not be mistaken as acceptance of those who might engage in what you consider inappropriate or immoral acts. One can be judgmental of unethical behavior and at the same time a tolerant person. It is quite common for someone to be both tolerant *and* critical.

Very Strong

Even though highly tolerant individuals have a remarkably open mind for differences, a potential conundrum exists: They often have great difficulty with, and are extraordinarily intolerant of, intolerant people. Extremely tolerant people tend to believe intolerance is both immoral and inappropriate.

Prejudices and bigotry are at odds with well-developed tolerance, so it is commonplace for tolerant people to clash with bigoted, intolerant people. Within our corporate work, those with extremely well-developed tolerance often feel and express high levels of frustration when exposed to such individuals, which unfortunately can undermine their good judgment.

Weak

Weak conceptual intrinsic judgment indicates a predisposition to feel prejudice toward others who are different, and to view and treat others as stereotypes and caricatures. No respect is shown for individuality of expression, appearance, perspective, belief, and so forth. If your tolerance is weak, you are apt to be closed-minded toward people who differ from you, and you probably have difficulty relating to such people.

Your lack of tolerance typically manifests into sexist, bigoted, negatively judgmental, and/or harsh attitudes and opinions toward those whom you perceive as different or "other." There is an arbitrary aspect to this intolerance, as you are only able to relate to and accept people who are very similar to you.

When intolerant individuals work with people or groups of people who are dissimilar, an underlying tension is likely in play. They may argue with the others just for the sake of arguing, sometimes even willfully choosing to take the illogical or contrary position to others in the group. This inability to get along with others diminishes team efficiency and effectiveness.

Being intolerant impedes both professional and personal success. Intolerant individuals are at risk for experiencing increased stress and distraction in every human interaction they have. Even something as straightforward as a phone conversation can become problematic if, for example, the other speaker has a foreign accent. While speaking with a customer service representative to resolve a product issue, a big dose of intolerance thrown into the mix undermines the entire interaction—and can even prove quite dangerous—such as when requesting help from 911.

Fortunately, with effort, determination, and a genuine desire to improve intrinsic conceptual orientation, anyone can improve their tolerance. There is no downside to humanizing and enriching your level of tolerance—and there is much to be gained if you do so. Our predictive statistical data reveals, without equivocation, that tolerant individuals are less stressed, less distracted, more content, and more successful. If your judgment currently shows weakness in this area, here are some suggestions to improve and strengthen your tolerance.

Success Tip #1: Recognize intolerance in your past.

Intolerant attitudes and behaviors are usually learned as the result of contact with negative people and their negative opinions—often people who were authority figures during our childhood. Examine those in your past who held the most aggressive, intolerant ideas and were vocal in expressing those beliefs around you and to you—and work on rejecting their ideas.

Intolerance also grows from negative experiences—or even a single negative experience—with people who were different from us. Consider whether any such experiences may have had an impact in your life, then try to determine what might have been the reasons behind them—and whether you have made an undeserved assumption about certain groups of people as a result.

After some reflection and contemplation, make an effort to reject those ideas and generalizations. If this proves difficult for you, consider seeking help from a therapist or other professional.

Success Tip #2: Reject the intolerance around you.

Today's reality television shows promote an amazing spectacle of anger, shouting, arguments, fistfights, manipulation, lies, backstabbing, and profane, immoral, or unethical behavior—much of it rooted in nothing more than an utter, complete lack of tolerance toward others. Do not let this unfortunate trend bias you toward honoring or respecting intolerance and bad behavior. Instead, realize and reject today's cultural mindset when it glorifies and celebrates blatant, simple-minded intolerance.

Fortunately, many people are becoming aware of the need to curtail such poor behavior and actions. For example, many children's sports leagues now require that parents heed limits and exert self-control as they watch their children play. They ask that both parents and children sign a contract, promising to display appropriate behavior.

Success Tip #3: Don't judge an entire group unfairly.

Refrain from judging an entire group or class of people by the actions of a few individuals. For example, if you or someone you know has had a bad experience while interacting with people from another city or a foreign country, or from another ethnicity or background, try not to assume that all the people from that other place or group would behave similarly.

Success Tip #4: Practice open dialogue.

Whenever possible, talk openly with people who hail from different backgrounds, socioeconomic statuses, and belief systems. You may find an honest dialogue with them exhilarating and intellectually stimulating. Do not let your differences manifest arbitrarily into negativity. Practice getting along with others, and attempt to be more agreeable, more accepting, and more tolerant as every day goes by.

Success Tip #5: Honor our internal similarities whenever possible.

The majority of people have similar motivations and needs in life: good health, safety for our loved ones, basic human freedoms, a need for justice, and so forth. Remember that on the inside—in our hearts and minds—most of us are much more alike than we are on the outside.

. . .

Whether you employ one or several of these suggestions, you'll start making more sound, people-based judgments and decisions about others. And when that happens, it leads more quickly to *your* success.

Intrinsic Actualization — *Compassion*

The *actualization* component of intrinsic judgment manifests as *compassion*. It determines the degree to which you act upon your intrinsic value tendencies.

A person may have a strong conceptual orientation and understanding of what tolerance and compassion are all about—but caring is not really caring unless and until it is accompanied by demonstrable applications of compassion in real-life environments. No matter what we believe or understand conceptually, to be a truly compassionate person we must *demonstrate* our intrinsic judgment by making caring decisions and performing compassionate actions. The strength of this area of judgment indicates the likelihood that we will undertake and accomplish actual actions that show we care.

In other words: Does our ability to care and empathize move beyond *conceptual* ideas to actual *actions* of care?

Authentic caring and compassionate actions are not that difficult to recognize, both in ourselves and in others. We project ourselves—our values and judgments—into situations with which we are involved. If we are nervous and scared, we tend to project nervousness. If we are happy, we tend to project happiness. Well, we project our intrinsic values and judgments, too. And as those who genuinely care project their intrinsic values and judgments, others rather easily and quickly notice them.

The power of such projections should not be underestimated. Well-developed compassion is highly predictive of success, because most of us prefer to be around people with strong intrinsic judgment. Such individuals are more caring and compassionate—and they make the rest of us feel good about ourselves. As a result, we are apt to notice, return, and reward their compassion and caring.

Some people who are interested in workplace success and performance disregard compassion, just as they might do with tolerance. Often this is due to their predisposition to concentrate almost exclusively on the technical aspects of their job. They lump intrinsic judgments under the term *soft-side issues*—to which they assign lesser importance.

If this is a tendency that characterizes you, you are making a mistake. As previously discussed, very little is ever done without interaction with others. Wrapped up in intrinsic judgment is your ability to interact with and relate to others, empathize and sympathize, follow through with caring action, and make others feel good. It's not hard to see how such positive effects can produce personal and professional success for someone with well-developed intrinsic judgment.

Compassion also correlates to our ability to help others solve their personal, or people-related, problems. Some people have made an entire career of getting ahead by getting along! That alone will not work in some fields, such as engineering or medicine, as you need the requisite skills to build a bridge or perform a surgery. Nevertheless, the ability to empathize, and to exhibit caring and compassionate behaviors, is predictive of success, bringing with it an unexpected richness and depth of experience to everything you do, both in and out of the workplace.

If your profession depends partly on the experience of authenticity and compassion in people, as most professions do, then you need well-developed judgment in this area.

Strong

If you have strong judgment in this area, you are a caring, compassionate, and empathetic person who attracts others to you. You inspire confidence and trust, convey concern, and offer up good advice to others. You place a high value on relationships. You are a "people person"—someone with strong social skills.

You are not necessarily an extrovert, but you do have confidence in social settings. You are likely to be sacrificial of your time and energy, as you are willing to put the needs of others on par with, or ahead of, your own needs.

Usually, strong intrinsic actualization reflects a positive upbringing full of close family relationships. If this is not the case for you, and yet you have strong intrinsic judgment, you have "made peace" with and moved successfully beyond any negative circumstances of your upbringing.

If you sometimes engage in uncaring and uncompassionate behavior, this is likely caused by burnout, stress, or negative outside influences. Thus, even though your behavior at times might be similar to someone with weak intrinsic judgment, the reasons behind your uncaring behavior are vastly different. You need to work *immediately* to determine the source of your negative behavior—and do something about it. So if a friend or close colleague is influencing you in a negative way, you need to talk to them about this or limit the time you spend with that person. At the same time, stop making excuses for your uncaring behavior, because *you know better.* Mitigate the burnout, the stress, or the negative outside influences, and revive your caring and compassionate values and actions. Stress and frustration are detrimental to the use of good judgment—but they should not be considered an excuse for it.

Very Strong

If you have an exceptionally well-developed actualization component of intrinsic judgment, there is the increased likelihood that you are sometimes overly compassionate and even naïve about people. You may give others too much benefit of the doubt. As a result, others sometimes are able to take advantage of you.

Success Tip #1: Don't ignore yourself.

To combat this, be aware of your inclinations to disregard yourself and your own needs, especially if you find yourself involved with selfish, egotistical, or narcissistic individuals. Take care that you do not lose control of your compassionate side. Do not let it become a domineering, energy-zapping, self-destructive negative.

Returning to the positive, we can expect people who have very strong intrinsic judgment to know the great joy and pleasure that is associated with the glorious human virtues of compassion and empathy. In a professional sense, actions of care may kindle what is currently simply a job into a fulfilling, lifelong career. Even on a smaller scale, many of the best workplace memories and experiences are directly attributable to a kind word or a generous deed. It bears repeating: Never, ever underestimate the power of the intrinsic.

Weak

If your intrinsic actualization is weak, it is unlikely that you prioritize actions of caring, compassion, and empathy in your decision-making and behaviors. You do not go out of your way to be overtly loving or kind.

This does not necessarily make you cruel or "bad"—but without a strong intrinsic component within your decisions and actions, the cold, hard truth is that it is to be expected that others view you as aloof or detached, lacking in people skills—and perhaps even as distant or heartless.

If you lack a strong intrinsic component in your decisions and actions, the likelihood is high that your decisions and actions are uncaring and unsympathetic. This greatly increases the chances that callous acts manifest in your behaviors, and that others perceive you negatively—which will diminish your chances for success in any occupation.

Some individuals who score poorly in this indicator do not care to improve it. Indeed, you may be one of those people who lack the motivation to improve upon their compassion and empathy. However difficult and unwelcome as it may seem, if you improve this area of your judgment, the benefits will be profound. Here are some ways to start.

Success Tip #1: Perform selfless acts.

Start making an effort to do things for others without consideration for how they will pay you back. Compassion has a great deal to do with motivation—and if you can come to terms with the idea that caring actions are ends *in and of themselves*—rather than a means to something else—then you begin to develop a better appreciation for the power of compassion. If you can do this, there is a much greater chance that your actions will be authentic and genuine. Others will notice, and it is likely they will respond in kind. Yes, your actions might not be genuine at first, but sooner or later the power of the intrinsic will win you over.

Success Tip #2: Strive for self-awareness.

Seeking conscious self-awareness through contemplation, meditation, or reflection can improve intrinsic judgment and the way we interact with others.

Compassion is the result of conscious decisions and a continual monitoring of the ego. When selfish interests prevail, they diminish our connection to our inner compassion—and it is more difficult to be caring when life becomes *all about me*. Yet until we consciously think on it, we are not always aware of how much *about me* life has become, especially if we find ourselves immersed in a fast-paced, hectic, stressful world. Nevertheless, with conscious self-awareness, we can improve our intrinsic judgment and the way we interact with others.

Success Tip #3: Pay attention to what others need.

Consider that your idea of caring and compassion might deviate from what others regard as caring and compassion. You may have a desire to care, but the way you want to show care may not be the way that someone else wants care to be shown. Therefore, in many instances, compassion requires attention to detail.

In fact, merely inquiring about another's concerns is likely to be seen by others as a form of caring in itself. And it is.

Success Tip #4: Learn by example.

Learn whatever you can from any person who you feel is especially caring or compassionate. Ask such people about their philosophy or the set of values they are living by in their own life. Inquire about their motivations, their caring lifestyle, and how they are received and responded to by others. Find out what makes them who they are.

Then ask yourself what you can use from their knowledge to motivate you to act in a similar manner.

Success Tip #5: Do it for yourself.

Remind yourself that you are doing this caring action for your own good. The statistical data reveals that strong intrinsic judgment is predictive of success. So think it through and say the words, even if you have to fake it! Choose intrinsic decisions and take intrinsic actions. You just may discover you like the feedback you receive, the reactions of others, and the positive outcomes you experience.

Let the joy of intrinsic values and feelings sink in and become part of you. Appreciate them. Soon you may not have to fake it anymore. When you discover the power of compassion, you will be thankful for it for the rest of your life.

. . .

As mentioned, the *conceptualization* and *actualization* components of intrinsic judgment (see page 44) manifest as *tolerance* and *compassion*.

Tolerance has more to do with what we *understand* intrinsically, whereas compassion has more to do with what we *do* intrinsically. It is possible to have well-developed tolerance and yet still lack compassion. This means that you have a conceptually positive attitude toward people—an attitude of tolerance and respect—but do not easily actualize that attitude into actions of care and empathy.

- If your intrinsic actualization is stronger than your intrinsic conceptualization, you are likely to be good at not only understanding an intrinsic predicament but also *resolving* it.

- If your conceptual judgment is stronger than your actualization judgment, you probably tend to think more about an issue rather than deal with it directly.

- Ideally, your compassion is *equal to or stronger than* your tolerance. If that is the case, you move beyond the ideas and concepts of tolerance to exhibit the actions of caring and compassion.

Remember that within our discussion of intrinsic judgment, there is no connection or relevance to introversion or extroversion, two classic definitions of personality traits relating to sociability. You may be extremely shy and introverted, and also extremely caring and compassionate, very much able to connect with others intrinsically. To be a caring person you must have strong intrinsic judgment, and whether you tend to be introverted, extroverted, or some combination of each plays no role. Your personality type is irrelevant to success.

. . .

Very few individuals find their desired level of success if they don't understand and manifest the human factor. Tolerance and compassion will advance your relationships with your peers, subordinates, and superiors alike. The understanding of compassion toward others can augment your success. Always remember, though, that caring is not actually caring unless it is associated with genuine *actions* of care.

The data reveals, unquestionably, that strengthening your intrinsic judgment will lead to improved decisions and actions—and greater chances of success.

The first time I ever spoke to Charlie was on the telephone. He had completed our judgment assessment, and I was asked to interpret his scores for him. Charlie, who was unknown to me at the time but a good friend to my partners, had expressed an interest in our work with judgment. Charlie had retired and didn't need to work, but nevertheless he had offered to help in any way he could.

When I called Charlie, he answered his cell phone while driving down the interstate. I knew that the interpretation of his scores would be more meaningful if Charlie could view the report, which he obviously could not do while driving, so I offered to call back later. Since I had called Charlie, however, and he knew it was a convenient time for me, he still insisted that now would be a good time for us to talk.

But first, before we discussed his judgment scores, Charlie wanted to know about me. He asked about my life story, how I knew my partners, how I got into the work with judgment, my family history, and such. When he found out that I was a recently retired U.S. Navy fighter pilot, he began to refer to me as "Captain."

Continued

I thanked him for that, but told him I'd retired after twenty years of military service as Commander, one rank below Navy Captain.

"Never mind all that," he said, and to this day he calls me "Captain."

After about fifteen minutes of Charlie asking me about me, we finally got into the interpretation of his scores. There he was, driving down the interstate, doing his best to pay attention as I explained to him the details of his value structure.

I immediately liked Charlie. He was kind and personable, and made me feel good. When at last I met him in person, at a business luncheon with my partners, he instantly smiled and shook my hand. He made it clear that he was genuinely glad to finally meet me and put a face to the voice he had heard over the phone.

Then Charlie, my partners, and I proceeded to our table, located at the far end of a large room. As Charlie made his way across the room, just about every single person stopped him, smiled, and wanted to speak. I've never seen anyone "work" a crowd like Charlie, and I use that term in a very positive light here because they all *wanted* to speak to him. Several began to stand up, but Charlie insisted again and again that they keep their seats, so as not to disturb their lunch. Charlie knew everyone, and everyone knew Charlie—and more important, Charlie liked everyone, and everyone liked Charlie.

During our lunch I asked Charlie how he knew so many people. He replied that he was blessed to have had the opportunity to develop so many wonderful relationships.

For the next several months, busy with my own work, I didn't think much more about Charlie. Through my partners, however, I learned that he was helping us arrange meetings with several potentially lucrative clients. As I got to know him better, it became obvious to me that Charlie helps for no other reason than because he wants to help.

I shouldn't have been surprised when, later that year, my wife and I received a very nice Christmas present and personal note from Charlie. This man, who knew everybody and whom everybody knew, took the time to send holiday cheer to someone he had known for only a few months—someone he had met in person only once. (Charlie's thoughtful Christmas tradition, by the way, continues to this day.)

After Charlie had arranged several high-level introductions for us, I finally asked my one of my partners, "Who is this guy Charlie? What is his story?"

"Oh, I thought you knew," my partner replied. "He's Charlie Price, the founder of Price/McNabb." Charlie's former company is a long-standing regional advertising and public relations agency—one of the most successful in the United States. Under him, the company acquired hundreds of clients, including many blue chip national accounts like Milliken, McDonald's, Nucor, Starbucks, and Biltmore Estate, with revenues in the hundreds of millions of dollars. "A few years ago he sold his company and retired," my partner continued. "He doesn't need the work. He helps us just because he is a nice guy. That's Charlie."

Over the course of Charlie's career he has won numerous awards and accolades. Of note, in 1988, he was the first inductee into the North Carolina Journalism Hall of Fame for Advertising, and in 2012, he received a Lifetime Achievement Award from the American Advertising Federation.

And to this day, when Charlie sees me, he smiles and says, "Hello, Captain."

TRUTH #2: EXTRINSIC JUDGMENT

It started small, on May 30, 1982, and at the time, not a single person in the world realized it. Nevertheless, it had started, and it would continue for years. And though it started small, it would eventually become a very big deal. Even so, until it finally happened—or at least until shortly before it happened, when suddenly it seemed the whole world was watching—he continually downplayed it. After all, he was just following the lessons he had been taught by his father: *Work hard. Do your best. Always give one hundred percent. Be dependable. Respect the job.*

Those were the sorts of things his father had told him—and taught him—his entire life. As an adult, he readily acknowledged the influence of his father, who had been born back in 1935. He said he felt lucky because the values so ingrained in those from his father's generation were now ingrained in him, too.

Possibly what he believed to be the most important lesson of all was his understanding of *the value and importance of work*. To him, working hard wasn't going above and beyond. Working hard is just what you do.

And so it was, and so it continued.

Continued

Then, over thirteen years later, on September 6, 1995, it happened: He broke Lou Gehrig's record.

The record had stood for almost fifty years. It fell when Manny Alexander, second baseman for the Baltimore Orioles, made the third out in the top of the fifth inning (making the game official). At that moment, Cal Ripken Jr. became baseball's new "Iron Man." Ripken now held the record for the most consecutive baseball games ever played: 2,131.

However, Ripken wasn't done yet. He played in consecutive games for another three years—a total of 2,632—before he voluntarily ended his streak on September 19, 1998, having worked straight for over sixteen years without ever missing a single game.[1]

Even though many Americans today hold values similar to those handed down from Cal Ripken's father's generation, many don't. They lack a high level of intensity with respect to the value of work. Nevertheless, even people who don't have a deep-seated respect and commitment to the value of work in themselves are more than likely able to appreciate a strong work ethic when they see it in someone else.

And everyone saw it in Cal Ripken Jr.

Play was paused when Ripken officially broke the record. He trotted over and acknowledged his family. He tipped his cap to the fans. A few minutes later he sat down, ready for play to resume. He seemed humbled and almost embarrassed by all the applause and commotion. After all, he was just doing his job.

But the fans would have none of it. At six minutes the cheering was still going strong. Ripken took several more curtain calls, stepping out of the dugout to thank the fans, and at one point touching his heart to show his appreciation.

Then he sat down again.

---

1   C. Ripken Jr. and M. Bryan, *The Only Way I Know* (New York: Penguin Books 1997), chapter 18.

But the cheering continued.

At nine minutes he took another curtain call.

The shouting continued, "We want Cal! We want Cal!"

At ten minutes, and with no sign of the fans letting up, his team-mates practically threw him out of the dugout, telling him to take a lap. He started off at a trot, as if he was thankful but wanted to downplay his achievement, hustle around the stadium, and get back to the game. Remember, to him, he was just doing his job.

Finally, when he was about halfway around the field, with the entire stadium cheering, it seemed to sink in for him. He started to recognize the impact that his record had on others. He slowed down and began shaking the hands of fans and waving to the crowd.

Everyone at the stadium—including the opposing dugout as well as the millions watching on television—appreciated Cal Ripken's work ethic and what he had achieved.

After no less than twenty-two minutes and fifteen seconds, the crowd finally settled down, and play resumed.

Extrinsic judgment is related to process, tasks, and work. Often referred to as "global extrinsic," "global E," or "E-judgment," it represents the second of the three broad areas of judgment, and our second global truth.

E-judgment is all about the completion of tasks. It is your tactical judgment, your "mission orientation." Extrinsic judgment is your process-, procedure-, and work-related judgment. It represents your judgment regarding all the "things" and "details" in your work and in your life activities.

The *conceptualization* and *actualization* components of extrinsic judgment (see pages 31 to 34) manifest as *trainability* and *dependability*.

Extrinsic judgment gives you the ability to make progress on an assignment or duty, and to advance a work process from point A to point B, moving toward its conclusion efficiently, effectively, and even economically. To accomplish work with such consistency, you must be *dependable*—a large component of extrinsic judgment.

Well-developed extrinsic judgment is highly predictive of success within the workplace. The great majority of occupations require that you perform and complete tasks—from start to finish—precisely and accurately. Extrinsic judgment provides that very ability to get things done.

Extrinsic judgment also relates to work ethic. The phrase *work ethic* often becomes lost in cliché or platitude. Here, however—specifically within the context of success—a *strong work ethic* refers to someone who understands the importance of work; who is trainable and dependable, with a quick learning curve; and who will be where they are supposed to be, when they are supposed to be there, doing what they are supposed to be doing (working!) with vigor. It is almost synonymous with extrinsic judgment.

Dependability, a strong work ethic, and the ability to accomplish the tasks at hand are among the top tier of characteristics employers ordinarily seek in their employees. Most employers maintain that a strong work ethic is a prerequisite for employment—an essential, indispensable characteristic—and it is quite common for employers to quickly terminate those who exhibit poor extrinsic judgment.

But there's more to it than that. A sizable percentage of our population is of the opinion that extrinsic judgment transcends far beyond the mere ability to complete tasks or assignments. They believe that extrinsic judgment is an obligatory and essential trait of a virtuous and honorable person. The predominance of such phrases and concepts as the *Protestant work ethic*, considered by some the primary defining characteristic of character and integrity, can be traced back many generations.

We might be tempted to develop opinions and ideas regarding a person's strength of extrinsic judgment based solely on his or her outward style—for example, deciding someone is a "lazy bum" or a "hard worker" based on not much more than the person's attire and appearance. But tens of thousands of judgment assessments reveal that extrinsic judgment is generally unrelated solely to appearance or style. People develop a particular "look" for a number of reasons—to reflect their desire or need to project a unique or distinctive appearance, to indicate regional or culturally based attire, to fit a work-related dress code, or simply to please themselves. It would be a big mistake to judge someone on whether their outward appearance consists of conservative, suit-and-tie business attire; tattoos, piercings, leather pants, and spiked purple hair; or cowboy boots, hat, jeans, and spurs.

In fact, contrary to general opinion, strong extrinsic judgment is often lurking in seemingly unlikely places—or *appearances*. For example, compare the stereotype of a loud, long-haired, tattooed, rock-and-roll musician with that of an executive in a three-piece suit. Your sensibilities might lead you to the conclusion that one of these individuals has weak extrinsic judgment and the other has strong extrinsic judgment, but that assumption isn't necessarily true. To extrinsically stereotype an individual based solely on their style or appearance is incorrect and often inaccurate. As for the rock star and the executive, either, neither, or both may have strong, or weak, extrinsic judgment.

Still, you should be aware that if you sport an unconventional or unusual style, some people will immediately draw arbitrary conclusions about your judgments, particularly your extrinsic judgments—your work ethic. This may be at least a temporary setback to your success.

In contrast to differences in appearance, our consulting business gained some insight on E-judgment through the study of *generational* differences. When we examined aggregate extrinsic judgment scores for those who have taken our assessment, we discerned extrinsic tendencies specific to various generations.

We observed weaker overall extrinsic judgment in the current generation of young adults (ages eighteen to twenty-eight) who have recently entered, or will soon enter, the workforce, compared with previous generations who entered the workforce in the 1970s, 1980s, and 1990s. As a whole, the older generations started off by placing more value on work—and thus on dependability, reliability, and work ethic—than younger generations do right now.

Do not take this as an indictment of an entire generation. While our findings do address an observation about overall generational strengths when it comes to extrinsic judgment, stereotyping specific individuals due to age is incorrect and counterproductive. Everyone is an individual, and everyone is unique. Many young adults have incredibly strong extrinsic judgment, just as many older adults display incredibly weak extrinsic judgment. Only behavior and actions—and not age, style, or appearance—can reveal whether an individual has well-developed tactical judgment.

Strong

Strong extrinsic judgment is indicative of dependability, reliability, and a solid work ethic. You understand the importance of work and of the completion of tasks and duties. You are considered a go-to type of person with a strong aptitude for processes and procedures. You adapt to new tasks and skills on a quick learning curve.

Strong E-judgment brings an effective tactical and mission orientation. You have a desire for accomplishment on the job, and you are able to move a process forward, from start to finish. You are adept at completing a high volume of assignments and undertakings, effectively and proficiently.

You have a penchant for details and lists, and you derive pleasure from the completion of tasks. Perhaps when you have already completed a task that was not on your list, you typically add it to your list so that you can mark it complete. This is due to your strong extrinsic judgment, which derives pleasure from the completion of tasks.

You tend not to be overwhelmed even if subjected to a plethora of minutiae, charts, graphs, data, and so forth. You are able to orient yourself quickly in the workplace and projects at hand. More often than not, you enjoy engrossing yourself in the specifics, details, and particulars of your work. Occupations that are awash in details, facts and figures—accountants, statisticians, engineers, architects and builders, reporters—are suitable for those with well-developed extrinsic judgment.

You clearly know the difference between being sick and feeling puny, and unless you are truly sick, you will be at work. Arbitrarily missing work makes you very uncomfortable, and is in stark contrast to your value structure.

In addition to dependability and reliability, your strong work ethic reflects a tendency for hands-on execution, and you are a quick study of the work environment. If you are adequately trained in your profession, and you possess the specific skills necessary for your job, your well-developed extrinsic judgment provides a tremendous, substantial boost toward your success.

Very Strong

If you have particularly strong extrinsic judgment, being reliable, dependable, and steadfast is much more profound, philosophical, and intense than merely exhibiting certain characteristics. Instead, this is part of *who you are*. As a result, you may clash—possibly severely—with those who display weaker extrinsic judgment, as they tend to be lackadaisical and unreliable in their approach to their work.

It may be impossible for you to coexist well with such individuals. No matter how much effort you put forth, you still may have difficulty understanding and relating to someone with the characteristics of poor extrinsic judgment: undependability, unreliability, and a lazy attitude toward work. If your difficulty in relating turns into frustration, actual conflicts may follow.

The frustration and conflicts that often arise between individuals of differing judgment strengths can greatly undermine the individual with strong judgment. Therefore, if you have strong extrinsic judgment, be careful. Guard and protect your innate work ethic, and do not allow frustration to override your good sense.

Another potential pitfall of strong extrinsic judgment is that you may become a workaholic—if you are not one already. Particularly with exceptionally well-developed extrinsic judgment, you may allow work to hijack your life, which can undermine your success. There is quite a difference, after all, between a *hard worker* and a *workaholic*.

If you desire success, you should be all about hard work, dependability, and fostering a strong work ethic. However, if you allow extrinsic judgment to excessively dominate your value structure—the way in which you assign value—it may be to the detriment of your overall quality of life. This can diminish your chances to be truly successful.

There are times, of course, when work should take priority over personal issues. However, if the domination of work is left unchecked and becomes permanent, without limits or constraints, you may develop destructive behaviors, such as the inability to do the following:

- Say no to work

- Enjoy time spent outside of work

- Go home at a reasonable hour

You also might be at risk of letting your exceptionally strong extrinsic values manifest into micromanaging behaviors—something that is rather common among those with exceptional, very strong E-judgment. This can become more and more of an issue for you, especially as you move further up the career ladder.

Consider the following guidance to ensure your E-judgment doesn't turn into a problem for you, both personally and professionally.

Success Tip #1: Don't be a taskmaster.

If you manage others, avoid the tendency to become the proverbial domineering taskmaster. Make sure that you are capable of delegating tasks to others, if appropriate. When applicable, allow yourself to "turn loose" of responsibilities. Learn to depend on others in your workplace. If you do not, others may view you negatively, which can quickly lead to frustration and stress and lower the performance of your team.

Success Tip #2: Lighten up!

Keep in mind that if your extrinsic judgment is (1) highly developed and (2) dominates your other areas of judgment, the emphasis you place on the extrinsic is likely much greater than most other people's. Although it may seem like it to you, someone who doesn't quite share your very well-defined extrinsic sensibilities is not necessarily entirely undependable or lacking completely in work ethic. Occasionally you may need to lighten up. Start by placing a little well-deserved trust in someone who clearly deserves it. Make sure that you bring the intrinsic into your decisions and actions (discussed starting on page 47) as well as the systemic, to be discussed in the next section (starting on page 111).

Easing up a bit on others is not the same as making an excuse or justifying laziness or undependability, but is simply a reminder that someone can be a very hard worker without being a workaholic like you—which leads us to the next bit of advice.

Success Tip #3: Know the difference between a workaholic and a hard worker.

Our data clearly indicates that those assessments that show more parity in their valuations and judgments are more successful. Among individuals whose extrinsic score is both highly developed *and* stronger than their intrinsic and systemic scores by a factor of two or more, approximately twenty-five percent struggle with mid-management and higher-level executive positions, primarily because of the way they treat their subordinates. These individuals grapple with understanding the difference between a committed, hardworking individual who values work, and a workaholic.

Knowing the difference is crucial to your success. For someone who is destructively extrinsic dominant, work-first-and-only habits can lead to crossing the line between a few late nights at work to finish a crucial project, and neglecting one's personal life entirely for no significant gain in one's working life.

In the trade-off between work and non-work, there comes a point at which success is not enhanced, but hindered. The damage to a person's success occurs when problems or challenges outside of working hours go unmanaged and become overwhelming, as the workaholic is either oblivious to or deliberately ignoring them. These issues might include

- Lack of adequate rest or medical care
- Neglect or abuse in personal relationships
- Mismanagement of finances (common among extremely E-dominant individuals)

However, any number of other issues might compound to the point of interference with the work itself, not to mention the individual's life.

Success Tip #4: Consider a variety of opinions and approaches.

For many occupations, strong extrinsic judgment is vital, particularly related to processes, procedures, tasks, and a strong work ethic. Extrinsic disagreement and conflict within the work environment may arise if strong-willed individuals differ on a particular course of action. Appreciate that the nature of success may require extrinsic disagreements and differing opinions. This type of give-and-take is acceptable in most workplaces, and perhaps even desired—when it is kept under control. Politely and professionally verifying, substantiating, questioning, or even opposing work-related decisions is part of the nature of success.

Extreme extrinsic conflict within the workplace, however, is unacceptable. It often leads to public displays of poor judgment, or to lapses and blunders in safety by individuals who should know better. These are the very same people who—if they were not experiencing great frustration or difficulty in understanding those workers who aren't as committed as they are, or who simply have a different tactical approach—would normally use outstanding judgment and be exceptional employees.

In many cases, multiple paths or courses of action are acceptable for the safe, effective, and efficient completion of your duties. Do not let strong extrinsic judgment lead you to a potentially erroneous decision or an angry conflict with someone for not being in total lockstep agreement with you. If you cling to the notion that one—*and only one*—specific course of action is acceptable, and all others are unacceptable, you will be missing out on countless opportunities to expand your understanding and increase your personal and professional success, not to mention sending your frustration and stress through the roof.

Moderate

If you have moderately strong E-judgment and you are challenged with a tactical problem, your solution will be acceptable *as long as the sun is shining and birds are chirping.* If the tactical judgment demands are slightly more complex, however, your extrinsic judgment strength may not be adequate.

A situation that is chaotic, urgent, complex, and stressful requires a higher degree of extrinsic judgment; without it, you will struggle, or even fail, to make effective decisions. The unfortunate truth is that rarely are the sun shining and the birds chirping during moments of high-level, important decision-making.

Moderately developed E-judgment is considered marginal for intense decision-making situations, including most mid- and executive-level occupations and many judgmentally demanding entry-level jobs. For example, midlevel and executive business managers commonly contend with broken equipment, employee issues, defective products, and so forth—stressful issues indeed. But corporate employees aren't the only ones who suffer without an infusion of extrinsic evaluative judgment. Physical trainers must be able to work with moody or demanding clients as well as those who have health issues that affect them when they exercise. Other judgmentally demanding jobs, such as construction laborer and grocery store cashier, can be overwhelming when task completion is not a forte. Those who have only average scores in extrinsic judgment may struggle with making the proper decisions and finding the best solutions.

Success Tip #1: Seek specific instructions.

Make sure that when you are assigned new tasks and procedures, you request and receive precise, detailed directions and instructions. The completion of any work can be much, much simpler if you only need to follow the instructions rather than use your extrinsic judgment to figure it out.

Success Tip #2: Know any routine work procedures completely and entirely.

Of course everyone should know the proper everyday procedures involved in their job, but this is true even more so for those with only moderately strong extrinsic judgment. Within any occupation, knowing the procedures inside and out will help reduce your dependence on your extrinsic judgment. Again, placing slightly more emphasis on proper procedures rather than only your judgment may help guide you toward more satisfactory completion of your work.

Be cognizant that if your intrinsic judgment dominates your extrinsic, you might be spending too much time and energy on *getting along* and not enough time and energy on *getting things done*. This is a very common issue for teams with overall strong intrinsic judgment and yet moderate or weak extrinsic judgment.

Weak

If your extrinsic judgment is weak, you wrestle with the accomplishment of tasks, jobs, and assignments. Handling all the details and fully completing work is a struggle.

For those who exhibit weak (or even moderate) extrinsic judgment, the details of work might seem rather petty—perhaps even inconsequential.

As a result of this attitude, however, both the execution and the delivery of your work are poor—chances are that someone along the way has advised you of this. You tend to miss work deadlines, and more than once you have failed to hand in requested projects, research, or reports on time.

People who show weakness in extrinsic judgment do not place a high value on the key attributes of dependability and reliability, and this is reflected in their work performance. This diminishes their chances for higher levels of success.

Someone may have a pleasant demeanor, wonderful talents and skills, and friendly relations with his or her workmates, but without strong extrinsic judgment, this person will not be taken seriously within most work environments. People with weak E-judgment are the ones often described as "a nice guy (or girl) who has lots of good ideas but never seems to get anything done." This typically includes

- Procrastinators
- Underachievers
- People with "potential" (but no clear progress)
- People who lack motivation

People with weak extrinsic judgment may find themselves passed over for promotions or not given a chance to advance at work because they are perceived as putting forth less effort.

Someone who does not comprehend the value of the details of work, or the value of striving to complete tasks—or who does not exert the effort needed to live up to the expectations of his or her workplace—is a consistent disappointment to others. And this attitude usually stunts that person's success.

Individuals who are very successful in a given profession view a lack of dependability in others as a huge negative. They expect precision and reliability in their employees and coworkers. People with well-developed extrinsic judgment quickly lose patience with those who take too long or fail to accomplish the task at hand. They become quite frustrated when confronted with signs of a poor work ethic in colleagues, team members, or partners.

Most people are able to improve the *conceptualization* component (trainability) of extrinsic judgment by gaining additional experience in the workplace. Unfortunately, they may find it difficult to improve the *actualization* component (dependability). Our data has revealed that if an individual, by the time he or she is a young adult, does not value being dependable and reliable, and fails to prioritize the importance of the proper completion of work and tasks, that person will have difficulty making substantial improvements.

However, even though extrinsic actualization is difficult to improve, it is not impossible. So, if you desire success as a business person, a home-maker, an entrepreneur, an aviator, an engineer, a college student, or what-ever your choose, you should spend a great deal of effort to develop your extrinsic judgment, because weak E-judgment is seriously detrimental to the task, process, and procedural environment of most work, and to your overall success. You can start by exploring our practical suggestions for improving your dependability and work ethic, on pages 101 to 109.

First, however, let's take a close look at how to improve the concep-tual component of extrinsic judgment: trainability.

Extrinsic Conceptualization — *Trainability*

The *conceptualization* component of extrinsic judgment manifests as *trainability*. It determines the degree to which you understand practical and pragmatic processes, tasks, and projects, and the general dynamics of a work environment. (For a review of conceptualization and actualiza-tion, see pages 31 to 34.)

Trainability is a measure of your ability to understand the nature of processes; your capacity to understand your work; and your skill at ori-enting yourself and "fitting into" a workplace or project.

If you are trainable, you learn the ropes quickly. Thanks to your short learning curve, you quickly become proficient and easily master new or recurrent training. Your colleagues and superiors perceive you as coachable and quick to pick things up.

Conversely, if you are weak in this area, you have difficulty picking up the necessary skills and knowledge. It takes you a while to get the hang of whatever is being asked of you at work—or maybe you just don't think the details are all that important.

That said, people who have an understanding of work and its demands often assume that everyone else understands the nature of work too. However, this is just not true. A stunningly high percentage of young adults moving into the workplace today have poor judgment in this area. Many do not understand work on a fundamental level, and many do not have an aptitude for it.

This is a generational shift. In previous generations, more people worked out of necessity, whether in the form of chores throughout their youth or in an actual job as an adult. But many young adults today are inexperienced in the ways of work, whether in the form of responsibilities around the house or a paying job; subsequently, they have less of an understanding of what it takes to complete the necessary tasks and duties. Such individuals tend to be less trainable.

In contrast, those young adults who are brought up doing chores—from raking the leaves to setting the dinner table to taking out the trash—have an upbringing that contributes to their extrinsic conceptual orientation and enhances their trainability. At the risk of stating the obvious, work—whether formal or informal—contributes to an individual's orientation in, or understanding of, the nature of work. We know this intuitively, and the assessment data bears this out overwhelmingly.

Doing work and chores is important because tasks help develop our sense of the importance of being responsible, and of the necessity to complete assigned tasks and duties—all concepts explicitly important to success. Those who, as a child or young adult, experienced either formal or informal work generally score much better in this area, and tend to be more trainable when they enter the adult workplace.

Our data also suggests that schooling is not necessarily a substitute for work, and thus does not automatically impart trainability. A sizable percentage of students (twenty-five to thirty-five percent and growing) do not view schoolwork as work, and therefore their education does not contribute notably to their trainability. Moreover, there is a vast difference between the knowledge of medicine, engineering, law, the construction trades, homemaking, or whatnot—and the actual implementation of it.

For example, to be a pilot, you must complete the appropriate ground school and, at a minimum, pass the FAA Private Pilot exam. However, there is little correlation between being able to pass an FAA aviation knowledge test and trainability in the cockpit. This scenario can be applied to most any occupation: For example, it's one thing to read about CPR technique and pass the written exam, but it's quite another thing to actually learn CPR well enough to apply it effectively as an emergency medical technician.

Generally, those individuals who have had jobs or internships while attending school score better in extrinsic conceptualization than do those who lacked any sort of work experience during their schooling. That is, recent graduates with work experience already under their belt typically are more trainable and experience a shorter learning curve when they enter the workplace.

Our data shows that it is also common for the less educated laborer at the construction site or the line boy at the local airport to be more trainable at any future job than the highly educated individual who lacks work experience. Education is important, and in many occupations it is a prerequisite for employment. Nevertheless, education alone is often not a substitute for hands-on experience. There is just no better substitute than actual work experience to prepare for the rigors of a high-intensity, demanding workplace environment.

Remember, it is tremendously important not only to *do* work, but to *understand* work—to have a general grasp of what work is all about, so that when work is performed, it is done competently, efficiently, and effectively.

The following story is about a client with (1) a weak extrinsic conceptual orientation, (2) an otherwise strong value structure, and (3) poor initial work performance.

After graduating with high honors from college, Dan immediately sought out a demanding, fast-paced "dream job" with a real opportunity for advancement in his chosen field of finance. During a job interview, Dan displayed ambition, enthusiasm, and high expectations, and he was personable and likable. A well-known banking company hired him without reservation. However, shortly afterward, Dan's dream job became a nightmare for him.

He missed deadlines and follow-ups.

He failed to fill out required customer applications.

He did not run some of the required financial reports.

He entered incorrect data and made numerous mistakes on other reports.

Dan was a nice guy. Everybody liked him! But as to his understanding of the requirements of his job, he was an abject failure. His notion of work was out of sync with the nature and requirements of authentic work.

Dan failed at his first job because he was not prepared for the work. He left that first job and gained experience in a much less demanding job—still in his chosen field of finance, as a clerk for a more experienced finance manager.

Two years later, Dan was hired back into his dream job.

This time, his performance was outstanding.

Dan's success now was not because he had acquired more intellect or specific job skills; he still possessed the same skills, the same intellect. Nor was it because his job was less demanding. The reason Dan excelled the second time around was that now he had a much better orientation toward work and tasks. The concept of work now made sense to Dan because of the experience he gained in his less-demanding job.

Strong

If you exhibit strength in this area of judgment, your high trainability and ability to conceptually grasp new processes, tasks, and the nature of work itself save you and your employer both time and money. You develop into a competent employee more quickly, and prove quite capable of finding your way around a workplace without constant monitoring or supervision. Training for you is much less onerous, and you generally have a positive disposition when faced with the concept of being taught.

You tend to feel at ease in the workplace, too. Over time, you relate well to any new information that comes in, such as the latest innovations associated with technically advanced machinery.

Many occupations, such as medicine, accounting and engineering, ask that their workforce always be learning. People in such fields frequently need to go back to school to take courses or go through new training to learn about the latest advances. If you're involved in the everlasting endeavor of learning, your well-developed extrinsic conceptual orientation is immensely helpful.

Moreover, groundbreaking, state-of-the-art technologies tend to excite and inspire you rather than frighten you. Your tactical orientation enhances your ability to grasp the multiplicity and complexity of new processes and procedures in your field. If you work in the business world, your innate comprehension of what truly matters in your field makes others more inclined to give you a boost up the corporate ladder.

Your well-developed extrinsic conceptualization allows you to see practical and process-oriented solutions to problems, and you are generally at ease in the workplace. You possess a clear understanding of work processes, and you have a natural ability to formulate those processes efficiently and effectively.

You tend to be resourceful because you have a better understanding of the necessity of work and the importance of the proper completion of tasks. A strong extrinsic conceptual orientation is associated more with problem resolution than with excuse-making.

Very Strong

Since you easily comprehend and grasp work processes, and you have a short learning curve, it may seem odd to you when someone else—perhaps a very intellectual or a very friendly person—is unable to acclimate to tasks and responsibilities as easily and as quickly as you do. This may lead to frustration for you (and for them, too). Be wary about letting this lead to diminished judgment on your part. Should you encounter someone with relatively weaker trainability, or who might understand work but just not as fast as you do, do not allow the difference to frustrate you.

Nevertheless, celebrate the fact that you are highly trainable. You are adept at coming up with resolutions to problems, and at figuring out the most efficient, effective techniques and methods to arrive at the conclusions. With your very strong tactical orientation, you comprehend work, tasks, duties, and responsibilities quicker than most.

Weak

If you are weak in this area, you have a slow learning curve and typically require a lot of hands-on training and supervision. It takes you somewhat longer to comprehend work, processes, and tasks, and it is likely that you struggle to keep up with others who naturally comprehend such duties. Often associated with weak judgment here is a naïveté of work environments of any kind: You are inclined to feel ill at ease, awkward, and somewhat uncomfortable with the very notion of assignments, projects, deadlines, and other work-related responsibilities.

One possible explanation for this is a lack of hands-on experience with work in the past. You may have spent much of your time in school or in job *preparation* rather than in actual job *participation*. Once you engage in actual work, however, you can improve upon your judgment here—and sometimes rather quickly.

Many individuals, particularly older generations of Americans, may have had their first paying job as young as the age of eight. Depending on the opportunities available, a young child could get paying work shining shoes in the city, delivering papers in the suburbs, selling eggs or produce at a roadside stand, mowing lawns, picking fruit, tending to livestock, and so on. People currently in their forties and fifties may remember their first paying jobs from their preteen years: babysitting, dog-walking, car-washing, selling door-to-door, raking leaves, painting houses. Those jobs helped instill strong extrinsic judgment.

Today many parents seek to provide their children with a life that is "easier" than their own. Their intentions are admirable, yes, but they often produce an unfortunate, unforeseen result: High numbers of young adults entering the workforce are lacking in practical work experience, so they lack understanding of what work is all about. In fact, it is downright astonishing how many young adults entering the workplace today show weakness in this area of judgment. If this describes your circumstance, all hope is not lost. Unlike some areas of your value structure that are difficult to improve, trainability is rather acute in its movement once you start working in a specific field—and usually improves substantially.

For example, say you are a student aviator who lacks work experience and scores poorly in extrinsic conceptualization. You will find that as you gain actual hands-on experience as a pilot, you will not only develop specific piloting skills and knowledge, but also gain an enhanced conceptual orientation of the *work* of flying. Whatever your chosen field, hands-on experience will help you become more effective and efficient with the details and nuances—and in all likelihood, your extrinsic orientation will improve quickly.

If you are not lacking in actual workplace experience and yet are weak in this area, you should consider some of the following ideas and suggestions.

Success Tip #1: Make a conscious effort to learn the details of your job.

Watch the movements of fellow workers, particularly those who seem very mission-oriented, as they go about their work duties. Observe not only *what* their jobs are, but also *how* they go about doing their jobs, including routines and specific task flows. Listen to your coworkers as they explain the details of what they are doing and how they do it. Then, ask them *why* they do it.

Consider asking for a hands-on demonstration, and pay extra-close attention to the details of what they do and how. It would be helpful to work with an exceptionally patient and easygoing colleague, as you will be generally slower to catch on to the multitude of details and the complexity of tasks. Do not let this reality trouble you. With experience, your extrinsic orientation will improve.

Success Tip #2: Let visualization be your guide.

In your mind, construct a mental map of the layout of your work environment, so that even with your eyes closed, you know the location of every piece of equipment—every switch, knob, dial, and instrument. Visualization is a great aid that allows you to familiarize with your workplace and any machinery, and it will prove especially helpful to you during periods of high stress. Your mental map helps you learn the flow of your work.

Aviators do this by engaging in "hangar flying," where they sit with other pilots and discuss the details of flying, or even envision the details, activities, movements, flow, and scan for each particular segment of a flight. You can do this in your own work environment too.

Success Tip #3: Practice, practice, practice.

People who excel in their field and rise to the top of their industry develop ways to stay sharp, and that usually involves some form of practice. Avail yourself of training and practice, and then more training and more practice. Such activities will improve your conceptual orientation of tasks and processes. Pilots have simulator software or flying video games to test their reactions and evaluate their performance. Perhaps something similar exists for you in your line of work.

Success Tip #4: Don't be afraid to ask questions.

It may be a cliché, but *Do not be afraid to ask questions* is something you can really hang your cap on. Engage as often as you can with more experienced workers—yes, the old-timers. They are an invaluable source of advice. Try to go beyond the intrinsic valuations of why they like or don't like their job, and instead inquire about the minutiae of work. No matter what your occupation, there are old-timers who can help.

Success Tip #5: Understand your environment.

Learn not only the specifics of each procedure at work, but come to an understanding of the workforce environment where you utilize those procedures. Remember, you want to improve your overall comprehension of what work is all about. This will help you better comprehend the daily workflow; when and where particular procedures are most necessary; and what you should do when you encounter unusual, stressful, or unexpected circumstances.

. . .

Trainability is much more than merely learning the steps of a process. Being more trainable allows you to grasp the overall work environment better; improves your job performance and work aptitude; allows you to better comprehend appropriate workflows; and leads you to become a more productive, efficient, effective, and ultimately more valued employee or worker in your chosen field.

Extrinsic Actualization—*Dependability*

The *actualization* component of extrinsic judgment manifests as *dependability*. It determines the strength of your work ethic, your sense of responsibility, and your dependability—not as concepts or ideas, but as real, tangible actions.

Remember, if your extrinsic *conceptual* judgment is strong, you are highly trainable. Here we go beyond conceptualization to *actualization—*dependability. (For a review of conceptualization and actualization, see pages 31 to 34.) From the point of view of most employers, dependability ranks as one of the most desired character traits of an employee—and, as such, a strong score in this area of judgment is vital to your professional success.

Whereas the conceptual component of extrinsic judgment (trainability) examines your orientation to the external world, the actualization component (dependability) examines whether or not you are likely to translate your extrinsic orientation into real, demonstrable actions, revealing true dependability and reliability.

Extrinsic actualization moves beyond the understanding of work processes to the fulfillment and execution of the work itself. It addresses the following questions:

▸ Will you actually get your work done?

▸ Will you be dependable in carrying out your work activities?

The answer depends on the strength of your judgment in this area. In its simplest terms, dependability (extrinsic actualization) can be viewed as a measure of the likelihood that you will be where you are supposed to be, when you are supposed to be there, doing what you are supposed to be doing—and doing it effectively at that.

The presence of dependability in your judgment has great impact on your professional reputation. Employers need employees who are consistently dependable in their activities, so make sure that *you are that person.* In most work settings and for most employers, the importance of dependability is unmistakable, and a lack of dependability is entirely unacceptable.

This area of judgment also determines the degree to which you are able to help others solve practical problems in the workplace.

There are individuals who have a reputation for being dependable and reliable—and those who do not. For some people, it is almost *expected* that they will miss work or deadlines, or fail to finish tasks or projects. This type of behavior is considered their norm, and there is tacit acknowledgment among their peers that this is simply who they are. Likewise, there are individuals who miss work or a deadline only if something is terribly wrong—an emergency or a crisis—and their peers know this.

Be open-minded to what your behavior reveals about your work ethic and dependability, even if you are not pleased with the results. However, unlike extrinsic conceptualization (trainability), which can improve rather quickly, poor extrinsic actualization (dependability) is often quite difficult to improve. Our data shows that adults who are weak in this area seem to have a difficult time becoming more dependable. Often this area of judgment seems altogether immovable, and very difficult to improve, in the habitually undependable individual. However, dependability *can* be improved, and if yours is weak it *must* be improved. Later I'll show you how.

Strong

Strong extrinsic actualization—what we often call *work ethic*—is vitally important in most business environments.

Possessing this kind of strong judgment indicates that you are particularly helpful in situations where task completion is important. If you say you are going to be somewhere and get something done—then you are at that place, getting that thing done. You are a responsible individual with a well-developed work ethic. If you are new to an organization, or involved with a new team at work, you are quick to develop a reputation for being dependable. In fact, it is likely you are one of the most reliable individuals within your entire workforce.

Very Strong

With a well-developed work ethic, you probably recognize that others view you as a first-rate worker pertaining to your effort, dependability, and task/project accomplishment. The majority of the best employees in all fields have strong judgment in this area, and many exhibit a *very* strong score. The downside here is that you might be something of a workaholic. Perhaps you lack balance. You may be unable to say no at work; set reasonable work hours for yourself; or put a task aside and tend to family and personal matters.

Also, very strong extrinsic actualization may lead to frustration. If you are a dependable person who is where you are supposed to be, when you are supposed to be there—and if you invariably and habitually complete all assigned duties and tasks—there is no greater frustration for you than dealing with an undependable colleague or employee. People with a poor work ethic absolutely infuriate you.

Unfortunately, the probability that you will be able to turn a consistently undependable person into a routinely dependable one is very, very slight. So instead of going to great lengths in an attempt to alter the habitually unreliable behavior of others, develop the personal mechanics required to manage and control your frustration. Remember that unlike *trainability*—which can be improved rather quickly with experience—*dependability* is difficult to absorb into one's value structure.

On the other hand, if you encounter irresponsible behavior in a workmate who is usually reliable, work with that person to help him or her determine the cause of their uncharacteristic behavior.

What if you happen to have a strong work ethic, and yet *your* behavior is not consistently dependable? In this case, you may be consciously *choosing* to be undependable. After all, being dependable is *who you are*. Therefore, if at times you are undependable, the cause is vastly different from the explanation behind someone with weak extrinsic actualization who places little value on dependability.

You value dependability, so if you are not a shining example of it, reflect on the root cause: Are you experiencing feelings of victimization within the workplace? Are you angry with a superior or colleague? Is there an unjust situation at play in your world? Once you have figured out what is going on, do whatever is necessary to alleviate the root problem so you can overcome your uncharacteristic behavior. Otherwise, your newfound lack of dependability could lead to your failure within the workplace.

Moderate

What if you are sometimes dependable, sometimes not? Moderately strong judgment in this area is generally an undesirable thing. The problem with hot-and-cold reliability is that other people never really know when they can depend on you. Thus, they begin to feel as if they can *never* depend on you. They are left to wonder: *Will you be there—or not?* Sure, you may be on a dependable stint right now, but if your colleagues have been burned by you before, do not expect them to have faith in you.

The bottom line is, even if you have moderate judgment in this area, others will eventually come to consider you as unreliable, or lacking in work ethic. After all, being dependable only *sometimes* is really not being dependable at all. If this describes you, heed the success tips listed in the Weak section below.

Weak

If you have not developed your value structure in this area by the time you are an adult, you are consistently undependable. You lack in work ethic, reliability, and follow-through. You do not put a priority on executing and finishing tasks and projects.

The sad reality is that most adults find it difficult to make substantial improvements in the area of dependability, reliability, and predictability. Yet such dependability is crucial for sustained high professional performance and work success. So you may possess all the job skills imaginable, be an intellectual genius, and have the most pleasant, friendly temperament in all of mankind, but if you lack a strong work ethic and are undependable, you are likely to fail miserably within most work environments. Without dependability on your side, you are unlikely to ever achieve your success.

Dependability, reliability, and follow-through are vital in workers. Weakness in this area raises a red flag, so make note of—and heed—the following advice: *It is time for you to have an epiphany, or a life-changing moment.*

Consider that if you are weak in this area, and you tend to be unreliable, then you probably do not even view this lack of dependability as a major concern, because to you it is of no major concern! Because of your value structure, you do not consider dependability in the same way as someone who highly values it. Accordingly, you must do your best to understand why dependability and reliability are essential character traits in successful people.

Take a moment to mull over the conundrum associated with undependability: Individuals with a strong work ethic often are unable to relate, even on the most rudimentary level, to those who lack a strong work ethic. It doesn't make sense to them; they simply can't understand it.

Remember, your value structure is not merely something you have, but *who you are.* The way people with a strong dependability score view the external world—their world lens—is quite different from that of someone with a weak score. If you lack a strong work ethic, what you believe is important extrinsically or tactically diverges significantly from what dependable people believe is important. And therein dwells the potential for enormous, exceedingly detrimental conflict.

You see, for most people, there is nothing more important within the workplace than a strong work ethic and dependability. If an individual is lacking in talent, skills, intellectual prowess, or even a friendly demeanor—and yet they are dependable and reliable—it is quite common that they be given *multiple* opportunities to correct and amend any mistakes and errors they may have made and to get their skills up to snuff. However, if employers are consistently hardworking and reliable, then undependability probably frustrates them greatly—and they will be inclined to offer an employee only a few chances to demonstrate his or her dependability. If the employee is unable to do so, the chances are good that this person will not be considered for advancement—and quite possibly will have his or her employment terminated.

If you lack a strong work ethic, your knowledge, skills, and talents are irrelevant. You should count on this being the case within most work environments: As both an employer and an employee, I have witnessed this scenario repeat itself over and over and over, from the entry level to the executive suite.

No matter how friendly or cordial your relations may be with your workmates, undependable actions cause others to view you as someone who does not live up to your potential—and in all likelihood, you will be passed over for promotion, limiting your professional success. High levels of trainability and a deep understanding of work are all for naught if they are not backed up with a strong work ethic and reliable actions.

As mentioned, it is not easy for most adults to improve the strength of their work ethic. If they have not developed this element of their value structure by the time they have reached adulthood, they will find that improvements in this area prove problematic—and any long-term success is an uphill battle. Self-awareness, mentoring, training, coaching, and counseling in this area may not produce the dramatic improvements that can occur in other areas of the value structure. However, some improvements can be made, and these are very important for your professional success.

Success Tip #1: Live up to the dependability standards of others.

Acknowledge and accept that your dependability is being evaluated by others, and on their terms. Whether you believe this to be fair or not is irrelevant; your dependability is being defined by *others*, according to *their* needs, wants, desires, and definition of dependability.

Consider that if you are not actively and mentally engaged with the process of your work, and are not present at the correct time and place—no matter the reason—there is the distinct possibility that others perceive you as undependable. So you must learn to evaluate the necessary levels of dependability as it relates to specific situations, and you must force yourself to live up to those standards and expectations. If *being late* becomes a part of the negative identity others have formed about you, do not shrug it off as inconsequential. If you are coming in to work late or finishing projects after the expected deadline, acknowledge that this is a major concern for your colleagues, and then avoid being late in the future.

Success Tip #2: Become a copycat.

Pay attention to, and try to mimic, the actions of particularly hardworking, dependable colleagues. Do what they do. Adopt their habits of reliability and follow-through. Make *their* routine *your* routine. Do this—and you will become more reliable.

Although mimicking others is not a panacea, it's a place to start. Adopting a mentor sometimes can help you develop better habits too.

Success Tip #3: Take corrective action.

If you sense frustration directed at you from someone you perceive to be dependable, acknowledge to yourself that the cause might be your own lack of dependability—and take concrete steps to correct that deficiency.

Place a higher priority on finishing your work. Physically complete and follow through with all tasks and responsibilities. Step by step, with dedication, you may be able to mitigate, or at least minimize, your colleague's sense of your lack of dependability.

. . .

As mentioned, the *conceptualization* and *actualization* components of extrinsic judgment (see pages 81 to 92) manifest as *trainability* and *dependability*.

- Trainability has more to do with what we *understand* extrinsically, whereas dependability has more to do with what we *do* extrinsically.

- Ideally, your extrinsic actualization is *equal to* or *stronger than* your extrinsic conceptualization. If so, you tend to not only talk the talk, but also walk the walk. You will likely move beyond the ideas and concepts of trainability to perform actions that reveal dependability and reliability.

- Having strong extrinsic conceptualization yet weak actualization means that you have a solid understanding of work but do not carry that understanding to execution. Even though you grasp what work is all about, you tend to be undependable when it comes to getting things done. Others will perceive you as a person who does not live up to your potential in the workplace.

. . .

Your fundamental dependability contributes powerfully toward your professional success. Recognize that dependability, in its simplest terms, means being where you are supposed to be, when you are supposed to be there, doing what you are supposed to be doing.

If you lack a strong work ethic, yours is not a situation where your values are merely different from someone else's, with both sides having equal value and equally valid points. Being undependable is worse, and being dependable is better—*period*.

> Herbert C. Christiansen, the son of Danish immigrants, was born in 1918. He attended Schurz High School on Chicago's northwest side. Upon his graduation, he was offered a job at Clark & Barlow, a hardware business founded in 1894.

Herbert took his job very seriously, and he moved up the ranks at Clark & Barlow. During the 1930s Herbert was placed in charge of the marine products division. During World War II, Clark & Barlow supplied parts used to help build Patrol Torpedo (PT) boats.

In 1939, at age twenty-one, he married his high school sweetheart, Marjorie. The couple began raising a family.

In 1945, at twenty-seven years old, Herbert left his employment for two years when he served in the U.S. Army during World War II. He was a sharpshooter stationed in Germany. Afterwards, Herbert returned home and resumed work at Clark & Barlow. He worked his way up to become the company's head purchasing agent.

From the 1950s through the 1990s, mild-mannered Herbert continued to work and raise his family. He and Marjorie had a son, two daughters, nine grandchildren, and eventually sixteen great-grandchildren.

In 1997, at seventy-nine years old, Herbert and his wife moved from the city of Chicago to the suburbs. However, Herbert continued to commute into the city, walking more than a mile each way from the train station to his office.

Sadly, in 2007, after sixty-eight years of marriage, Herbert's wife Marjorie died.

About a year later, at ninety years old, Herbert C. Christiansen retired. A number of national news organizations interviewed and wrote articles about Herbert. They all wanted to tell his story. You see, Herbert retired not only at the ripe old age of ninety, but also after working for Clark & Barlow for seventy-one years—without missing a single day of work!

His daughter Beverly said, "He liked the attention, but didn't understand why all the fuss. He was proud of having worked all those years, but even more proud of his perfect attendance. Luckily, he only got sick on the weekends . . . What kept him going was his love of the job and his loyalty to the company. He used to say, 'They

Continued

helped pay my mortgage. They kept food on our table. Where would I be without them?'"[2]

Herbert C. Christiansen died on May 7, 2014. He was ninety-six.

2   J. G. Kates, "Herbert C. Christiansen, Purchasing Agent, 1917-2014," *Chicago Tribune* (May 20, 2014): 1, http://articles.chicagotribune.com/2014-05-20/news/ct-herbert-christiansen-obit-20140520_1_christiansen-herbert-c-hardware.

TRUTH #3:
SYSTEMIC JUDGMENT

In the 1990s, Vice Admiral Gerald Hoewing (since retired) was Commanding Officer of VFA-81, my U.S. Navy F/A-18 Hornet squadron at the time. We were onboard the aircraft carrier USS *Saratoga*, enforcing the embargo during Operation Desert Shield and preparing for what would later become full-blown combat during Operation Desert Storm. Yet despite the high level of intensity at that time, I never saw Commander Hoewing really angry—except once.

For most of us, it was our first involvement with a hostile nation. Our preparations revolved primarily around the tactics of war, which for a Navy fighter pilot includes launching from, and trapping back aboard, the aircraft carrier in both daytime and nighttime.

Between the launch and trap was the business of destroying our assigned target.

The hours turned into days, and the weeks into months, as my fellow pilots and I studied in exacting detail what we thought to be every possible scenario. This contingency planning, along with lots and lots of flight time, made us good—very good.

I felt confident and perhaps even a bit cocky, yet at the same time there still existed a bit of nervousness—probably that fear of the unknown.

Continued

During one of our many Ready Room meetings, Commander Hoewing asked us pilots if we were ready. And we all said that we were.

One of our junior officers (JOs) began a discussion of one of the mirror-image routes we were flying, listing weapons load, fuel requirements, and other such details . . . and that's when Hoewing interrupted.

"That's not what I'm asking," he said. Instead, he wanted to know whether we were ready for something to go terribly wrong—for instance, if one of us had to divert, or had engine failure, or got shot out of the sky and had to eject.

If we had to leave the jet, would we be ready?

It quickly became obvious that most of us had spent the bulk of our time thinking about the mission, and precious little time on the implications of an ejection. Still, we responded, "Yes, sir, we're ready." After all, we had been briefed by the Intel guys and the Navy Seals on the Safe Areas, and on all the various protocols and passwords, and on how to get picked up by the snake eaters (our affectionate term for the Special Forces crowd).

I suppose we were rather casual in our response to "leaving the jet." None of us felt that anything like that would happen to us. We were U.S. Navy fighter pilots, flying the latest and greatest F/A-18 Hornet, for goodness' sake.

Well, our casual response didn't sit too well with Hoewing. One unfortunate JO (thankfully not me) was ordered to the Paraloft to bring his gear for inspection—immediately. His survival gear was lacking, to say the least. And Hoewing got angry.

I had never seen him yell like that before. I've never seen him yell like that since.

It got our attention.

Hoewing's face was red and his voice was loud. He reminded us that the moment we pull the ejection handle and bail out, we would no longer be fighter pilots. We would exit the jet and float to the ground in the parachute as soldiers. And for fighter pilots, who have very little formal "soldier" training, that was a scary proposition indeed.

Within twenty-four hours my survival gear was double-checked and squared away, and although it was already in pretty good shape, I made sure it remained so for the rest of my Navy career. Thanks to Hoewing, we maintained a heightened awareness of our survival mentality. And if we didn't fully appreciate even then, we soon did, because during Desert Storm four jets from the USS *Saratoga* were shot down—one of them from my squadron.

Many years later Gerald Hoewing would retire as a three-star Vice Admiral.

His last job was Chief of Naval Personnel—one of the most strategic jobs in the entire U.S. Navy.

Systemic judgment represents the third of the three global judgments, and our third truth. Often referred to as "global systemic," "global S," or "S-judgment," it encompasses the long-range and far-reaching aspects of your judgment, your "big picture" strategic judgments.

Systemic judgment looks at things from a more expansive vantage point regarding long-term, big-picture strategies. For most people, their systemic judgment is weaker—often much weaker—than their intrinsic and extrinsic judgment. And for many people, their systemic judgment, in and of itself, is weak. As such, systemic judgment is often an untapped resource. If developed, it can greatly enhance a person's overall judgment and decision-making process, because it provides a broader perspective on the world at large, and thus boosts success.

To use systemic judgment is to consider the implications and consequences of our actions. Systemic evaluation allows us to ponder the effects of our current decisions on future outcomes. When we use systemic judgment, we ask questions such as

▸ Why?

▸ What for?

▸ Is this really what we want to do?

▸ What could go wrong?

Metaphorically, systemic judgment takes the broader view from thirty thousand feet up, as opposed to the narrower, detailed view at ground level. With systemic judgment, we observe the whole forest—not just individual trees.

Systemic judgment is your ability to understand and comprehend the interrelationship of seemingly disjointed ideas and events; the future repercussions of current decisions; and how various situations and scenarios relate to, interact with, and combine with each other. By applying your systemic judgment, you can then use those interactions and relationships to help you derive better plans and strategic solutions.

The *conceptualization* and *actualization* components of systemic judgment (see pages 31 to 34) manifest as *understanding strategies* and *using strategies*.

So your systemic judgment determines how well you both *understand* and *use* strategies to help formulate and guide your choices and decisions. It takes the long-range view, beyond the immediacy of the current task, and thus it is an extremely important element of success.

Mathematician and meteorologist Edward Lorenz, the father of chaos theory, coined the now-famous phrase *butterfly effect* in 1972, when he gave a talk titled "Does the Flap of a Butterfly's Wings in Brazil Set Off a Tornado in Texas?" The butterfly effect theorizes that a small change early in a process may trigger vast, often unexpected outcomes later in time.

In Ray Bradbury's 1952 short story "A Sound of Thunder," the accidental killing of a butterfly by time travelers during a trip to the past caused great and harmful changes in the present.

Butterflies are not the only thing these two points have in common. Both are systemic concepts.

Systemic judgment brings attention beforehand to the appreciation and consideration of potential future consequences. So even though we are unable to predict the future, using systemic judgment greatly improves our chances of success because it permits us to consider the impact our current choices will have on future outcomes. Through considering the implications of our decisions, we can attempt to diminish the potentially negative, unintended consequences.

Without systemic judgment, we leave the impact of future outcomes to luck or chance.

Entry- and midlevel jobs often do not require the use of high-level systemic evaluative judgment. In fact, depending on the nature of the work, in some situations the use of systemic judgment—the consideration of implications and consequences—may seem to get in the way of the immediate accomplishment of a top-priority duty or assignment.

But as a person advances throughout the course of his or her career, moving up the corporate ladder and into positions of higher responsibility, each job may become less focused on the details, specifics, and minutiae of various tasks and assignments (the extrinsic), and become more about administration, overall corporate vision, creating plans and goals, and general organizational guidance (the systemic). Therefore, as higher and higher seniority is achieved, there is a corresponding need for the superior systemic judgment required to make higher-level strategic decisions.

People in the workplace use systemic judgment to set appropriate policy, develop a corporate vision, and streamline direction, all of which help ensure a business's continued success. And without this type of judgment, organizational success is put at risk.

The need is great for systemic judgment in positions of corporate leadership, yet unfortunately, it is sometimes difficult to find executives and employees who exhibit it. Systemic judgment, for most people, is a bit more difficult to understand than the intrinsic and extrinsic domains, partly because the value structure of most Americans does not emphasize it. Our society tends to place more emphasis on the intrinsic—being social. We focus also on the extrinsic—being diligent and hardworking. Generally, we are not taught to develop our ability to comprehend far-reaching implications, consequences, and big-picture realities.

This makes strong—and especially dominant—systemic judgment quite unusual in the population today. Most people do not place as much emphasis or value on the long-term view and on the scrutiny of repercussions and consequences. Of course, this does not apply to all situations, but our culture tends to move quickly on to the next step, and to condone and participate in more reactive *leaping* as opposed to deliberative *looking*. As a nation, we often celebrate, praise, and value a somewhat irresponsible and carefree notion of trial-and-error and fiscal experimentation. We are not usually as concerned with, respectful of, or appreciative of systemic judgment.

However, the more integrated and complicated your work becomes, the more you will need systemic judgment. Otherwise, without the long-range view, and the thoughtful consideration of the implications and consequences of your decisions and actions, you will overlook important factors in ways that can make an entire work activity vulnerable and defenseless. Simply put, systemic judgment is crucial when making decisions and taking action.

The effect of cultural influences on systemic judgment cannot be overstated. Consider, for example, the immediate, instantaneous nature of our modern world, which unfortunately is very much to the detriment of strong systemic judgment: We want it *right now, right away*, and *without question*. Many people today dwell in the backward mode of *Ready . . . fire . . . aim!*—so much so that a systemic thinker is sometimes viewed as a contrarian, even a stick-in-the-mud who opposes accomplishment and progress.

Merely pausing to question a course of action can elicit angry complaints from individuals lacking in systemic judgment. Meanwhile, those who make decisions without the use of systemic judgment will tend to take action—*any* action—without worry or consideration for implications and consequences. They just want to do *something*.

It is quite easy to understand why systemic judgment so often lies fallow in the minds of today's workforce. In our current work environment, people often find early success if they are likable, friendly, and easy to work with, and if they accomplish a high volume of quality work. These are typical intrinsic and extrinsic realities. Yet the very success of people in these scenarios limits their ultimate growth. After all, if your career path is infused with characteristically intrinsic and extrinsic duties and responsibilities, there is the distinct possibility that your systemic judgment has been somewhat disregarded, sidelined, even marginalized.

For some people, the culprit is nothing more than their fundamental disinterest in forming a long-term vision involving their career and/ or the organization. Those who have a narrowly defined, repetitive, task-oriented job, such as an assembly-line worker or a cashier, may find that the job meets their needs both financially and intellectually, and so they never pursue the systemic decision-making component of their value structure.

Other employees blame their lack of systemic development on their employer: "They never let me think for myself." Superiors and colleagues might be unable to recognize the difference between simple laziness and a pause in the action—an intentional break in order to apply systemic judgment, to help better resolve a problem or reprioritize workflows. Employees are told, "Quit thinking about it, and just do it." This negative attitude toward the systemic, whether it originates from an employer or from an employee, does little to promote the development and use of systemic judgment.

Someone hired into an entry-level job is likely to be given specific tasks to be completed in a specific manner and time. No matter how the employee feels about doing the tasks, he or she must meet the expectations in order to keep the job. Keeping the entry-level job may be more important to the employee than whatever sense of satisfaction one might derive from expressing dissatisfaction and frustration about the tasks at hand.

In such situations, employers demand little in the way of systemic thinking, and any pursuit of it is left to the individual. The reality is that thoughts like *Why are we doing this?* during working hours may be counterproductive to accomplishing the tasks necessary to keep the business running. Pauses for contemplation may appear as an unnecessary delay on the part of the employee. An individual who stares off into space, contemplating, rather than completing a specific task may not last long in an entry-level job, where such tasks are typically simple and expected to be completed without a great deal of reflection.

Many employers would express frustration or suspicion toward any suggestions from the entry-level employee as to how to improve a system, or toward questions as to why a process occurs. For example, an entry-level employee who pipes up with a suggestion to change priorities or who questions the organization's practices is likely to experience an unwelcome retort from an experienced employee: "Are you trying to tell me my job?" or "Shut up and get back to work!" or "We've been doing it this way since before you were born!" These employees may become discouraged when superiors or coworkers misconstrue their systemic thoughts. They may shut down that part of their judgment development and fail to practice it further.

However, although both employees and their superiors often don't realize it, a systemic understanding and the use of strategies *are* valuable even when a job involves, say, manual labor or entry-level work with specific outlined procedures already in place. The most resilient and determined individuals will come to accept that this may be neither the time nor the place to express systemic suggestions, and nevertheless will pursue their systemic agenda in another manner.

There might be many reasons—financial, familial, geographical, educational—you work in an undemanding, "small picture" job rather than having reached the higher stage of your career at this point. Perhaps your responsibility to have and maintain this employment transcends any other emotional or intellectual fulfillment you might otherwise seek. Even so, developing your systemic judgment in preparation for the desired job of your future is crucial if you wish to advance beyond entry-level work. Find a way to do deep systemic thinking without interrupting your current work. In fact, it may be best to pursue any advancement of your strategizing and decision-making skills outside of the workplace entirely.

Keep in mind that even if you feel that you are being systemically "crushed" or suppressed by the job or those around you, it is not helpful to assume the role of systemic victim. You may have been misunderstood, chastised, or actively discouraged by coworkers or superiors, or perhaps your great ideas and long-range thinking weren't fully appreciated—"Just do it this way!" Maybe you were not allowed the forum to pursue your ideas due to the limitations of your job. Regardless, you still should continue to develop your systemic thinking. Just save your big-picture thinking for a time when it will be appropriate and appreciated.

Have your great ideas at the ready for when and if a promotion becomes available. This is especially helpful if you are working at a job where advancement is possible, but you are currently limited by either a time frame or minimum-skill requirements. Your superiors may not appreciate a brand-new whippersnapper telling them that their long-held views need improvement. But they may be far more willing to promote a praiseworthy entry-level employee who has established a working knowledge of company goals and who respectfully suggests useful ways to achieve greater performance. (Of course, do not forget that your systemic ideas may have already been tried.)

If advancement is not likely, at least not in the time frame you would prefer, it may still be beneficial to take time to think strategically as you prepare for the opportunity to change your circumstance. If and when that chance occurs, your resilience and determination will come in handy.

You already will have pursued your systemic development on your own terms and your own time, and you can then use any newfound strategic judgment to impress potential employers at job interviews.

Here is an illustration of this.

While visiting a hotel owned by one of our corporate clients, I found myself searching the halls for a recent hire who held one of the lowest-tier jobs in the hotel: an assistant to the assistant maintenance technician. I sought out this individual because something about him had surprised me: On our judgment assessment, he had systemic scores that were more in line with executive management.

He was also a college graduate—a qualification that was not required for his job, which involved changing light bulbs, painting over scratches in the walls, moving furniture, and other exceedingly straightforward tasks. When I found him and asked why he had taken the job, he explained that he had applied with the company at higher levels, but had been told that the hotel chain nearly always promoted from within. So, after failing to be hired from outside the company to a management position, he had accepted an entry-level job within the chain. He had thought about it, and felt that the best way to make an impression and gain the opportunity at a higher-level job of his choice was to start at the entry level and get to know the company on the way up.

He had a plan—a long-range, detailed plan: to do the best he could at the simple tasks, and to be ready when any promotions were in the offing.

While working at the entry-level job, he took every opportunity to shadow the higher-level employees, offering to help with tasks and asking about how they were performed. He also kept a detailed journal at home, writing down questions he wanted to ask, suggestions he might have for improvements, and areas in which he saw inefficiency. As an entry-level employee, he made sure to maintain a good work record.

Sure enough, not more than a year after he was hired, he received a raise and was being trained for a higher-level job within the hotel. I continued to follow his progress as he later transferred to a larger hotel, moving into a midlevel management role with more responsibilities and a bright future.

This young man worked—on his own time—on developing strong systemic judgment. Although he did not need big-picture perspective directly within his first job, he parlayed it into future professional success, all because he had vision.

For an employee who moves into higher-level positions of responsibility, the consideration of implications and consequences becomes more and more important. This is particularly true within executive-level positions that demand vision and strategy for overall corporate direction. A lack of systemic judgment can be devastating—to the employee, the team, and the corporation.

If intrinsic and extrinsic judgments overshadow the systemic, or if systemic judgment is weak, an employee may end up struggling in the higher-level position. This is quite common, and it can be disastrous given the high-level, intense nature of executive-level decision-making. Obviously, it is helpful for the individual to uncover any systemic weakness beforehand and to strengthen that judgment prior to being burdened with systemßic demands. Discovering so after the fact makes high-level success much more difficult to achieve.

Imagine how an engineer, physician, nurse, teacher, coach, housewife, accountant, politician, CEO, or COO—essentially, anyone with considerable responsibility—might need to infuse strong systemic judgment into their awareness and behavior. Success in many such careers requires a fundamental ability to both comprehend implications and consequences and use that understanding to formulate and guide decisions and actions.

Do not indiscriminately assume that merely because someone has achieved a responsible position within their profession, that person naturally possesses strong systemic judgment. Unfortunately, and very often, this is entirely not so. In my work with corporations, the data repeatedly uncovers poor (sometimes *extremely* poor!) systemic judgment at even the most senior executive levels. There are plenty of examples of hardworking, compassionate individuals who unwittingly obliterate multimillion-dollar organizations because of their lack of systemic judgment—their inability to understand long-term implications and consequences, or to make sense out of complicated, interconnected events, trends, and impending developments.

Of course, there are many reasons why businesses fail, but poor systemic judgment by those in charge is high on the list. Within the aviation field, for example, the *poor judgment* listed as "Probable Cause" in many accident reports is frequently an instance of *poor systemic judgment*. A pilot might be intrinsically aware and extrinsically capable—but if the pilot is not systemically astute and the forces of providence and circumstance conspire against them, a flight can quickly turn tragic. As author, aviator, filmmaker, and sailor Ernest K. Gann so powerfully pointed out, fate is the hunter.

In occupations where mistakes can be catastrophic—construction, for example—systemic judgment may help prevent an impending accident by anticipating the future consequence and thus breaking the "accident chain." The contemplation and consideration of likely and even unlikely outcomes that may occur at a later time due to the decisions and choices we make now provides tremendous insight that helps guide our decision-making process. Systemic judgment provides input into the decisions we make now so that future outcomes are decidedly better.

Horrific accidents, such as the sinking of the *Titanic*, have been caused by placing too much emphasis on the intrinsic (getting along with others) or the extrinsic (completing the task), all while entirely ignoring the systemic necessity of considering the future consequences of present actions. With so many variables to consider when making complicated decisions within a complex task—and with so many possible outcomes, some good and some bad—the use of a systemic component in asking those broad-based, long-range "what if" questions is imperative.

How many times have you watched the news or read the newspaper in utter amazement, wondering, *Why did they do that?* or *What were those idiots thinking?* Often, the answer is as simple as the lack of systemic judgment.

Occasionally, a client (usually someone with weak systemic judgment) argues with me against the need for strong systemic judgment. The person lets me know—sometimes rather emphatically—that their job is purely about the accomplishment of tasks, processes, and procedures that are very extrinsically oriented. Considering implications and consequences and taking the long-range view, this person claims, is both irrelevant and an unnecessary distraction in their day-to-day workplace.

On the surface, that may seem correct. After all, if there is a written procedure, wouldn't it make the most sense to just follow it? You'd be doing and completing your task, right? However, when you undertake extrinsic tasks without a systemic component, and just *do* without *thinking* first, the results can be, at the very least, inefficient and ineffective—and at the most, haphazard and even disastrous.

Systemic judgment helps prevent the "do over," because it considers repercussions and answers the question *What will this decision look like in the morning?*

Thinking ahead improves even the most extrinsic-oriented and task-driven work environments. Incorporating systemic judgment into your approach enables you to operate on a higher extrinsic level. There is no downside—only a marvelous upside: more effective, sustainable, and well-thought-out decisions.

Strong

If you have strong systemic judgment, you consider implications and consequences as you make decisions. You *think* before you *do*; you are a forward thinker.

You consider and reflect upon the broader perspective, employing an all-encompassing viewpoint as you seek solutions to problems. You have an understanding of how a decision will look in hindsight, and you use that understanding to help guide your decisions.

Strong systemic judgment enables competent brainstorming, which you tend to enjoy because you are an ideas person. You are quite comfortable with long-range planning and integrating your ideas and plans into your actions. This enhances your decisions, because you are infusing your evaluative judgment with a strong strategic component. Be grateful and appreciative for your strong systemic judgment, because it provides a wonderful boost to decision-making in the intense workplace environment.

Most work requires strong intrinsic and extrinsic judgment—but even if you get along with others and perform tasks, processes, and procedures well, in the absence of the systemic aspect of judgment, your decisions are just as likely as not to be arbitrary, ill-conceived, and ineffective. Strong systemic judgment keeps you from rushing to judgment; it helps you pause and think things through before you act. This is particularly important in situations where it is difficult to remediate a bad decision, and where the realization of a particular outcome on the first attempt is crucial.

People with strong systemic judgment should be aware of a rather common scenario, however, that can diminish the effectiveness of strong strategic thinking: Should either (or both) of your I- and E-judgments be considerably stronger than your S-judgment, the former two will tend to overshadow and diminish the use of the latter, no matter how strong. Systemic judgment may be moderate or even strong, yet still be relatively weak when compared with a person's very strong intrinsic and/or extrinsic judgments. In fact, very strong I- and E-judgments are much more common within the population.

Therefore, make sure that you exert a conscious effort to use your systemic judgment, because even though it might be strong, your two other global judgments are apt to overpower it. If this happens, your systemic judgment will be undervalued and underutilized as you make decisions.

Very Strong

Bear in mind that very strong systemic judgment is rare. Although it is wonderful to have developed exceptionally strong systemic judgment, because of its rarity, the potential for negative issues and conflict is high.

There is often as much or even more pushback and conflict between individuals of differing strengths of the systemic as there is with differing strengths of intrinsic or extrinsic judgment.

Moreover, as previously discussed (see page 115), our society tends to be motivated intrinsically and extrinsically rather than systemically. Exceptional intrinsic and extrinsic judgments, while not commonplace, are much more common than exceptional systemic judgment. So while most of us encounter individuals with very strong intrinsic or extrinsic judgment, rarely do we interact with very strong systemic judgment. Therefore we are less experienced and are less accustomed to dealing with individuals with such an unusual value structure.

The E-dominant individual (quite common in the population) is predominantly tactical-, task-, and mission-oriented. Should an exceptionally strong S individual pause to ponder the implications and consequences of a scenario or task—behavior that is completely natural to that person—that behavior can be frustrating for the E-dominant individual, who typically wants to take immediate action. This is a recipe for extreme disagreement about the best way to proceed. E-dominant individuals may feel as if they are getting nowhere, whereas S-dominant individuals may feel as if they are screaming down the wrong path.

If you have exceptional strategic judgment, you must maintain a keen awareness of the reality that not many people have such extraordinarily strong systemic sensibilities, and others are likely to misread you and your actions. You are likely to be perceived as disturbingly slow to decide and as unable to just get on with it already. In actuality, however, thinking before we act is a positive tendency indeed. What's more, an inability to make a timely decision is generally a problem only among people who are overwhelmingly systemic dominant, not just systemically strong.

Fortunately, as long as you are aware of the potential for frustration in others and you strive to keep the lines of communication open, you should be able to minimize or even squelch nascent frustration. Direct, straightforward communication about big-picture concerns can prevent these "lulls" in decision-making from being regarded as laziness or an inherent inability to make a decision. With good communication about such issues, long-range, big-picture suggestions typically come to be highly regarded and even welcomed by others.

If you have exceptional S-judgment, you probably have already noticed that your evaluative judgments and decisions receive a fabulous reception at times. This is due to the rare quality of powerful systemic judgment, and the uniqueness of your viewpoint as compared with most others. In simple terms: Those with exceptional systemic judgment think differently from a sizable percentage of the population.

Although your extraordinary judgment is enviable, be aware that you might also encounter conflict with the general nature of your day-to-day work world. You might be very decisive, but you bring a contemplative component into your decisions and actions. If you contrast that with the instantaneous nature of our cell phone, data overload, social media, *speak-before-we-think, who-cares-about-the-consequences, I-want-it-now* culture, it is easy to conjure up the potential for frustration. You are better equipped to keep frustration at bay if you maintain a conscious awareness of these glaring differences.

Weak

If you have weak systemic judgment, you tend to tackle problems without thinking them through. Your actions display a lack of consideration and thought that causes your work to be inconsistent and haphazard, and you may find that you often need to redo tasks.

Decisions made without first considering outcomes may cause more harm than good, especially at times when you are unable to remediate a poor decision. So to become successful at your chosen occupation, you must learn to take time to consider the implications and consequences of your actions *before* you act.

Weak systemic judgment lends itself to mindsets of blind ambitious action without reflection. You impatiently do things—*anything*—without deliberation, single-mindedly and fervently moving ahead without the slightest consideration for potential outcomes. In other words, you tend to throw it at the wall and see if it sticks.

In the complicated world of business (and life in general), the strongest and most well-developed intrinsic and extrinsic judgments may not be able to overcome the adverse impact of poor systemic judgment. For example, a city planner must consider a wide variety of consequences: traffic, future growth, noise, zoning, maintenance, cost, revenue, community desires, environmental impact, and on and on and on. During the entire lifespan of a project, a city planner must continue this systemic process, examining changes, new information, extenuating circumstances, and additional variables in order to update decisions and actions appropriately. Someone without a grasp of the systemic, and without an ability to interconnect each of these variables into a cohesive plan, can easily omit important information and, subsequently, make decisions and choices that negatively impact the entire community.

For high-level decisions such as these, you must learn to pause, consciously take time to consider all aspects, and then—*and only then*—decide on a course of action. If you lack systemic judgment, this updating and contemplating process does not come naturally for you.

People who lack systemic judgment often feel that that things get out of control in a hurry—that they are, in effect, blindsided by life. Certainly that may be possible in some cases, but it is much more likely that such a person is rather oblivious to consequences and lives in a way that allows bad things escalate quickly.

You might think of a series of actions or events that lead to negative consequences as links in a chain. This accident chain, if not broken, ultimately leads to disaster. Yet people with poorly developed systemic judgment do not see this chain stretching out before them. They are unable to see what they did to cause their latest mess or predicament. They do not perceive the interrelations between all the decisions they have made that led up to the catastrophe. They see only the catastrophe itself and feel that it showed up out of nowhere.

We all have known people in our lives to whom bad things seem to "just happen." Should we thoughtfully examine each of their misfortunes, however, chances are that we would see the links in the accident chain. For such people those links are invisible, leaving them to feel that they are simply unlucky or a victim of circumstance. But this lifelong recurrence—a pattern of accidents and hardships—reveals that in all likelihood, the individual lacks systemic judgment.

Fortunately, it is possible for anyone—yes, *anyone*—to learn to look before they leap. So if you lack systemic judgment, take heart: It does not have to be that way forever. Many individuals are able to pinpoint a specific event that shaped the development of their value structure—an "aha" moment. This is particularly true with developing systemic judgment. You can improve your chances of success by heeding some memorable advice.

Do You Even Know What You Did?

Here is an example of an "aha" moment as told to me by a client:

When I was fourteen years old, several of my friends and their older siblings were learning how to drive. My friend Leslie had an older sister named Patricia. Patricia was sixteen and had just obtained her driver's license.

One Saturday, Patricia borrowed her mother's car and drove Leslie and me to visit another friend who lived at the end of a cul-de-sac. After our visit, we jumped back in the car to return home. All three of us—including the driver, who had begun to turn the car around—rolled down our windows and waved out the window at our friend, shouting, "Bye!"

Suddenly, there was a loud metallic noise, and the car lurched sideways and halted. Confused, Patricia stepped on the gas. The engine roared and the car rocked forward, but it didn't go any further. We stepped out of the car and saw the problem right away: One of the wheels was stuck on a sewer grate.

Patricia had not turned sharply enough, and had driven

ever-so-slightly off the pavement and onto the curb. Then the front passenger wheel had gotten wedged in the grate when Patricia stepped on the gas. Worst of all, the tire was punctured and losing air.

There was no way we were getting home in that car. Patricia called her mother, who then called a tow truck.

As we waited, Patricia was completely distraught and hysterical. Leslie seemed not at all surprised at what had happened. I tried to comfort Patricia, saying that this was a "simple accident" and that her mother would understand. Nothing I said seemed to calm her down.

When their mother showed up, she seemed irritated with Patricia—and yet, like Leslie, not at all surprised. She looked at the car and the way Patricia was reacting, and then said in a crisp tone, "Do you even *know* what you did to cause this?"

Patricia's response was simple: "It would have happened to anyone!" She claimed over and over that this was a completely random accident.

I quietly asked Leslie why Patricia didn't just apologize since it was obviously her fault.

Leslie's response was this: "This is just the way it goes with her. An accident just seems to always happen. Patricia always claims it's not really her fault. She never sees it coming, and she never takes responsibility."

Now, I was so young at the time that I hadn't fully put together the idea of systemic thinking. Still, I definitely knew what Patricia did to cause this situation (even if she didn't know it herself). I clearly saw the chain of events that had led to this moment:

Link #1: Patricia lacked training and experience in her driving. She was new behind the wheel.

Link #2: Patricia had pushed things beyond her proficiency due to her desire to show off her new driver's license to her friends. Clearly, Patricia wasn't ready just yet to drive with friends in her car.

Continued

Link #3: Part of Patricia's nature was that she was easily distracted. So when she had taken the time to wave goodbye to our mutual friend, she hadn't really watched what she was doing when bringing the car around the cul-de-sac.

Link #5: Patricia had an inappropriate reaction to the initial problem when the car wouldn't move. She should have gotten out of the car then to check on what was wrong. It wasn't a good idea to gun the engine before she had figured out the problem. As it turned out, this had caused the wheel to jam in the sewer grate and then puncture and lose air.

Link #6: Patricia was unwilling to take responsibility for her actions leading up to the accident. She was the driver, so the accident was indeed her fault. (The car would never have done this on its own!)

From that point on, at many times in my life, I've asked Patricia's mother's question, sometimes of myself and sometimes of someone else—sometimes out loud and sometimes just in my head: *Do you even know what you did to cause this?*

Success Tip #1: Recognize the accident chain.

Work-life situations that are truly blindsiding are the exception rather than the rule. If you are habitually in the wrong place at the wrong time and if the craziest things happen seemingly "out of nowhere," it is time to take a cold, hard look at your decision-making process and seriously consider that you are lacking in systemic judgment.

Yes, it can be difficult to take this honest look. For many, it is less threatening and easier to believe that they are a victim of bad luck rather than reckless in their behaviors or lacking in a bit of common sense. But if you can come to acknowledge the reality, it is the first step in actually seeing the accident chain of decisions that led you to your latest fiasco.

Success Tip #2: Pause before you act.

On a very up-front and conscious level, you need to slow down, pause, and ponder the upcoming decision or course of action. Is it the right one? Why or why not? Do not leave outcomes to luck or fate just because you fail to consider implications and consequences.

Success Tip #3: Ask yourself about the consequences.

Talk to yourself out loud (not too loud!) about the issue at hand. The resulting dialogue can go a long way toward guiding you to a well-thought-out decision.

What should you say? How about this: "Hey, let's wait a minute here, and think through the ramifications of doing X or Y. What if this happened? What about that? Is it good for the company? How might it affect me and my career or my family?" Then answer the questions and address any concerns that come to mind.

Yes, this might seem a little uncomfortable at first. But our data reveals that *many* individuals lack even a basic consideration of implications and consequences—and you have to start somewhere.

Success Tip #4: Ask others for their opinion.

If you can't figure out the likely answer to a scenario or dilemma, learn to ask this question of others: "What do you think?"

Unfortunately, when you have only weak systemic judgment, it may lead you to bogus solutions even if you *do* pause to consider the implications of your actions. Repercussions and likely consequences might not be readily apparent, even if you try to think of them. To combat this, seek additional advice from others, especially those more experienced than you.

Rather than making high-level decisions on your own, learn to ask, "Do you see any problems with this decision or course of action?" People who have stronger systemic judgment than you may offer helpful thoughts or perspective. It is likely that you will hear worthy suggestions from them. Once you do, seriously consider incorporating their advice or ideas into your decisions and actions.

Success Tip #5: Don't give in to immediate pressures.

Avoid the temptation to make decisions purely on either intrinsic or extrinsic considerations—or even worse, due to internal or external pressures.

Success Tip #6: Avoid rushing into things.

Don't give in to your personal inclination to rush into decisions. Take a breath first, and fight your proclivity to embark hurriedly on whatever mission is before you. Don't cut corners on a task; do things the right way, giving them their due consideration and process.

Success Tip #7: Ignore the details.

Learn to ignore the details temporarily as you learn to see the big picture. Here's how:

1. Figure out where you want to be in the big *systemic* picture.

2. Use your imagination to conjure up what could go wrong.

3. Only then determine what *extrinsic* tasks you must complete to get there.

4. Finally, perform each task with *glorious and fulfilling intrinsic* passion.

. . .

Adapt this advice to your own particular work and circumstances, and you will approach the heart of success.

Systemic Conceptualization—
Understanding Strategies

For approximately eighty-five percent of the population, systemic conceptualization is the weakest of the conceptualization components in the three areas of global judgment. (For a review of conceptualization and actualization, see pages 31 to 34.)

The *conceptualization* component of systemic judgment manifests as your *understanding* of strategies. It determines your forward-thinking ability to comprehend and appreciate implications and consequences, and your appreciation of the big picture.

Your systemic understanding is related to theoretical and abstract issues, and to analytical, mental, and cerebral interactions. It assesses your ability to understand and appreciate ideas and plans, and the benefits of adopting a broader, more comprehensive point of view. It also reveals whether or not you are a forward-looking thinker.

This area of judgment determines your ability to discern an overall pattern and relationship from within a throng of details, and to see the entirety of the situation. Systemic conceptualization provides your ability to see the broader view from thirty thousand feet up, rather than from a position down in the weeds.

To fully grasp systemic conceptualization, we must understand the true meaning of the word *appreciation*. *Appreciation* is a "head word"—it is conceptual in nature—but this does not make it any less of a reality affecting our behavior. When we *appreciate*, we *look a bit more closely*, taking all we can perceive into consideration, and then stopping to observe in an even more detailed manner. Appreciation for our work situations and other environments serves us well as we formulate our choices and decisions, especially if the effort to enrich our situational appreciation is conscious and purposeful.

Here is a simple example that illustrates the meaning of *appreciation*.

I grew up in South Carolina, where the summers are hot and the winters are relatively mild. The lakes do not freeze, deep snows are uncommon, and there is no such thing as ice hockey. We know that there is a sport called ice hockey, and you could probably watch it on television, maybe, but growing up in South Carolina in the 1970s, I did not care one tiny bit about hockey. You could say we did not *appreciate* hockey.

Well, one summer when I was a young teenager, my family visited our relatives in St. Louis, Missouri. As I learned, ice hockey is taken very seriously in St. Louis. It is practically a matter of life or death.

During the visit, my cousin Willie took me to a hockey game, saying, "We're going to a fight, and maybe a hockey game will break out"—an old joke for you hockey fans, but funny to me at the time.

Watching the plays was very exciting, and I kept asking questions about the rules, players, teams, scoring, and so forth. Willie felt completely at ease watching the hockey game and answering my questions. He himself was a good hockey player, and he had a rich, in-depth, extensive appreciation for hockey, one that went far beyond merely knowing the rules. He knew when good things were happening and when bad things were happening. He sensed shifts in momentum, and knew when to cheer and when to boo—whereas I had no clue.

At first, I could not even follow the hockey puck. It was just a blur of madness.

However, by the end of the game, hockey began to make sense to me—not a lot, but a little bit—and I developed a burgeoning awareness of what hockey was all about. I had even begun to develop an appreciation for the game, and as we left the stadium, I considered myself a brand-new hockey fan.

Now, at that point, I would have been able to make slightly better hockey decisions than when I first entered the stadium—not just because I had learned the basic rules of hockey, but because I now had an understanding of and appreciation for the game.

Truth be told, to this day I do not understand all the various regulations and strategies of hockey. But because of that one experience as a spectator at a St. Louis Blues game in the early 1970s, I have a greater awareness of and appreciation for hockey. This type of appreciation is a positive influence on decisions.

Within systemic conceptualization, to appreciate is to consider the future consequences of our current actions. Of course, we need to consider the near term, too—the immediacy of our situation—but we also need to explore and ponder long-term implications and consequences; consider how events will unfold and evolve; and chew over what a decision will look like in the morning. The more we appreciate a circumstance or predicament, the stronger our mental engagement in it—and thus the better our judgment in that particular instance.

When we mentally engage in a situation and take on a perspective that *appreciates* everything about it, we often uncover that seemingly random events are not so random after all. Indeed, this larger strategic viewpoint can help us sort out these events into a connected, workable relationship. It can be of tremendous benefit, particularly if we are involved with high-level decision-making.

Never underestimate the interconnectedness of seemingly random events. People often take for granted that the resolution of problems, or even just the natural progression of life, will take place automatically and inevitably, "just because." This assumption does not take into account the big picture, and thus it causes enormous problems. Simply, avoid assuming what should not be assumed.

A broader, more comprehensive understanding of our world reduces the number of mistakes that we might make—particularly when compared with the volume of mistakes we might make if we adopt a narrower, less expansive viewpoint. An appreciation of strategic implications causes us to slow down our decision-making, even if only slightly, as we give greater weight to "thinking time"—the time taken to deliberate and ponder before taking action.

The importance of this strategic awareness, in business and in life, cannot be overstated. There are many examples of situations where proper procedures were followed and yet, lacking strategic direction, caused more problems than they solved. Yes, proper procedure must be followed—but to solve some dilemmas requires more than merely following procedure.

For example, consider a company-mandated procedure for ordering inventory—when stock reaches specified reorder levels, new inventory is ordered. Including strategic awareness takes that process one step further and asks, "Is our reorder level set correctly?" or "It seems we are ordering too often. Is inventory being misplaced or stolen?" or "Do we even need this inventory?" Some companies have operated for years with internal theft because the individual in charge of ordering lacked any systemic awareness of inventory control.

It is important to always keep in mind that past and present actions very often have a major impact on future results and outcomes. As a broad-minded employer or employee, you must be intensely aware of this interconnectedness of present actions and future outcomes.

This may sound entirely obvious, yet many people are lacking in this area of judgment. Insufficient systemic awareness and inadequate appreciation of implications and consequences have been a primary cause for countless poor professional and personal decisions, especially when the decisions were made under periods of high stress. Systemic thinking is quite simply one of the many and varied characteristics an individual must possess to be successful over the long haul.

The familiar phrase *cannot see the forest for the trees* describes those who have difficulty understanding strategic implications. If we are engrossed in a multitude of details at the expense of all else, we are apt to overlook higher-level priorities and or long-term ramifications. Executives, homemakers, college students, medical interns, aviators—every time we "fly," we must maintain both tactical and strategic viewpoints.

Understanding strategic implications can manifest in a variety of positive ways. First, it can operate as a beneficial "safety valve." For example, if it is unnerving for you to ride a bicycle without a helmet or walk along the edge of a cliff, it is likely that your systemic orientation or understanding is signaling *danger* to you. If you instinctively feel that the implications of these choices can be life-changing in an instant, then your systemic understanding is functioning. People who feel only excitement and exhilaration when participating in such activities have a less well-developed systemic appreciation. This "appreciation gap" is perhaps nowhere wider than among young people. Teenage girls, as a group, score much better in this area of judgment than teenage boys, who are, on average, slower to develop systemic conceptualization.

Second, an appreciation of the systemic can alert you to undertakings that are not necessarily inherently dangerous, but flawed in their direction or purpose. If you are actively engaged in a task—and yet lacking in systemic awareness—you are prone to just keep going, without ever pausing to make certain you are proceeding in the right direction or in pursuit of a worthy objective. For example, a ditch digger might be capable of digging the best ditch in the world, but that person needs to make sure first that the ditch needs to be dug, and then that it is being dug properly.

Strong

Strong systemic conceptualization indicates an ability to evaluate theoretically and abstractly. It does not necessarily indicate the ability to *accomplish*, but it does indicate the ability to *envision*—an aptitude for the free association of ostensibly unrelated thoughts and ideas.

If your systemic conceptualization is well developed, you have a talent for brainstorming and long-range strategic planning. You bring broad perspectives into a decision-making process, and an ability to see implications and consequences. You have a pronounced proficiency in understanding global and/or far-reaching problems. You understand that the effects of past and present decisions and actions can be far-reaching, sometimes even generational, in their implications.

As you make your way through various situations and circumstances, you tend to project your view of the potential consequences into the future, with a keen awareness of cause and effect. You realize that the smallest decision, though it may appear to be made "in a vacuum," in actuality may have sweeping consequences that may affect the stability and sustainability of an organization—and indeed, its very existence as a viable entity in the future.

You know that the myriad of decisions you make in the early stages of your preparation and task completion affect the successful and safe completion of that task. This awareness is particularly advantageous during abnormal and unusual situations where far-reaching, longer-term solutions might not be transparent. As a manager, a parent, a landscaper, a small business owner, a coach, an accountant, a minister, or in any profession, you are aware that the choices you make now sometimes have long-lasting influence on the future.

You understand danger: Your mind considers the consequences of falling off that cliff and the potential for injury to an unprotected head. With well-developed judgment in this area, your strategic awareness is strong. If so, pay attention to it. If not, you need to develop it.

Well over fifty percent of the population believe they are more strategically oriented than they actually are. I once had a client who claimed that he had strong systemic judgment because the word *strategic* was in his job title, and could be found on his business card. (Turns out he was wrong.) To avoid deceiving yourself about your strategic sensibilities, be as objective as you can about the true nature of your strategic awareness. Base any determination you make about yourself on your *actual* values, not on your *desired* values.

If your systemic understanding is developed and active, it influences your evaluative judgment no matter the scenario:

- Would you actually feel danger—not just excitement and an adrenalin surge—when standing at the edge of a cliff?

- What goes through your mind when you see someone riding a bicycle without a helmet?

- Do you ever consider putting in a pair of ear plugs when you're around loud music or equipment?

▸ When driving through a safari park, would you consider opening the windows despite instructions to keep them shut for reasons of safety?

▸ Before going for an ocean swim, do you notice whether lifeguards are on duty, think about the currents, or consider swimming with a buddy?

Base your answers here on your awareness of implications and consequences, and not on whether or not you have, for example, a fear of heights. Be honest with yourself. It doesn't matter whether these examples apply to your life in particular; if they don't, just think of some that do.

The bottom line here is: What typically goes through your mind when you are presented with a new idea, challenge, opportunity, or crisis? Does your personal radar ever genuinely sense danger—and if it does, do you listen to it or just shrug it off? Do you regularly and consistently consider the future (whether that's in minutes, months, years, or generations), or are you almost exclusively concerned with immediate issues?

The question to answer is whether or not you genuinely consider and appreciate the bigger picture beyond your immediate actions. Unfortunately, many people do not—and even worse, many who do not . . . think that they do.

Very Strong

Very strong, highly developed systemic conceptualization is quite rare, found in approximately only fifteen percent of the adult population. If you are one of the fortunate few, your strategic awareness is significantly more acute than that of the vast majority of the population.

However, along with the wonderful positives of astute strategic awareness, there are a few potential negatives. As long as you are able to avoid these pitfalls, your exceptional systemic conceptualization will provide extraordinary input to your evaluative judgment.

Success Tip #1: Sweat the little stuff.

Avoid spending *too much* time in protracted consideration or contemplation. You are vulnerable to overly pondering, reviewing, and assessing—especially in the exceedingly rare case where your systemic score dominates your intrinsic and extrinsic judgments. This may cause such extreme examinations of every possible imaginable scenario that you have difficulty adopting one of your many and varied plans. As valuable as strategy is, don't focus so intently on the big picture that you are unable to accomplish the task at hand.

Success Tip #2: Be mindful of your effect on others.

Frustration—for both you and your colleagues—is another potential negative outcome of exceptionally strong systemic conceptualization. Your tendency to ponder and evaluate, especially if you are systemically dominant, may be in stark contrast to an individual or team that tends to act quicker due to their more intrinsic or extrinsic sensibilities. Others may view you as the contrary one or the person who is always pondering and picking apart every scenario rather than taking action. At times, the frustration and friction between you can lead to stress. Fortunately, if you are mindful of your uniquely strong systemic awareness, you have a head start in mitigating any future frustration or stress.

Weak

With weak systemic conceptualization, you do not devote appropriate consideration to the implications and consequences of a decision or process. Typically, you fail to take into account the outcomes of plans and upcoming actions. You often disregard (or fail to discern) relevant, higher-level issues that may lie beyond the realm of minutiae and detail. Weakness in this area is a serious detriment to your chances for high levels of success.

Insufficient systemic understanding diminishes the effectiveness of any plans, strategies, and long-range goals—that is, if you have long-range goals at all. Often, long-term plans and goals do not interest you; they annoy you or seem irrelevant to you, and so you do not take the time to develop them.

It is typical for you to lack an understanding of the aggregate situation; to have an inadequate appreciation for wide-ranging, all-encompassing perspectives; and to become overly and excessively concerned with detail. Of course details matter—but with weak systemic conceptualization, it is likely that the details command overly important significance in your approach. You wrap yourself up in minutiae but miss the big picture—and colleagues who have a stronger systemic orientation may frequently have to be on call to explain the relevant points to you. The reality is, details and big-picture, long-term strategies are *not* mutually exclusive. To achieve success in your chosen profession, it is vital to maintain both perspectives.

Many times, your inability to grasp the strategic implications leaves you entangled in difficult and problematic circumstances. While it may seem to you that these predicaments appear "out of nowhere," they are often due to actions not being backed up or supported by a broad perspective on the situation at hand. Your propensity to focus on narrowly defined symptoms rather than on the root cause of problems may exacerbate, quickly and repeatedly, the underlying cause of the dilemma.

Technological advances that create instant, sometimes overwhelming quantities of communication and information overload can further exacerbate systemic weakness by fostering the tendency to act before we think. The consequences of such behavior can be detrimental to your success, if not downright dangerous and deadly.

A person lacking development here will be more likely to start a project without checking for the necessary equipment; run multiple errands without a sensible plan; or make business decisions without considering potential economic pitfalls. This approach is akin to shooting a gun without considering where the bullet will go. You can get away with this in some occupations, but not many.

Improving strategic awareness is not easy to do, but it can be done—and it is important that you do it. Here is how.

Success Tip #1: Slow down.

Before you act, take time to observe and assess. In all likelihood, you typically act too soon, without reviewing potential outcomes or appreciating the implications and consequences of your choices. Stop to smell the coffee, whether you're making a decision, performing a task, or embarking on a new endeavor. Don't just plunge in; take the temperature of the situation first.

Adhere to this long-standing and still useful cliché: Slow down and count to ten before making a decision. Then, while counting to ten, mull over the big picture.

Success Tip #2: Ask yourself about the consequences.

Develop the habit of asking systemic questions so that you can improve your systemic awareness. For example, ask yourself

- ▸ *Should I be doing this?*
- ▸ *Is this the best course of action?*
- ▸ *Is this what I really want to do?*
- ▸ *What could go wrong?*

Even just probing the who, what, when, where, and why of a problem or predicament will improve your overall understanding of the situation.

Success Tip #3: Back away from the details.

Try to employ a sweeping perspective of the issue before rendering a decision. Put on your systemic-thinking cap and ask yourself big-picture, strategic questions before you act. Throughout the course of a project, event, or opportunity—and particularly in the early stages, when important decisions must be made—briefly stop asking "How?" and spend a few minutes asking "Why?"

If you work in an office, literally slide your chair away from your desk and consider your project in terms of *Why?* and *What for?* The point is to regularly disengage temporarily from the details and reflect on the broader view.

Success Tip #4: Reject instant gratification.

Do whatever it takes—turn off your phone, regulate your online time, switch off the TV news—to cut down on information overload. Take the time to consider cause and effect, not just the knee-jerk reaction to the latest buzz. The routine of instant gratification develops the tendency to act before we think. Garner an appreciation for long-range implications and for longer-term consequences. Doing so improves decision-making and problem-solving, and leads you further toward your success.

Systemic Actualization — *Using Strategies*

The *actualization* component of your systemic judgment manifests as your ability to *use* strategies. It determines your ability to incorporate and act upon your knowledge of implications and consequences—and thus your ability to apply comprehensive strategies. For most people, however, the systemic element is the weakest of the three global actualization components. (To review conceptualization and actualization, see pages 31 to 34.)

Furthermore, an individual may have a strong strategic *awareness*—an appreciation of varied and numerous ideas, plans, and strategies—as well as a finely tuned warning system that alerts that person to potentially hazardous, unproductive, uneconomical, and objectionable consequences, and yet fail to heed the warning or apply that knowledge to his or her decisions. While systemic conceptualization determines your ability to *understand* strategic implications, systemic actualization determines your ability to *use and act on* that knowledge—and the presence of the former does not guarantee the latter.

The differences between these two areas of judgment may seem negligible at first glance. After all, if a person can *understand* strategies, it seems natural that he or she would *use* those strategies. Unfortunately, this is not always the case. The reality is that it is commonplace for people to understand the implications of an agenda—all the while ignoring them during actual decision-making and action. Most of us at some point in our lives have been guilty of such contradictory behavior and faulty decision-making. If there are substantial differences between a person's strength in *understanding* strategic implications and their strength in *using* that understanding, the impact on decision-making and problem-solving can be profound—and often, not for the better.

Consider the following questions:

- Do you actually use big-picture implications to direct and influence your decisions and actions? For example, if you are standing next to that cliff and your strong understanding of strategic implications signals *Danger!*, do you exhibit follow-through by heeding that warning and stepping away from the edge?

- Has there been a time in your life when you had an awareness of implications and consequences, but did not allow that awareness to guide your decision-making?

- Have you ever downplayed or pushed aside your systemic awareness rather than use it in formulating your professional and personal decisions and choices?

▸ Have you ever known that you should not do whatever you were about to do—and then done it anyway?

For many people, the failure to *use* their systemic awareness is a big issue, and one that negatively influences their daily judgment and decision-making. Furthermore, for most people, systemic judgment is the weakest of their three global judgments. At times it is overpowered, quickly and effortlessly, by intrinsic and extrinsic pressures—and sometimes also by chaos, confusion, and stress (we'll talk about this in Part 3). Failure to heed their inner systemic awareness can lead to poor decisions as they interact with people, situations, problems, and opportunities.

One characteristic of someone with well-developed systemic actualization is the regular practice of *validation and verification*. This is prompted by what is sometimes referred to as "personal radar," "red flags," or "the caution factor." If we do not work to verify and substantiate strategic implications, then they remain just that: implications, or thoughts in our head.

Only when consideration moves toward validation and verification is there a real impact on real outcomes. The conceptualization component of systemic judgment triggers an alarm, and then the actualization component of systemic judgment prods and nudges us to action: to validate and verify. We experience, sense, or feel the need to verify—and so we do.

For example, before I make a potentially foolhardy decision and jump off the cliff into the lake below, the conceptualization component of my systemic judgment alerts me to impending danger and the unacceptable consequences of injury or death. Moreover, the actualization component of my systemic judgment is strong enough so that if I decide I actually am going to jump off that cliff, first I will walk down to the water to *validate and verify* the depth.

If you are a Bering Sea crab fisherman, it would be your systemic awareness that alerts you to a line of impending weather along your fishing route—along with any dire implications and consequences associated with that weather. Then your systemic actualization causes you to act on that understanding: to query the weather forecaster for updates, find another fishing route, turn around or divert to calmer seas, or perhaps even cancel the trip.

This anecdote may not seem to have much relevance for you, but other examples of the actualization component of strategic judgment are countless, wide, and varied. Think of examples within your own field of endeavor.

There are many, many situations where validation and verification are vitally important—where decisions require more than thinking about your predicament or merely understanding the systemic implications and consequences. Effective and appropriate decisions require that you use your systemic awareness in the actions of verification—the actions of *making sure.*

There is another benefit to having an active systemic actualization component within our decision-making: Not only does it improve the decisions we make, but it also helps us avoid the commonplace tendency to postpone or procrastinate—those times when we are not making decisions we know we *should* make. For example, our strategic actualization prompts us to purchase that life insurance policy, put new tires on the car, mend the fence, update our will, replace aging machinery, eat healthier, avoid a dangerous stretch of highway, repack the parachute, and so forth. The strength of our systemic actualization determines whether we have the tendency to move beyond *thinking* about the decisions, and actually *make* those choices.

What about you? Do you have life insurance, new tires on your car, a mended fence, a will, safe equipment, and a healthy diet? The answers speak directly to your systemic actualization.

Strong

Strong systemic actualization indicates that you use strategic implications and broad considerations to help guide your decisions. You incorporate big-picture awareness into the problem-solving process, and this improves the result. You often avoid the negative consequences associated with shortsightedness and snap decisions. It is natural for you to examine, analyze, and apply "what ifs" and various possible scenarios before you take action—*which you then do.*

Because of the strong actualization component of your strategic judgment, you tend to think before you do, and you bring an expansive view to the solution of problems. You are not frightened or fearful of problems of a more abstract or suppositious nature, because your tendency to use strategies in your decisions is pleasurable for you, and puts you at ease when examining the "what ifs" before you act.

You naturally grasp that pondering implications and consequences, while better than not pondering, still does not guarantee outcomes. Therefore, you attempt to *validate* your instincts, moving beyond the mere consideration of potential repercussions to the actions of making sure. You check the depth of the water before taking the plunge—which, ironically, may cause people with weaker systemic judgment to view you as contrary or hesitant, or even as something of a "wet blanket."

The majority of the population does not have strong systemic actualization—and so if you do, it means most of your workmates are not quite as gifted as you in considering the solutions to large-scale, long-term problems. In fact, they are quite likely to seek out your advice concerning the solution of long-range, far-reaching, or speculative issues—even if they think you are a spoilsport when it comes to the thrill of jumping off the bridge.

Systemic actualization is less developed and is underutilized in a substantial portion of the population. For most people, the realm of the systemic is relatively weaker than the intrinsic or extrinsic. This means the overwhelming majority are either intrinsic or extrinsic dominant, and as such are generally wired to get along and/or get things done. Bearing this in mind, it is important to note that some scores that are only moderately strong in the intrinsic and extrinsic therefore are considered relatively exceptional in the systemic.

Very Strong

Should your systemic use be exceptionally well developed, it can manifest somewhat quickly into powerful and problematic levels of frustration. The reality is that our culture does not generally encourage systemic thinkers, with the value structures of approximately sixty percent of the population not including a strong systemic actualization component.

The frustration that erupts between the tactical thinker and the strategic thinker can be enormous. As your evaluative judgment is so likely to clash with that of others, you must acknowledge that most people do not have a powerful actualization component to their systemic judgment, and then take care to listen to the intrinsic and extrinsic suggestions of others *even when they do not listen to your systemic suggestions.* You may have great suggestions, *better* suggestions—but hey, *you* are in the minority.

Considerable conflict can occur within a team that comprises some intrinsic-dominant individuals, some extrinsic-dominant individuals, and some systemic-dominant individuals. Within my corporate work, I have witnessed this occurring firsthand many times. If the team members—executives, coaches, coworkers, volunteers, members of the PTA, or whoever—have not developed the mechanisms to handle frustration, they may be at odds over not only consequential decisions, but also trivial and inconsequential decisions and choices.

Make the effort in your workplace to use what is, in all likelihood, a diversity of opinions to broaden and improve any decisions. Take care so that frustration over how your workmates act and reflect does not undermine the effectiveness of your own decisions.

Moderate

Moderate systemic actualization is rather common. It indicates that while the use of strategies has some prominence in, or bearing on, decisions and choices, the ultimate decisions may still be based more on immediate needs, routines and habits, and outside influences than on long-term considerations. Outcomes tend to be a mix of positive and negative, a result that shapes the next series of choices accordingly.

When your systemic actualization is only moderately strong, considering implications is not your first instinct. The moderate-scoring individual likely embodies the saying *Good judgment comes from experience—and experience comes from bad judgment.* Those who have access to a wise mentor are more likely to make better choices based on their mentor's good advice, and retain the learned ability to make good choices, and pass on their wisdom. Those who are not so lucky as to have a mentor are likely to learn from the experience of their previous bad decisions. In other words, having moderately strong systemic actualization at least provides an ability to learn from one's mistakes.

As objectively as you can, try to determine if moderate systemic usage describes you. If it does, be open-minded to the possibility that your life can improve by exploring further study in this area. Many helpful books have been written on the subject of developing and using helpful strategies.

It is also a good idea to discover if, within your family or inner circle of friends, you have access to at least one person who is able to pass on big-picture advice and wisdom for your benefit.

Weak

With weak systemic actualization, your ability to incorporate big-picture, strategic concepts into decision-making is essentially nil. You make the same mistakes over and over and over again.

If you manage to implement a positive and effective strategic decision, it is the exception, not the rule. Any good strategic choices you make are likely due to good luck or maybe a strong work ethic rather than a well-developed systemic actualization component within your value structure. You may even have a strong appreciation for strategies and the big picture, but weak systemic actualization indicates that when it's time to *use* that appreciation, you do not perform as well.

If this describes you, trust that you are weak in this area, and be fore-warned that unless you improve it, you are going to continue to make abysmal strategic decisions in the future.

An unfortunate characteristic associated with weak systemic actual-ization is the proclivity to believe that bad decisions are easily remedi-ated with a redo or an impulsive attempt using a different method. (This tendency is especially common among individuals who are very strong extrinsically and very weak systemically.) Rather than ponder, consider, validate, and verify beforehand, you move forward with a quick decision, see what happens, and if the results are not to your liking, just try another approach. Your motto is *Do it over, and sooner or later I'll get it right!*

Inadequate systemic actualization indicates you have a tendency to make hurried, reactionary decisions as a matter of habit. You throw it at the wall and see if it sticks. This can lead to consequences that are perma-nently life- or business-altering. Some mistakes can never be remediated.

An executive or manager who proceeds to try something new with-out using strategic judgment first may cost his or her company thousands of dollars. A business entrepreneur who makes a rash decision may drive his or her enterprise into bankruptcy. The hard-core reality is that many decisions made hastily and without a systemic component actually are irreversible and sometimes result in tragedy. Organizational decisions made without a systemic component can, and often do, lead to debilitat-ing corporate failure.

Fortunately, you can strengthen weak systemic judgment—and if you do, your decisions will improve. Here is how you can start.

Success Tip #1: Slow down your decision-making process.

Go beyond appreciation, and make a conscious effort to *incorporate* those big-picture understandings into your decisions and choices. Do not fall prey to the belief that systemic awareness is enough. It is not. Actions speak louder than appreciation. So listen, listen, and listen again to that inner voice of systemic awareness. If your strategic understanding of the implications and consequences of a particular action tells you to do it, then do it.

If it tells you not to do it, then *do not do it.*

Success Tip #2: Let big-picture questions guide your actions.

Make sure to consider not only the relational, short-term, and tactical aspects of an issue or problem, but also the strategic, long-term, comprehensive aspects. People often become so intrinsically or extrinsically dominant that they do not even allow systemic ideas, thoughts, and questions into their mind. *Let them in!* Avoid the tendency to pay lip service to the systemic and then ignore it in your decisions. Do not stop at those good ideas and intentions, but make a purposeful, conscious effort to go beyond that point and actually *use* them.

Ask yourself the far-reaching, broad, comprehensive systemic questions—and then use the answers to guide your decisions.

Success Tip #3: Look before you leap.

Do not merely take a quick peek at the consequences and hope for the best. Develop the habit of taking the extra time to substantiate your systemic ideas.

If you know in advance that you will be unable to unequivocally validate and verify an idea or speculation, do not use this knowledge as an excuse to avoid the verification process altogether. Just an attempt to verify something can offer greater insurance than acting on impulse and leaping before you look.

Learn to verify—physically, as well as you are able—the depth of the water before you jump. Do not merely take a quick glance and hope for the best. Even if you are unable to measure the depth with exactitude, at least give it a genuine long, hard look.

Success Tip #4: Heed red flags.

When your personal radar clues you to danger or vulnerability, listen to it. Even the tiniest red flag can provide a crucial warning. The pressures that can influence a decision are many and varied—and if your systemic actualization is weak, you are more likely to succumb to those pressures. Know this about yourself—and pause, think, follow through, and verify *before* you act.

Now, there are situations where stopping to validate an instinct or speculation is easier said than done. For example, in the business world, you might experience extrinsic pressures from a business meeting or a tight schedule to do something *right now*, before you or your business is ready. You might feel pressure to take a risky course of action, adopt an untested process, or cut corners where you know you shouldn't. Resist such pressures, and listen to your inner radar.

Success Tip #5: Incorporate strategy in your decisions.

Consciously include a systemic component in your decisions. Do not allow competing intrinsic and extrinsic interests to dominate and obliterate the systemic issues involved in a given situation. People with undeveloped systemic actualization often make decisions overly weighted in the intrinsic and extrinsic, without regard for systemic implications and consequences. A quick glance at the daily news—accidents, bankruptcy, scandal, criminal acts, horrific tragedies, and more—bears this out. Do not let your desires to please and gel with others (intrinsic) and your desires to do something (extrinsic) override all other factors.

Success Tip #6: Calculate the odds of success.

Consider your situation or potential solutions to your problem from both a best-case and a worst-case scenario—and calculate the odds of these outcomes for each solution.

For example, if you are a pilot planning a flight, and conditions change—whether because of a delay, anticipated maintenance, or unexpected weather—consider best-case and worst-case outcomes for the flight depending on the new information: *What are the best- and worst-case scenarios if I launch in this weather? What are the best and worst cases if I do not stop for fuel? What are the best and worst cases if I divert?* Then answer each question as best you can by pondering the various scenarios, and using your best judgment to help render your decisions.

A conscious and dedicated contemplation of best-case/worst-case outcomes will get you in the habit of actually using systemic judgment to affect your decisions—and that approach is rare and valuable indeed, and something that will drive you toward your success.

. . .

As mentioned, the *conceptualization* and *actualization* components of systemic judgment (see pages 31 to 34) manifest as *understanding strategies* and *using strategies*.

- ▸ If your conceptual judgment is stronger, you *think* more about an issue or strategy rather than dealing with it directly.

- ▸ If your actualization is stronger than your conceptualization, you are likely to be good at not only *understanding* strategies and their implications, but also *applying and employing* strategy as you make your decisions.

- ▸ Ideally, your use of strategy is *equal to or stronger than* your corresponding understanding of strategy.

If you have strong conceptualization and poor actualization, it means that you have a solid grasp of implications and consequences, but do not follow through and use that understanding to guide your decisions. You may have many good ideas; be able to distinguish a strong plan from a weak plan; and benefit from excellent personal radar. But you do not use your strong mental blueprints to implement your decisions and actions. Thus, others in the work world are likely to perceive you as someone with good ideas who fails to satisfy the positive culmination of those plans.

Many of our clients who completed our judgment assessment, and who have a respectable score in conceptualization and a weaker score in actualization, admit that when engaged in questionable activities, they often think, *This is a bad idea* . . . but then do it anyway. A telltale sign of a disparity between *understanding* strategies and *using* strategies is a feeling of regret and remorse immediately following a decision. If you have ever had a hunch that you should not be proceeding in a certain fashion, and yet you make that ill-conceived decision anyway, then you are well aware of the negative implications and consequences of disregarding your systemic awareness at decision time.

Of course, there are many reasons why we make particular decisions at a given time, but if there is a major disparity between your systemic conceptualization and actualization judgments, pay extra attention to your systemic judgment when making decisions. This will aid you greatly on the journey toward your success.

At the end of 1991, I left active duty in the U.S. Navy, joined the Navy Reserves, and was hired by American Airlines. Life was good. Then in 1993, when I was one of the most junior pilots in their workforce, AA laid me off (in the airline industry, we call this a "furlough"). For the first time in my adult life, I found myself without a job.

I decided to try my hand at running my own business. I did my homework, got a loan, and opened a "quick lube" shop. It was profitable within three months' time.

Over the course of the next several years I opened five more quick lubes, a full-service automotive repair shop, a convenience store, and several car washes. I was quite busy, and depended heavily on my employees. We had frontline staff, managers, and district managers. Over the course of about twenty years, I hired and fired over five hundred people.

My shops employed some excellent automotive mechanics. If a

vehicle needed brakes, tires, an oil change, alignment, preventive maintenance, or whatever, my mechanics repaired it enthusiastically and professionally. My employees and I demanded a high level of automotive competence from every technician in our shops; otherwise, they were quickly weeded out.

Even so, as good as most of my mechanics were at automotive maintenance, there was one particular mechanic who stood out above all the rest when it came to those obscure, intermittent, complicated, and difficult-to-diagnosis automotive problems. That would be Bubba.

Well, in fact, Bubba was not his real name. However, if the name "Bubba" conjures up for you the image of a good ol' country boy, then that name has provided for you an accurate image of Bubba.

Bubba was one of those employees we hid from our most hoity-toity customers. How shall I put it? He didn't always present well. His accent was so thick and countrified that often I could not understand him, even after three or four tries. A few times I had to have him write down on paper what he was saying so I could figure out what it was. Usually then, after spending a few minutes deciphering his terrible spelling, I would understand.

In the automotive shop, we used "tickets" to relay information from the customer to the mechanic. The service writers created the tickets and then handed them over to the mechanics. Each ticket came in its own plastic pouch and included an outline of the work to be performed on the vehicle; a list of the parts and labor that would be necessary; the car keys; the vehicle's location on the lot; a disposable floor mat and steering wheel cover; and the customer's description of any vehicle problems.

Bubba was quite demanding when it came to the service writers. If the ticket was not written out in detail, describing everything that the customer noticed about the vehicle, he would demand more information. If any details were left out, Bubba would insist that the service writer call the customer for the information. The service

Continued

writers learned that to keep Bubba happy, they needed to query the customer about every little quirk relating to their automobile, even if it seemed utterly irrelevant and unrelated to the problem at hand.

At first, I wasn't so sure about the wisdom of hiring Bubba. Adding to this feeling was the fact that my office had a window with a view into the service bay area, and sometimes I would see Bubba just standing there, staring at a customer's vehicle. Bubba was a smoker, and I didn't allow smoking in the shop. So he would stand at the bay door, just outside the shop, staring and smoking.

My initial impression at moments like this was that Bubba was taking yet another smoke break to avoid work.

Soon, though, I began to notice a pattern to his behavior. Bubba would read the ticket slowly and carefully, taking much longer to do this than the other mechanics. Then he would move to the bay door, light up a cigarette, stand in silence, smoke, and stare. Several times I wandered into the shop and stood beside him as this went on. We stood there in silence, him smoking and both of us staring at the car in question.

I quickly realized my impression was entirely misplaced. Bubba's behavior didn't follow the pattern of the typical lazy employee, the ones who hid from view and smoked while perfecting the art of doing nothing. (Those employees didn't last long.) No, Bubba stood in plain sight, not hiding, and his demeanor didn't change when I walked up, the way it does when you've been caught doing something you shouldn't. Bubba just stood there, smoking and staring, arms crossed and seemingly unperturbed by my presence.

Normally I became irritated when an employee stood around, doing nothing, staring. There is always something to do in an automotive repair shop. However, even though Bubba stared at cars, his productivity was good. Still, I was curious—why did he do this?

So one day when he was staring, I nonchalantly asked him how things were going.

He said, "Fine."

So I nonchalantly asked him what he was doing.

He said, "Thankin'."

That puzzled me. Who on earth was he thanking?

After a bit of back and forth, I realized what Bubba was saying. He wasn't thanking; he was *thinking*.

I asked him what he was "thankin'" about. He said he wasn't exactly sure, but he needed this "thankin'" time before he picked up a wrench.

Before Bubba's arrival, my shop had already developed a reputation for being able to solve even the most hard-to-pinpoint automotive issues. Often the troubled vehicle had worked its way through several shops around town—including the car's dealership, no less—with none being able to repair it. Drivability issues are by far the most difficult because of their obscure nature, and often they're not even very profitable, but we took pride in their resolution.

One day a vehicle arrived that we knew was going to be difficult: The customer had been to several shops, including the dealer, with no luck. The customer's vehicle had one of those tiny, annoying intermittent skips that can be almost impossible to find, and yet can downright ruin the driving experience.

As it happened, our most senior Master Technician, whom until that point we had considered our best diagnostician, was busy with work for the entire day. So we took a breath and a leap of faith, and handed the ticket to Bubba.

This was Bubba's first bona fide serious drivability repair job in our shop, and yet he seemed entirely in his element. He took his time, did some "thankin'" about it for several minutes, diagnosed the issue correctly, and then repaired it. It turned out to be a bizarre combination of problems with the computer, the electrical wiring, and the coolant. The customer was thrilled.

Bubba was impressive, and he was consistent. He followed his methodical pattern every time. When lesser mechanics at other shops were raising hoods and swapping out parts in a flurry, only to

157

Continued

learn later they had swapped out the wrong parts, Bubba was taking his time, diagnosing properly, and achieving the right repairs the first time he worked on a vehicle. He saw automotive relationships that few others could see. He understood the complexity of modern vehicles and had an amazing grasp of the distinction between symptom and root cause. Sure, he was very skilled and quick with a wrench . . . but he never rushed.

We were never able to show Bubba off to our most highbrow customers, and I always felt bad that I couldn't convince him to stop smoking. But we sure were lucky to have him.

GLOBAL JUDGMENT
INTERACTIONS

Now that you are familiar with the three global judgments—intrinsic, extrinsic, and systemic—it's time to emphasize the importance of paying close attention to these three areas of judgment not only individually but, even more important, in combination.

When we move beyond stand-alone analyses, and view a person's strengths and weaknesses in these areas of judgment *in totality*, it reveals additional and supplementary meanings. In fact, the examination of how you use your global judgments not only by themselves, but also in interaction with each other, provides the very deepest understanding of your overall evaluative judgments.

Specifically, and significantly, situations or problems often arise where a particular area of judgment—I, E, or S—is more necessary for an appropriate resolution. Because of this reality, and due to the makeup of your unique value structure, you may be better positioned to resolve certain types of issues. So

Intrinsic dilemmas will require . . . intrinsic judgment.
Extrinsic dilemmas will require . . . extrinsic judgment.

(Get the picture? I think you do, so I will not belabor the point.)

Thus, if our value structure is skewed toward a particular area of judgment, those are the solutions we are more apt to solve effectively. On the flip side, we are less apt to find solutions in areas where our judgment is weaker.

Still, there is a caveat here: Most decisions, to be good decisions, require some level of each area of judgment.

For example, the discipline chosen to address an employee's mistake ends up being the most effective when the employer employs

- a strong *intrinsic* component to understand the employee's motivations (whether they were good or bad),

- an *extrinsic* component to help work out the actual details of the discipline, and

- a *systemic* component to ensure the employee appreciates the longer-range implications and consequences of the discipline.

How our values and judgments are interrelated and interact with one another makes a difference for every single one of our decisions . . . and ultimately, for our success.

Judgment Dominance

Within the three primary areas of judgment—I, E, and S—most people have a dominant, a less dominant, and a least dominant judgment.

Your *dominant*, or strongest, global judgment indicates the area of judgment where you are the most comfortable and the most adept. You employ this area of judgment first as you approach a situation, tackle a problem, or go through your decision-making process. Your *less dominant* area is your second strongest area of judgment, and your *least dominant* is the area of judgment you consider last.

For example, if it turns out your global judgments are in this descending order of dominance—*dominant I, less dominant E, least dominant S*—then when you are confronted with a dilemma or predicament, you

- consider the people involved, how they are impacted, and the affected relationships *first*;

- consider the task or mission, and its tactical details, *second*; and

- consider the big-picture, far-reaching, all-encompassing strategies and considerations *third*.

The *differences in strength* between your three global judgments play a huge part in your order of consideration, but so does the *amount of emphasis* you give to each area of judgment. Specifically

- When the disparity of strength among your global judgments *grows or is large* (e.g., if you are incredibly strong in big-picture thinking, and are extremely weak in terms of the human factor), you place more emphasis and priority on your most dominant judgment(s), and less value and priority on your least dominant judgment(s).

- When your global judgments are *equal or nearly equal in strength*, you bring each area of judgment into your decision-making and problem-solving process—a desirable scenario.

The data tells us that individuals with parity among their global judgment strengths make consistently more well-rounded decisions—a sure-fire way to achieve success. Their decisions fulfill the concept more often and more effectively, which helps guide them quicker toward their success.

In a perfect world, an individual's I, E, and S judgments are all strong, and also relatively equal when compared with each other. When the three areas of judgment are balanced in relation to each other, a person is likely to

- bring solid intrinsic, extrinsic, and systemic evaluative judgment into decision-making and problem-solving

- give appropriate value and priority to all areas of judgment

▸ never overlook, neglect, or deprioritize any of the three primary areas of judgment while tackling problems and predicaments

Avoid the temptation to believe that your judgments are in actuality the way you desire them to be. Maybe they are—but maybe they're not. You are going to have to examine your judgments for what they truly are: the way that they manifest into your *real* decisions, not the decisions you *wish* you would make.

Do you honestly include intrinsic, extrinsic, and systemic considerations in your decisions and choices? A cold, hard, honest look at yourself allows you to take stock of any judgment shortcomings, and then do something about it. This is not a time for wishful thinking—this is a time for *honesty*.

An objective analysis will go a long way toward your success—and soon we'll figure out how to do just that.

Global Judgment Patterns

Within the three areas of global judgment—I, E, and S—there are thirteen possible combinations of interaction and interrelation. These patterns are influenced in large part by the values of our society and culture.

Your own personal global indicator pattern might be entirely different from the typical patterns we see. However, the three that follow are the most common:

▸ **Most Common Pattern:** *Dominant I; Less Dominant E; Least Dominant S.* Intrinsic scores are often stronger because of our cultural emphasis on social skills, being well liked, and valuing others. Social dexterity is viewed as a highly positive attribute. Chances are, you may know someone who has had a very successful career of getting ahead by getting along.

▸ **Second Most Common Pattern:** *Dominant E; Less Dominant I; Least Dominant S.* This pattern is typically influenced by the value and importance assigned to hard work. Many people go so far as to associate hard work with godliness. This emphasis, priority, and value placed on hard work contributes to strong extrinsic scores.

▸ **Third Most Common Pattern**: *Equally Dominant I and E; Weak/Much Less Dominant S.* Many people place sole emphasis and priority equally on intrinsic and extrinsic values and judgments. Thus, their ability in these areas of judgments evolves and comes to dominate their weak systemic judgment.

The most unusual pattern is *Very Dominant S; Weak/Much Less Dominant I and E.* Generally, not as much value is placed on the long-term view and the consideration of implications and consequences. Therefore it is a rare individual indeed whose S-judgment dominates their I- and E-judgments. (And although it is rare, in some people I and S dominate their E, and in other people E and S dominate their I.)

Remember, good judgment and great success occur when you maintain parity among your global judgment indicators. Danger lurks when there is great disparity in strength among the global indicators. A notably greater strength in one or two indicators can overshadow any relatively weaker areas of judgment, even if you are strong in all three of the primary judgment areas. Should you have this disparity among judgment strengths, devote additional attention to your weaker areas of judgment, making sure they are considered when you make decisions and solve problems. This will help you avoid tunnel vision during your decision-making.

Commonly, this scenario occurs when *exceptionally strong* intrinsic and/or extrinsic judgments come to dominate what would normally be considered strong systemic judgment. In such an instance, you must make a judicious effort to be doubly sure that you are considering strategies and big-picture considerations when making very important decisions.

When it comes to teams or groups, as with individuals, the most effective are those with each judgment area (I, E, S) represented in the various members.

Of course, there are going to be differences of opinion or even conflicts between persons who are strong in differing judgments. But such differences, if depersonalized, help make the group perspective that much stronger.

As is the case with individuals, weak teams often have judgment that suffers from tunnel vision. This circumstance prevails when one of the three domains (I, E, S) is overly dominant within the group. I see this often in my corporate work. For example, it is quite common for an individual tasked with hiring to select individuals who all have similar value structure. The hirer is often oblivious to the negative impact that this choice will have on the company and, eventually, even on his or her own success.

Self-Assessment: Your "Comfort Zone"

Using this book, you can undergo a reflective, three-step self-assessment. Here's how:

1. Examine your relative strengths in the three primary areas of judgments (I, E, and S) as objectively as you can, paying close attention to both your decisions and your decision-making process. Here are some questions to ask of yourself—but make sure your answers are unflinchingly honest:

   > Which areas are you more likely to emphasize and place priority on when making decisions and solving conflicts?

   > What area(s) are of less concern to you when you go about your problem-solving?

   > What drives your judgment?

   > Do you emphasize the intrinsic more than the extrinsic and systemic? Do you care about what your colleagues or customers think and feel, and how they might react to your decisions?

   > Do you emphasize the extrinsic more than the systemic or intrinsic? Are you overly concerned with the task at hand and

the details involved in its successful completion? Do you do whatever you can to complete the endeavor without really considering or reflecting on how it might affect others and/or what its successful completion means for the long term?

> Are you predominantly a strategic thinker? Before you do anything at work, do you reflect on how the resolution or solution is going to affect the company days, months, or even years down the line? Do you try to imagine the unintended consequences, and how that decision might impact your surroundings or even the world at large?

> Do you bring all three areas of global judgment into your decision-making?

> Do you emphasize one or more areas at the expense of the remaining areas of judgment?

Remember, when answering these questions about yourself, *be as objective as you can.* Examine *what* you do—not what you *hope* to do or what you would *like* to do, but what you *actually* do. Yes, that can be hard to do. But have faith that you can do it objectively. If you desire to get an actual read on yourself, your values, and your judgments—and thus your path to success—it is a necessary step.

2. Examine several important and recent decisions you have made, particularly those made under duress or in urgent or chaotic circumstances. Analyze those choices through the lens of the questions presented to you in Step #1.

We tend to fall back on our strongest areas of judgment when under stress, often discounting what our weaker areas of judgment are trying to tell us. Choosing recent, stressful decisions you have made, and the process you used to make them, will help you determine the likely true nature and character of your judgment.

Again, employ not wishful thinking about who you would *like to be*, but who you *actually are* and what you *actually did*. Regarding evaluative judgment, what matters most are the decisions you make, not the decisions you wish you would make.

3. Test yourself in light of the following examples.

Scenario #1

A vehicle travels the wrong lane through a construction area on a roadway and causes a great deal of damage. The driver was not an employee of the construction company, nor was he impaired or intoxicated in any way.

What are you likely to think first and most strongly about this situation?

1. *Someone should study why this happened! Possibly the construction zone needed better signage, flashing lights, or more employees to enforce the travel rules in the vicinity.*

2. *That's going to be expensive! Someone's going to get sued, or probably the taxpayers will end up just shelling out money to fix this mess.*

3. *I hope no one was hurt! Is the driver okay? Was there a medical reason this happened?*

Make a note of your response, and at the end of the exercise, we will examine the results.

Scenario #2

Margaret is a veterinarian who often cares for injured animals in her home. She sometimes keeps animals who were given up by their original owners. As a result, Margaret has modified her home to accommodate far more animals than would normally be allowed in a typical home in her neighborhood.

Now seventy-three, Margaret is planning on retiring soon. She lives alone and has no children. She has assured her neighbors that she has set money aside for a successful transition of the animals should something happen to her. Still, Margaret's neighbors have expressed concerns about the potential negative impact on their neighborhood of so many animals in such a small space with an aging caretaker.

What are you likely to think first and most strongly about this situation? Be sure to note your honest and immediate reaction.

1. *Margaret should have a backup plan in place before she retires.* She should use her funds to train an assistant, and make contact with another location that could transport and care for these animals should she become disabled. She should have an emergency amount of money also set aside if there is a sudden need for someone else to perform her duties.

2. *Margaret should work on adapting her home facilities to allow for her decreasing physical capabilities.* She should invest in automatic feeding and watering, easy cage-cleaning devices, bulk purchases of food and supplies on delivery, and safety railings and ramps to prevent injuries.

3. *Those nosy and selfish neighbors just need to leave Margaret alone!* She has dedicated her life to the well-being of these animals, and she knows how to best handle their future.

Answer Key

For both scenarios, you should have decided whether you supported answer 1, 2, or 3 the most depending on how you are most likely to respond. Sure, you might feel there is validity in each of the three considerations, but be honest here: Which response was most characteristic of your pattern of judgment?

Here's the key to what those responses have to say about your judgment:

Answer 1 = Systemic

Answer 2 = Extrinsic

Answer 3 = Intrinsic

Your comfort zone is the judgment area that you *first* considered for your decision-making. This is often revealed by your first thought after hearing of a dilemma or concern. Your first thought may not be your final deciding factor, and you might bring other factors into consideration, but your first and most relatable thought is usually the area of your judgment that is the strongest. What you consider next is usually the second strongest, and so forth.

If you had several thoughts in mind almost simultaneously, then you likely have equal or near equal parity among multiple components of your value structure.

Now that you have taken a first step in estimating your global judgment pattern, go back and review the intrinsic (pages 48–75), extrinsic (pages 81–109), and systemic (pages 113–154) descriptions.

Remember that the range, scope, and variety of possible global judgment interactions, groupings, and strengths weighed against each other are limitless. If your particular global judgment pattern seems a bit skewed or out of kilter, do not worry. But understand that there are particular areas of judgment that you might overemphasize, and other areas that you might underemphasize.

Then, to springboard yourself to success, start to use what you believe to be your particular pattern as a guide in the future. Using this guide, you can better understand and improve the judgment areas that might be lacking in your decision-making, and you can start incorporating a new emphasis and importance as needed.

STYLE MATTERS

Quite separate and distinct from our decision-making *ability* is our decision-making *style*. Our decision-making style influences our decision-making ability, and affects whether we will use that ability in a *consistent* or an *inconsistent* manner. Our style is determined primarily by the relative strengths of our global judgments, and may either enhance or undermine our decision-making ability.

Some people have only a mediocre ability to make decisions, yet function day to day on a higher level because of the unremitting and steady *consistency* of their decision-making style. This helps them exploit their decision-making ability to its fullest potential. The opposite is also true: Some people possess formidable decision-making abilities, yet their haphazard and *inconsistent* style gets in the way, undermining their inherently good judgment and frequently causing them to bungle decisions.

There is nothing magical or even particularly noteworthy about the terms *consistent* and *inconsistent* as used here. Other word pairs, such as *effective* and *ineffective, enlightened* and *unenlightened, decisive* and *indecisive,* or *systematic* and *haphazard,* can just as easily describe a certain style of decision-making. For the sake of explanation, however, I'm going to divide decision-making style into three categories:

1. Consistent reactionary

2. Deliberative

3. Inconsistent reactionary

Keep in mind that even though we tend to make our decisions predominantly using one particular style, we are capable of implementing each style—and some of our decisions fall at the fringes or somewhere in between.

Although they are extremely different from one another, consistent and inconsistent decisions do share a common trait: They are both *reactionary*. Specifically, consistent and inconsistent decisions can be made quickly and even automatically—either without thinking about them or *seemingly* without thinking about them.

The third category of decision-making, *deliberative*, refers to the style of making decisions more slowly, and with contemplation and reflection.

Consistent Reactionary Decisions

The vast majority of our decisions—perhaps over eighty-five percent of them—are *reactionary*. Every day we make hundreds, perhaps thousands, of decisions, such as when to wake up, what clothes to wear, what to eat for breakfast, the route we take to work, whether to bring our lunch or dine out, and so forth. This process is repeated throughout our day as we make decisions automatically, without much effort, engaging minimal areas of our brain—all day, every day.

Nevertheless, a decision is not unimportant solely because it is made automatically. Some reactionary decisions are *very* important—for example, those we make in response to an emergency or a life-threatening crisis, or even the reactionary decision to stop for a red light.

Within reactionary decisions, there are two subcategories: *consistent* and *inconsistent*. A *consistent* reactionary decision, while *seemingly* made without thinking, is actually a well-thought-out decision. This might seem counterintuitive, but even a reactionary decision might have been pondered many times prior to being made at a particular moment. For example, a top-notch football quarterback can size up the entire defense, taking in intrinsic, extrinsic, and systemic cues from the opposing team within seconds, and then change the play as the clock is ticking down, implementing a well-developed plan that he has practiced over and over with his team. This is the "art" of decision-making. Some quarterbacks have it; some don't.

A decision that you have already made many times in the past may seem to require no thought, yet it is likely that you previously gave consideration to each of the three areas of global judgment—intrinsic, extrinsic, and systemic—and so in fact are making a decision that is consistent, effective, and enlightened. You make it quickly, *seemingly* without thinking, and yet you are incorporating areas of global judgment as needed.

So, *seemingly without thinking* is not the same thing as *without thinking.* The *consistent* reactionary decision is made with a type of reactionary mode that is decisive, purposeful, and resolute—standing in stark contrast to the *inconsistent* reactionary decision. Described starting on page 175, inconsistent reactionary decisions are unenlightened, arbitrary, and ineffective. As a result, they are often detrimental, destructive, and dangerous. Should the proverbial knee-jerk reactionary decision turn out to be an effective solution to a complex problem, it is just as likely due to good luck as it is to good judgment.

Intriguingly, people with strong judgment are often reactionary decision-makers. Remember, we can make our decisions in a reactionary mode and yet still allot the proper consideration to each of the three areas of global judgment. If we have strong judgment, it may take us only a few seconds to thoroughly mull over an issue or problem, reflect on the impact through the lens of each global judgment, sort through the various choices, make an effective decision, and take appropriate action. Therefore, the decision might be reactionary, but it is also well thought out.

If we have a consistent decision-making style, others likely will perceive our decisions as effective, insightful, and reliable—hallmarks of consistent reactionary decisions. We give consideration to an idea until we believe all relevant information has been explored, and only then do we decide. Should we change our mind, it is not because we failed to consider the existing evidence or the dynamics at play, but because we have ascertained new information.

Training, experience, and familiarity each play a huge role in the consistent reactionary decision. As we gain more expertise within a particular realm or endeavor, we are able to move our decisions to a posture of *less thinking, more action*, and yet still maintain their consistency and effectiveness. Thus we make potentially thousands of effective consistent reactionary decisions every day, especially within those areas of work and life where we are familiar and at ease.

If you work in aviation, for example, consistent and effective reactionary decisions often are a part of the joy of flying: They are the feel-good, second-nature decisions you make constantly as you pilot an aircraft. Your aviation training and experience have helped to make such reactions effortless, efficient, confident, smooth, and graceful. This applies to many other occupations and endeavors, whether you're a doctor, a schoolteacher, an accountant, an actor, a cowboy, a homemaker, an athlete, or a garbage collector—and whether you're mowing your lawn or driving your sports car.

There is, however, some risk associated with a consistent, decisive style: the reactionary trap. When we make reactionary decisions one at a time, we are okay; our decisions include a healthy mix of the intrinsic, extrinsic, and systemic components. The problem arises when financial pressures, work deadlines, client and employer demands, information overload, and other such urgencies push the consistent reactionary decision-maker into making less effective, inconsistent decisions. We may retain the reactionary component but, in an attempt to move faster within the workplace, discard the practice of considering all aspects before making decisions. Decision-making panic may even set in as our pace changes and we become too reactionary, too haphazard. Afterward, we might scold ourselves: *Why did I do that? I knew better!*

So if you are in a fast-paced, high-stress, need-it-right-now environment, be very careful with your decision-making style. Avoid the reactionary trap, which launches you from one end of the spectrum to the other.

On the other hand, many dilemmas are too complex to be solved without thinking them through. If our training, experience, and familiarity do not lend themselves to a quick, effective solution for the problem at hand, then to make a wise decision we should slow down, deliberate, and consider various options. Otherwise, our decision has a much higher chance of being weak and even disastrous.

Deliberative Decisions

In the middle of the consistent (strong) and inconsistent (weak) reactionary styles is the *deliberative* style. When we make a deliberative decision, we pause, consider, and contemplate before we decide. We might talk to other people, seek out additional advice and information, or just think about it for a while.

Deliberative decisions are *not* automatic, and sometimes they require great effort. They engage more areas of the brain. We might mull over these dilemmas, going back and forth as we consider how to proceed. Our goal during such deliberation is to examine choices and potential ramifications, and to utilize the best *judgment* possible so that when the time arrives, we make the best *decision* possible.

Of course, this is not always easy to do: Deliberative decisions engage more areas of the brain and so usually they take longer. They require more time and typically are the bigger decisions: which occupation or job to pursue, how to handle a delicate situation at work, whether to get married, where to live, which house or automobile to purchase, whether or not to launch an aircraft into iffy weather. Many decisions require deliberation, but lucky for us, many do not—for if every decision involved extensive deliberation, life would grind to a halt.

A major problem arises when decisions that should be made *deliberatively* are instead made *reactively*. Within most work environments, and in conjunction with training, experience, and fundamentally strong decision-making ability, we may successfully make the majority of our decisions in a consistent reactionary mode. The flow is such that as issues arise, we know what to do, and so we do it. However, it is essential to distinguish between problems that can be solved reactively and those that need to be solved deliberatively. Should you be overly reactive to issues that require at least a modicum of deliberation, your problem-solving will be less than stellar. If this becomes habitual for you, your success could suffer.

Deliberate decision-makers are a unique bunch. Our data has revealed some interesting characteristics about their global judgments.

Compared to those who employ a consistent reactionary style, deliberate decision-makers have slightly less parity of strength among the global judgments. Specifically, one of their global indicators is slightly stronger than the other two. They are more comfortable making decisions with their dominant global judgment, which they consider first when problem-solving; they are slightly less adept at incorporating input and guidance simultaneously from all three areas of global judgment. Fortuitously, the dominance is not so great that these individuals entirely ignore the remaining two global judgments. They merely turn less quickly to the relatively weaker global judgments for input when making decisions. They develop a slower, more protracted decision-making style.

Deliberate decision-makers employ more personal reflection and even dialogue and collaboration with others as they decide on an issue. Such deliberation can lead to more reliable and better-quality decisions, leaving one school of thought to view this slight disparity of global judgment strengths as the preferred state. Furthermore, unlike consistent reactionary decision-makers, people with a deliberative style are less likely to leap unintentionally to an inconsistent reactionary style. This is a second reason why some people believe that a slight disparity among the global indicators adds a factor of reliability and safety during high-stress decision-making.

Inconsistent Reactionary Decisions

An inconsistent reactionary decision-making style is *very* common, negatively impacting almost fifty percent of the population. As mentioned on page 170, there is a vast difference between inconsistent decision-makers and consistent decision-makers, though both are in a reactionary mode: The decisions that accompany an inconsistent style lack the proper consideration; the decision-makers tend to act before they think. They exhibit less understanding of the issue at hand, and generally do not use all three areas of global judgment as they problem-solve. Often one or more of the global judgments are *entirely* excluded in the decision-making process.

Inconsistent reactionary decisions tend to be unenlightened, less effectual, haphazard, arbitrary, even careless. When we use this decision-making style, often we know that we've made the wrong decision. We may see immediately that it is ineffective, even counterproductive, and we may feel that we should've known better than to proceed in this way. Afterward, the decision-maker often wishes to take it back or do it over.

We sometimes refer to this as the "foot-in-mouth" style of decision-making. If this describes you, you need to consciously slow down your decision-making process and consider all aspects of an issue in order to improve the quality of your decisions. You should consider counting to ten (literally!) before you make a decision. If you employ the practice of deliberation, you can improve your decision-making style and see a noticeable improvement in the quality of your judgment and thus in your overall success.

Here is how you can go about doing this.

Success Tip #1: Choose your response.

Acknowledge that it is not practical for everything to be a top priority. Let the nature and immediacy of problems guide you in your style of response. If a problem is less urgent, do not solve it in a reactive style.

Likewise, if a problem is urgent, do not use overly lengthy deliberations to resolve it. Prioritize what is essential versus what may not be as important.

Success Tip #2: Decide on immediacy.

Determine if you need to deal with a task or problem by deciding first whether it must be handled right now (or can be addressed later or disregarded indefinitely), and then whether it can be delegated. The simple act of deciding whether you need to deal with a problem forces you to pause, which encourages a deliberative decision-making style.

Success Tip #3: Hold on a second.

Problems often come at you fast and furious, so a momentary pause can help tremendously in improving the quality of the global judgments you consider, and then use, in your decisions. Consciously attempt to disrupt the intensity and speed of your reactive decision-making style. If you can use a phrase such as *Hold on a second*, then you have won half the battle! By pausing, if only for a split second, you break the knee-jerk reactive chain.

Success Tip #4: Get smarter.

In some jobs—combat medic, pilot, athlete, parent—often there is no time available for lengthy deliberation. However, even decisions that need to be made quickly can eschew the knee-jerk reactive style. One way to reduce inconsistency in your decision-making style is to "get smarter"—through the right education, careful preparation, additional training, and practical experience.

If you have briefed a scenario thoroughly, mulled it over in your mind, talked about it, and trained for it, there is much less likelihood that you will be caught off-guard; fall prey to an inconsistent reactionary style; and make a poor, ineffective, reactionary decision when the instance arises. Do not let a lack of knowledge goad you into making reactionary decisions.

An inconsistent decision-making style is *not* written in stone. You can contravene this reactionary style and avoid making knee-jerk decisions if you pause, deliberate—and only then solve the problem at hand. Improving your decision-making style will lead to an enormous increase in your chances of success.

THE ART OF NOTICING

The *art of noticing* is grounded in your value structure sensitivity, how well you observe subtleties, your mindfulness of beneath-the-surface realities, and your ability to recognize the different dimensions of situations.

Some people, when they look at a situation, are aware of only what is occurring on the surface of things. They do not grasp what is in play *below the surface*, sometimes spreading out unseen in treacherous ways. They see *just the tip of the iceberg*—the ten to fifteen percent that rises above the water—and miss the eighty-five or ninety percent below the surface.

The *Titanic* was sunk not by the surface dimension of the iceberg, but by the "invisible" danger beneath the surface of the water. The crew may have seen the iceberg, and yet it may not have appeared particularly threatening because the true threat was mostly unseen. We know now, however, that lurking beneath was the perilous dimension that brought down that seemingly invincible ship.

People, situations, and events—whether problems or opportunities or crises—are often shaped similarly to an iceberg: There are both obvious surface realities and the hidden beneath-the-surface realities. The majority of outcomes regarding people and events are driven by these subtle, underlying dynamics beneath the surface, and not by that which is obvious. To use good judgment and make wise decisions, we must be able to detect realities both above and below the surface.

Some people, when placed in a situation or among other people, are able to discern surface realities and size up those dynamics. They are tuned in to the obvious. Others are more gifted at seeing beneath the surface; they are intuitive and have more developed sensitivities. They are tuned in to nuance and subtlety, and they just seem to pick up on things. Generally, these exceptionally good "noticers" have overall proportionately stronger judgment and tend to be more successful.

Within most professions, it is tremendously beneficial to be aware of all that transpires within the associated environment, both above and beneath the surface. Imagine the devastating impact to business owners and executives, engineers, parents, teachers, and coaches who are oblivious to their surroundings. Skim the daily headlines, and you'll learn of personal and professional failings that indicate just how serious inadequate noticing can be. After reading the stories, we are apt to remark, "Didn't they see it coming?" or "Wow, it happened right under their nose!" or "They must have been clueless."

An ability to notice a subtle change in the weather or in an aircraft's performance, such as a tiny mechanical hiccup or a slight shift in the pitch of engine noise, could be the first step in recognizing impending catastrophe, and therefore the first step in the decision-making process that guides the pilot away from disaster and toward a successful outcome.

On average, within the entire population, women have a slightly more well-developed ability to notice than men. Of course, this aptitude does not apply to all women or to all men. Some women notice very little, while some men notice very well. But make no mistake: Women's intuition is real. Just think about your own mother or grandmother: Didn't she seem to notice everything? It may seem tough at times while a child is growing up, but parents' powers of observation can provide a tremendously positive influence on their judgment.

The benefits of having good observational skills and sensitivity to the world around us impact everything we do, from the dynamics in play at the office to navigating the cockpit of an airplane. Think about how the art of noticing comes into play in the following scenarios:

- At a family gathering
- Walking to your car in an unlit parking lot
- Driving a Humvee in Afghanistan
- Playing a round of golf
- Sensing something is "off" with your body's health
- Going for a Sunday drive
- Negotiating a contract
- Camping out
- Coaching a friend or colleague
- Having a successful first date

Essentially, in *everything* that we do, the ability to notice is vitally important.

You should pay particular attention to your noticing capabilities—strong, very strong, moderate, or weak?—and consider what this implies about your judgment. Your level of noticing has ramifications for your judgment, and it is important to fully understand any potential advantages or hazards you must navigate.

Strong: Trust Your Gut

Individuals who are strong in the noticing arena have a well-developed ability to observe: They are quite aware of what is going on around them. If this describes you, then you

- Possess an ability to see beneath the surface
- Notice a host of both subtle and obvious details in a given circumstance
- See in-depth situational and relational realities
- Understand nuance and subtlety

You are intuitive. You have well-developed gut instincts—and you should trust in them.

For example, an intuitive foreman who walks onto a job site can quickly size up the situation and discern when something is wrong, even if it is not apparent to others. What causes the foreman to sense that a problem exists? It might be the flow of work, the movements of the workers, the tone of the employees' voices, or the pace at which work is being completed. This problem might be subtle and not so easy to detect, such as a slight change in the attitude or body language of the workers. The foreman might not even be able to articulate what is wrong; he may "just know" there is a problem. But once his formidable intuition has raised his awareness, it helps him swiftly identify problems and their cause. This allows him to bring them to the forefront quickly and, with any luck, before they rise to the level of a crisis.

If you possess a strong ability to notice, small problems are less likely to grow and become as detrimental than they might otherwise. This, in turn, prevents subsequent solutions from becoming more costly.

Some people have such well-developed intuition that very little escapes their notice. Their personal radar is uncanny; they sense things happening to them and around them. This ability is rather common, actually, occurring in almost twenty-five percent of the adult population (with a slightly higher occurrence in females than in males).

If the art of noticing is a quality that you have, then your talent for observation will serve you well, for people with well-developed intuition usually have overall stronger judgment than others and tend to be more successful at their work.

Very Strong: Don't Overpersonalize

However, there are a few potential pitfalls in regard to extremely well-developed intuition. Probably there are situations in which you notice too much, overpersonalize, or have an overly emotional response. This is quite common in people with a very strong ability to notice.

You also occasionally place *too much* emphasis on your gut instincts. When your strong intuition has served you well in the past, you are likely to rely too much on it, and at times this can lead you astray when facing a tough situation, problem, or decision. Be aware of this hazard, especially in the midst of a difficult decision when your gut says something contrary to the obvious facts at hand.

You also need to avoid the inclination to worry too much, which arises from your tendency to notice everything around you, including the abstract and intangible. Others may even term you a "worrywart" because of your tendency to read so much into situations. Though you may worry more than most people because you notice more to worry about, be sure not to read more into a situation than actually exists.

Try to be grounded, levelheaded, and factual in your decisions; do not let strong intuition completely take over the decision-making process. Be wary, and avoid overpersonalizing your judgments and choices.

Moderate: Show Me the Facts

Slightly over fifty percent of the adult population falls into the moderate category, which means they have a slightly lower level of awareness of nuances and subtleties. If this describes you, then you tend to place only moderate emphasis on insight and intuition, and sometimes you miss some of the underlying dynamics. At times, this tendency can undermine your success.

If you are in this category you should trust your gut . . . *sometimes*.

With important decisions to make—when merging your company with another, preparing to go into combat, deciding whether to fire the underperforming employee, calling plays in the Super Bowl, or apologizing to your spouse—it is beneficial to gather the facts and to notice and comprehend all that you can before making any decisions. Decisions should be based on knowledge and awareness, not on ignorance of facts and a lack of insight. It's important to ground decisions in as much relevant information as possible, and the subtlety, undercurrents, and nuance surrounding an event are often relevant, critical factors in high-level decision-making.

Unfortunately, many people miss the subtle interplay of dynamics during an event or in a given situation. Someone with only a moderate ability to notice will occasionally miss some of the underlying dynamics. On the positive side, however, possessing moderate observational ability is not always detrimental to the problem-solving process. If you are slightly less tuned in, you are less prone to noticing *too much* and allowing gut instincts to rule an important decision. You are more of a "show me the facts" type of person when there is a critical decision to make. In some situations, your moderate level of intuition can provide a welcome balance to, and a positive, calming, or stabilizing influence on, an individual or a team that possesses a very strong aggregate ability to notice.

The best of both worlds is to have very strong judgment and be a great "noticer," but to not overpersonalize, worry, or fret over situations and decisions—to keep a strong ability to notice under control. That is not always easy to do. Therefore, collaborations between someone with a very strong intuition and someone with a moderate ability to notice can offer some distinct advantages.

Be forewarned, though, that often frustration can arise between someone with very strong intuition and someone with only moderate intuition. Remember that if you understand each other, it is possible for each of you to bring value to the decision-making process. The element of stability you offer can counter the effects of a very intuitive person who worries too much.

As for those decisions that you make "solo" rather than as a group effort, your moderate score demands that you try to notice more of the underlying dynamics and observe that which is not obvious. Your tendency is to place emphasis on the *obvious*, sometimes at the expense of the *not so obvious*. With practice, you can easily learn to observe the "iceberg" below the surface. If you do, you will notice an improvement in your intuition and, eventually, in your overall decision-making.

The more insight you can develop, the better your capacity to notice the subtle dimensions of people and situations—and the better your overall judgment.

Weak: Not Clued In

Individuals who habitually fail to notice rarely see beyond whatever is right in front of their face. They have a general inability to observe and evaluate circumstances in an articulate and comprehensive manner. Their intuition is limited, and they typically fail to grasp nuances and subtleties, which undermines their ability to make consistent, effective high-level decisions. When involved in high-level decision-making, they often find themselves surprised or caught off-guard. They often do not feel clued in to the underlying dynamics of a situation, or sometimes feel that they just do not "get it."

The following scenario, based on a scene from the movie *All Good Things*, represents people with varying degrees of the ability to notice:

Adam and Alice are a married couple sitting at a table in a café, staring stone-faced at each other while their untouched food grows cold. Their friends Bob and Barbara enter the café and spot them.

Bob charges up to the table, and greets them heartily. "Hey guys! How are you? Glad you're here. We'll join you!" He hustles a waiter over and instructs him to bring over two more chairs.

Adam and Alice say nothing and look at them blankly.

Barbara says to the couple, "I'm sorry. He's an idiot," and drags Bob away.

With which person do you identify? Are you more often Bob or Barbara?

If this unfortunate portrayal of clueless Bob depicts you, you tend to make decisions without a strong grasp of the underlying dynamics. This reduces the strength and effectiveness of your decisions. So if you lack development in this area, do not trust your gut instincts. That is a hard notion for many people to accept, given how often we hear well-intentioned phrases such as *Just go with what you feel is right* or *Do what your gut tells you.*

If you are Bob, however, do not despair! There are ways to improve upon your ability to notice. In fact, these tips can help everyone, no matter how strong or weak your current ability to notice.

Success Tip #1: Dig deep.

Consciously examine as many of the particulars, details, nuances, and subtleties as you can before making a decision. If you are clueless, acknowledge that underlying dynamics are crucial—and often more so than the obvious dynamics. Know that your weaker intuition and observational skills may cause you to miss nuance and subtlety, which could be the primary driving force in a particular situation, and then strive to uncover the information you need to make more suitable choices. Decisions made without considering as much crucial information as possible are often less appropriate ones.

Success Tip #2: Consult with others.

Ask others what they see or think about a situation—their answers might surprise you! Others might call attention to important details and factors that you have missed. Or they might present you with ideas that you had not considered—ones that can alter and improve your decisions.

Developing stronger intuitive capabilities is a result of diligence, discipline, and, just as important, time. When you see value in, and develop discipline about, improving your overall intuition and awareness, then *noticing more* is a natural and likely outcome.

Success Tip #3: Slow down your decision-making process.

Slowing down does not mean extending endless delays before rendering a decision. A change of pace can be merely a series of momentary pauses to gather additional information and pay more attention to your surroundings as you go through the decision-making process.

Success Tip #4: Set aside private time.

Find a private location or a dedicated time in which to think things over. Many people have been successful in improving their observational ability simply by establishing a space or time for contemplation. You naturally notice more when you are not rushed, so briefly pause to gather your thoughts before you start your day. Or employ a short midmorning or afternoon respite, or consider an end-of-day debriefing.

For ideas on what might work best for you, read about or investigate what other people have done to encourage contemplative or meditative practices in their lives. Incorporating and honoring such routine practices, even if they take only a moment, can help you develop the habit of slowing down and paying more attention as you learn to notice things before making decisions.

Remember, it is easier to notice when you do not feel rushed. If noticing becomes a habit or part of your routine, you will find that you naturally incorporate your newfound higher level of enriched awareness, and the additional information it provides for you, into your decisions. Sure, you might not find time to relax, meditate, or contemplate every time you are faced with a difficult decision. But by developing better observation and intuitive skills and habits during slower times of contemplation, you will build improved noticing skills to aid your decisions during periods of heightened chaos, confusion, urgency, and stress.

. . .

The art of noticing is critical, and your ability to notice *can* be improved upon, sometimes even rather quickly and reliably. The sustainment of noticing over time involves taking some of the suggestions here and turning them into long-term disciplines and habits. It takes some diligence, but it's worth the effort. Developing this area of your value structure has a strong correlation to improved work performance and increased success within most occupations.

As you will see in the next chapter, the first step in decision-making is noticing (observation).

THE BUSINESS OF
MAKING DECISIONS

My consulting firm has administered hundreds of thousands of judgment assessments, completed thousands of individual and 360-degree interviews, and conducted over one hundred in-depth best/worst performer studies. This large body of work points to an irrefutable, obvious, and intuitive truth: *Being able to make good decisions is extremely important for success.*

Many occupations involve an ongoing series of decisions, one after another. So the ability to make competent, timely decisions—especially during periods of heightened complexity, urgency, and stress—is crucial to progressing toward success. In other words

- ▸ Those who use their good judgment to make consistent, high-quality decisions tend to find greater success.

- ▸ Those whose judgment is lacking are unable to make consistent, high-quality decisions, and thus they rarely find success.

For example, within aviation, pilots are judged on their ability to safely, consistently, and efficiently complete all aviation-related tasks and responsibilities. In addition to the required skills such as navigating and controlling the aircraft, a pilot must possess well-developed decision-making abilities, because piloting (like many occupations) involves decision after decision. An ability to make competent, timely decisions, especially while under pressure, is crucial to a safe and enjoyable flight.

In fact, the Federal Aviation Administration in Advisory Circular 60-22 even goes so far as to establish the expression *aeronautical decision-making* (ADM) and define it as "a systematic approach to the mental process used by aircraft pilots to consistently determine the best course of action in response to a given set of circumstances."[3] Aviation psychologist Dr. Richard Jensen, considered by many to be the preeminent authority in the realm of ADM, prefers the term *aviation judgment*. He defines it as "the *mental process* used to formulate aviation decisions."[4] Whichever term you prefer, *aeronautical decision-making* or *aviation judgment*, all pilots know that decision-making is a top tier issue in the field of aviation.

Of course, the need for strong decision-making applies to every occupation and every situation, and in everything we do. So let's take a closer look at the decision-making process.

A Three-Step Process

The decision-making process can be broken down into three key steps:

1. *Observe.* Receive information from a variety of sources (i.e., pay attention, notice your surroundings).

2. *Assess.* Consider, assimilate, and prioritize what has been observed (i.e., create a plan).

3. *Utilize.* Finally, and most importantly, *apply* what has been observed and assessed (i.e., take action).

Yet many of us are unaware that this three-step process is in play,

---

3   T. C. Accardi (ed.), *Aeronautical Decision Making*, Federal Aviation Administration Advisory Circular AC 60-22 (Washington, DC: Government Printing Office, 1991), ii.

4   R. S. Jensen, *Pilot Judgment and Crew Resource Management* (Burlington, VT: Ashgate, 1995), 6.

especially when we are making simple, inconsequential, repetitive decisions. The use of the three-step process becomes more apparent when we have a bigger—and perhaps even a life-or-death—decision to make.

For example, after a glance at the weather, we make a seemingly instantaneous and unthinking decision about which clothes to wear. For many of us, this daily wardrobe decision is utterly inconsequential, a snap decision.

But what if we are going on a hike through desert terrain where people occasionally get lost? What if we are about to drive our car through a mountain pass that has snow-covered roads? What if we are flying a small plane in the middle of winter in the dead of night? Or, you could even argue, what if today is the day of an important job interview? Now the ability to make an appropriate wardrobe decision, or at least to know when more emphasis should be placed on our wardrobe decision, becomes much more important, potentially a matter of life or death.

The ability to articulate and think through the three key steps—even if they are performed seemingly without our thinking about them—are part of what guides us to better decisions. And the cold hard truth is that *some people are better at decision-making than others.*

If this area of your value structure—your ability to make decisions, which includes your intrinsic, extrinsic, and systemic judgments—is well-developed, then high-level solutions and actions tend to occur effortlessly for, and instinctively within, you.

If instead you tend to struggle with making solid, consistent, high-quality decisions, admit and accept it *for the moment*—and then plan for it using the suggestions that follow later on in this process. Doing so will help mitigate any bad decisions that could derail your success.

Enhancing the Process

Your decision-making ability does not happen in a vacuum. This ability can be enhanced, and at other times diminished, depending on the interaction and influence of your other judgment tendencies. For example, if your overall ability to cope with stress is strong (which we will discuss later), this may enhance your decision-making ability. On the other hand, if you are unduly influenced by stress, this may detract from the strong decisions that you know you can make.

Try to analyze—as objectively as possible—which of the three key decision-making steps (observe, assess, utilize) showcase your particular strengths, and which might reveal an area of weakness for you.

For example, some people enthusiastically engage in step one—*observation*—and then, unfortunately, do not go much further. When you observe, it is as if you are a spectator at a sporting event: You might enjoy the event at hand, and even be stimulated by the viewing, but doing this alone does not make you a good decision-maker. It is a good first step, but it is not enough. Observation, while important, is the least engaged phase of decision-making.

Other people move beyond observation to the second step, and are excellent at *assessing* and *planning*. They are full of "big ideas." Yet while the formulation of ideas is a higher level of engagement than observing—and it is impressive to brainstorm and conjure up creative or meaningful ideas and plans—if you do not follow through and act to implement the visions, they cannot be considered quality decisions. You must follow through to the third step of the decision-making process: You must utilize and apply the plan you have created based on what you have observed.

For most people, a focus on the end of the decision-making process—*utilizing and applying ideas*—helps influence the very beginning of the process. People need to direct their attention toward the *application* of ideas and the potential impact on real-life situations. This is because too much brainstorming can become a substitute for action, while too little brainstorming can lead to ill-conceived decisions. Planning for every scenario is impossible, of course, but nevertheless, it is essential to gauge the influence any possible decisions and actions will have, then decide on a course of action, and then act accordingly. (Of course, the decision might be to take *no* action!)

Another thing to consider is that to be a good decision-maker you must have the ability to see associations and connections—something that Albert Einstein felt was the true mark of genius. This means you should look beyond the immediate surface of an event or situation. Ponder the surrounding issues to understand the contributing and influencing intrinsic, extrinsic, and systemic variables that make the event or situation what it truly is. When you are better able to see variables and interrelationships, you are better able to make intelligent, informed decisions.

Even so, for most decisions—particularly small, inconsequential ones—cognizance of each of the three decision-making steps is overkill. A problem arises, however, when decisions are complex and consequential—and yet they are made without appropriate observation, planning, and application.

Strong

Someone with excellent decision-making and problem-solving abilities will intuitively observe and receive information from a variety of sources; process and synthesize that information; determine appropriate solutions; decide on a course of action; and ultimately complete the task or solve the problem. For people with strong decision-making skills, the general approach is to appreciate—and then act upon—that which is relevant in complex situations. They take care to observe the various intrinsic, extrinsic, and systemic dynamics within an event or situation, and then integrate what they have observed into a plan or solution. Then they make their decision, and act.

Strong decision-makers successfully incorporate each of the three areas of global judgment into their decisions: intrinsic, extrinsic, and systemic. As they problem-solve, they include

- ▸ Intrinsic judgment, a people-oriented approach comprising gut instincts, body language, tone of expression, and other nonverbal clues

- ▸ Extrinsic judgment, which tends to be more data-driven, and may rely on and involve cold, hard facts, such as charts, graphs, and research findings

- ▸ Systemic judgment, whose sensibilities may include a consideration of the implications and consequences of differing schemes, proposals, and policies

A good decision-maker has an ability to incorporate all of these types of information into his or her decisions, and to make good decisions even while under stress.

Those who effectively and routinely follow the three-step process when making high-level decisions at work can be characterized as careful decision-makers and competent problem-solvers.

In our corporate work we regularly find individuals with incredibly strong judgment, who are fantastic decision-makers, working in what others would consider rather simple jobs. These individuals are content, their lives are great, and they are doing what they want to be doing, and doing it in excellent fashion *because of* their strong judgment, not *in spite of* their strong judgment. So be careful not to stereotype an individual's capacity for judgment according to the work they do. Someone might have a certain job because that is the extent of their capabilities, or because they were drawn to it and they enjoy it, or because it is a stepping-stone to higher levels of success.

Moreover, through our consulting business we continually encounter teams where a subordinate has stronger judgment than the superior. For example, in some executive suites the executive assistant has stronger judgment and is a better decision-maker than the executive. This might lead to certain difficulties, or what we call *negative weighting*, but it does not automatically lead to problems. Often the executive assistant thoroughly enjoys being the assistant, and the executive appreciates having a consistent sounding board at his or her disposal.

The point is, you never know where you will find incredibly strong judgment and decision-making ability. Sometimes it is found in that youngster up to his elbows in mud, digging a ditch. People of all occupations, from all walks of life, and in all types of work exhibit excellent judgment.

If you are an excellent decision-maker overall and you typically make extraordinary decisions, be aware of the downside: the potential for you to experience job boredom and frustration. Without the stimulus of challenging and stimulating decision-making as a regular component of your work, your job satisfaction may suffer.

This is usually not a problem for individuals in jobs that require a great deal of judgment, such as surgeons, engineers, senior executives, professional athletes, and people in high-risk occupations, to name a few. In jobs such as these, the need to make high-level decisions is routine, often occurring many times within a single event.

However, jobs that are not judgmentally demanding could be less fulfilling for these individuals. For example, the third-shift manager at a small hotel may be happy with the pay and benefits, but disappointed with the job, as the most difficult task might be staying awake during the very slow early morning hours. The boredom and the lack of judgmental stimulation can result in frustration, and ultimately can negatively affect the manager's job performance. Therefore, an ability to manage frustration must be part of the judgment repertoire here; otherwise, you may need to choose another job that is more personally interesting and enjoyable.

Now, if a personally interesting and enjoyable job currently is not available to you as a strong decision-maker, look for the positive in the job that you *do* choose. For example, if your job pays the bills and offers you the freedom to search for fulfillment in other ways, then you can search for your ideal job as time allows. Appreciate that your less-than-ideal job allows you to enjoy a paycheck while you focus on your future success; make connections that may come in handy later; look for opportunities that might not have been available otherwise; establish your reputation with your coworkers and superiors; and develop your value structure.

Moreover, rather than insulting your current employer with a negative attitude and a dismissive manner, take the job as an opportunity to exceed expectations and perform above your current demands. Your ambition may be beyond what your current offers present, but performing admirably on a job improves your chances of a better job situation in the future—and certainly more so than refusing the job or performing dismally after accepting it.

Very Strong

If you are typically a *very strong* decision-maker, there may be even greater potential for you to experience boredom at your work. Thus, it is doubly important for you to make sure that you find a way to thoroughly enjoy your work on a personal level.

Whether or not you consider your job to be personally interesting and enjoyable is intensely personal. After all, one man's trash is another man's treasure. People are different, and so our likes and dislikes are different, from one end of the spectrum to the other. Many individuals with incredibly strong judgment fit well into judgmentally simple jobs because they *like* their job. Genuinely enjoying what you do will help offset problems for a very strong decision-maker currently in a less judgmentally demanding job.

Conversely, our data also reveals that if you are a very strong decision-maker and your work *is* judgmentally demanding, then that alone can provide the necessary stimulation—even if you do not really *like* your job. A deep-seated personal liking of your job is often less important if your job regularly and consistently challenges your judgment. Often we hear that it is not necessarily the *specifics* of the job that matter, but it is the *challenge* of the job that provides the necessary judgmental stimulation and keeps the job fulfilling and worthwhile.

One of our corporate clients owned a private mailbox service company with several satellite locations around a major city. The demands of the different jobs at the different locations varied greatly. Some locations had long lines of customers to serve and large piles of mail to be sorted. Such locations required multiple employees to be available for customers throughout the busy workday.

One location, though, was in a much quieter, out-of-the-way plaza, and so it needed only one employee. The requirements for that one employee were to be always on time; able to handle long stretches of inactivity; and ready to assist at any moment, with a willing attitude, should a customer arrive.

Our client had hired William for this location, and he seemed overqualified for the position. But a year after taking the lonely job, William was still doing well. Yet I knew that his very strong overall judgment scores put him at risk for frustration in his less-demanding occupation.

I was able to speak to William and asked him for his feelings about "job fit." He mentioned that years before, he would have been coming out of his skin with frustration if he had to spend several hours every day with no customers and no specific duties. But he was at peace with it now, and he wished to stay in this job as long as the employer would have him.

I had to wonder: What as his secret?

William told me he had learned to fill his quiet time with cleaning, organizing the displays, and reading. He concentrated hard to stay alert so that he could greet the few daily customers with a smile and a cheerful *hello*. He felt a sense of duty toward having his work location run smoothly and being as consistent, positive, and reliable as possible for the company's regular customers.

William so valued his employment that he did not allow any possible feelings of disappointment to affect his work performance. Plus, fulfilling his responsibilities accurately and well gave William such a sense of fulfillment that he no longer craved the bustle of a busy location.

Weak

If you are in a judgmentally demanding job, and invariably struggle with high-level decision-making—especially during periods of high stress, urgency, and chaos—here are some suggestions for improvement.

Success Tip #1: Follow the three-step process.

Be extra-careful not to make a sudden or ill-considered decision. Always, always engage in the three-step decision-making process first (see page 190). Decisions made without contemplation often result in a worse outcome than if no decision had been made.

True, some decisions need to be made *right now*, but most lack that urgency. So be sure to consciously consider the three key steps first before committing to a solution:

1. *Observe* what is taking place.

2. *Assess* the situation and devise a plan.

3. *Utilize* your best judgment of the implications and consequences of your plan—taking care to include intrinsic, extrinsic, and systemic components—to make a decision and act.

Success Tip #2: Continually review the three steps.

As time passes and environments and particulars change, continually review the three key steps that you use to make your high-level decisions. Observe the situation, assess the consequences, and apply your solutions, actions, and decisions. Then, if necessary, revise your plan and try again. This process is especially important to do if you often struggle with high-level decision-making.

If you practice this decision-making process, you will discover that, over time, problem-solving will become more natural for you, and quality solutions will begin to present themselves in a timelier and more appropriate fashion.

Success Tip #3: Go at your own pace.

Do not let the preferred pace of others dictate the speed of your decision-making. Among those with strong decision-making ability, there is often a tendency (however unintentional) to rush other people into making their decisions. Do not let this happen with you.

Take your time.

Slow down.

Think through.

Rely on your training.

Do not panic.

Observe, assess, and devise a plan.

Consider not only your decision, but also how you arrived at your decision. What judgments and information were incorporated into your decision?

Now—*and only now*—act.

Frustration may develop when there is a gap between your and your colleagues' decision-making abilities. Ultimately, you may arrive at the same conclusion as a person with inherently strong decision-making ability—only you took longer to get there. And this, my friend, is okay. Do not let the urgency of a situation goad you into making a regrettable decision and implementing an undeveloped plan—especially if the situation is stressful. Make sure that you consider all input, and then consider it again, before making a decision.

Using the three key steps to help guide your decisions does not necessarily take hours or even minutes. Well-thought-out decisions can be made very quickly indeed. So if you know that you tend to struggle with high-level decision-making, give yourself pause to consider *consciously* the three key steps—even if for only a moment. This will ensure that your decisions are based on the dynamics of the situation, and not on a guess, a haphazard reaction, a response to someone else's urging, or a desire to do *something*.

Success Tip #4: Rely on routine.

Make an extra effort to rely on procedures and processes, rather than excessively on judgment, when making high-level decisions. Develop your job skills with any new training that is necessary. If you can't find time during a busy workday, spend extra time after work learning new procedures and processes to do it. One day you will find that this no longer requires additional hours or exertion but instead has become routine.

Realize that a generally poor or undeveloped decision-making ability does not indicate that you are any less skilled than your colleagues—or any less intellectual, emotionally balanced, or socially adept. Nor does it suggest that you tend to proceed in ways that are dangerous. More so than most, however, you must be an absolute expert in your chosen work, because only in this area can you make up for your lagging decision-making skills.

Success Tip #5: Envision multiple scenarios.

Reflect on as many worrisome potential scenarios as you can beforehand. What complaints or concerns do you usually hear from customers or clients? Think through the possible solutions so that when the perturbed client is in front of you or on the phone, you have already considered a particular scenario before it occurs and will have a workable solution at hand. That way, high-level judgment becomes less necessary at the time of the actual decision-making, because you have already considered and weighed the possible solutions.

Weighing all the worrisome and "what if" scenarios beforehand provides you with a boost for making good decisions in the future, wherein you rely slightly less on your judgment and slightly more on your training or knowledge.

Success Tip #6: Seek input from an expert.

Use the good judgment of others to help walk you through various potential outcomes. Look for acknowledged experts, and talk to them *before* you embark on a course of action. You also might engage in additional conversation or shop talk with old-timers, or seek someone outside your particular work environment. But choose someone with a lot of knowledge in the area particular to the difficult decision before you, especially if the resolution lacks a defined procedure or process.

Never let ego get in the way. At times, even seasoned and experienced senior executives should seek advice from a trusted colleague or peer before making high-level corporate decisions.

Realize, too, you don't have to *take* the person's advice. Nevertheless, it may well provide fresh and innovative insight that you have not considered.

Success Tip #7: Find a mentor.

Engage with a mentor for long-term improvement. Many of our corporate clients have set up in-house mentoring programs with great success. The mentoring process is not easy; it takes substantial effort and might be impractical for you, depending on your particular circumstances. We have seen reliable results, however, that through the mentoring process, decision-making can improve predictably.

Obviously, your mentor should have a strong decision-making ability. Find a mentor who seems wise and has good judgment. Your mentor should have an abundance of common sense, be a good problem-solver, unearth solutions to difficult situations, and offer a plethora of good advice.

A vibrant mentor/mentee relationship can improve your high-level decision-making, particularly if you adopt the following ideas for the best results:

- Meet regularly.
- Share actual problems relating to specific issues you've encountered since the previous conversation.
- Focus on *how* to approach and solve problems, and not merely on the final solution.

▸ Ask your mentor for advice on any *current* problems, again focusing on *how* to approach and solve them.

▸ Request a critique and commentary on your chosen approach.

If setting up your own mentoring program is too difficult, at least try to engage in regular conversations with someone of strong decision-making ability, as described earlier. Our data suggests unequivocally that if such conversations take place over a time period of twelve to eighteen months, then both the judgments and the decision-making of the mentee and the mentor alike will improve. Specifically, the dialogue works to raise awareness; help the mentee tackle current and future work-related issues, and address issues in general; and improve the mentor's judgment by exercising inherently strong decision-making skills that may have gone somewhat dormant.

. . .

People can—and, with a little time and effort, often do—become much better decision-makers and problem-solvers. There is no greater boost toward success than improving the ability to make steady, reliable, consistent, quality decisions.

Remember, how you reach your decisions isn't a foregone conclusion. Your judgments evolve and grow throughout your entire life, and with hard work, you can improve your decision-making prowess. And going about the business of critical decision-making with clarity and confidence, especially in times of urgency and stress, is crucial to your success.

PART 3

JUDGMENT ASSASSINS

THREE JUDGMENT KILLERS

Part 2 of this book revealed the first three truths at the heart of success: intrinsic judgment ("human factor" judgment); extrinsic judgment (work-, task-, and process-related tactical judgment); and systemic judgment (big-picture strategic judgment). These judgments are the primary factor in our ability to make decisions, find solutions, and solve problems—in essence, to discover our success.

But sometimes, even when our judgment is strong and well developed, our decision-making fails us, and we don't succeed at what we set out to do or solve.

The sad reality is that there are some truths about judgment that work *against* us. Known as the *judgment assassins*, they are the remaining three truths at the heart of success:

- ▸ **Truth #4:** *Stress*
- ▸ **Truth #5:** *Frustration*
- ▸ **Truth #6:** *Clutter*

You must always be watchful of the judgment assassins and guard your judgment against them. And if you become aware of them, you must destroy them.

Your success may depend on it.

You've probably heard or used these colloquial phrases triggered by one or more of the assassins:

- ▸ *Jim was in over his head!*
- ▸ *It was too much for Sam.*
- ▸ *Kate couldn't handle it.*
- ▸ *Ben wasn't up for it.*
- ▸ *Michael cracked.*
- ▸ *Shannon lost it.*
- ▸ *Joe couldn't deal with it.*
- ▸ *What was Pete thinking?*
- ▸ *Mary is usually better than that.*
- ▸ *What got into Frank?*
- ▸ *"You did what?"*

Have any of these phrases ever applied to you? For most of us, at some point in our lives, they have. But what exactly does it mean to be *in over your head*? What causes someone who is typically "up to it" to find themselves "not up to it"? What does *can't handle it* imply? And if someone is *in over their head* most of the time, does that mean they just don't "get it"?

Then again, there are also people who are rarely, if ever, in over their head. These are the individuals who always seem to find a way to work out the problem; who handle the crisis with precision; and who "make it happen." They "get it," and our data tells us unambiguously that they are much more successful than those who don't "get it."

Too, there are times when people who normally "get it" find themselves in a situation where they don't. Someone normally "up to it" may find he or she is "not up to it." Have you ever said, "Why did I do that? I knew better," or "That's so not like me! I just lost my head"?

The explanations behind these colloquial sayings and their impact on our success lead back to our value structure and our evaluative judgment.

Normally successful problem-solvers are *in over their heads* when their judgment capabilities are not strong enough to resolve a certain dilemma. In such circumstances, the strength of their judgment is weaker than the judgment demands of their situation.

When this happens, our evaluative judgment is not strong enough to provide a workable solution—we therefore find ourselves *in over our heads*. There are two key issues in play here:

1. *The strength, nature and character of our evaluative judgment.* The stronger our evaluative judgment, the more likely it is that a workable solution will present itself.

2. *The level of judgment necessary to resolve the situation.* The judgment required varies tremendously with each circumstance we encounter. Some situations require almost no judgment, and others require tremendous judgment and consideration.

Of course, many decisions—approximately eighty to eighty-five percent—are just made seemingly without thinking (see the discussion of reactionary decisions on page 170), and with no need for us to evaluate them first. Examples of these situations are as follows:

- Walking into a meeting, you place your cell phone in silent mode.
- When inventory gets low, you order more.
- On the first day of the month, you begin last month's financial reports.
- Sitting in your car at a stoplight—the light turns green, you step on the gas.
- When your dog whines, you let it outside.
- When your alarm clock rings, you reach over and hit the *snooze* button.

- Your team scores a goal, so you cheer.

- When the microwave dings, you remove your hot coffee.

In contrast, many other situations require an enormous level of evaluative judgment to resolve appropriately:

- A business executive deciding whether or not to expand in a new corporate direction

- A young married couple weighing the pros and cons of having children

- A cancer patient conflicted over whether to continue chemotherapy

- An employee deciding whether or not to accept a promotion in another region of the country

- A factory manager considering if the time is right to purchase expensive new equipment

- A woman deliberating over whether or not to continue life support for her elderly mother

Judgment Surplus—*Preferred Situation*

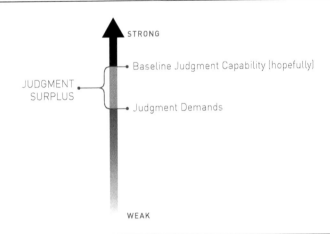

Figure 1: Judgment Surplus

- ▸ A combat soldier deciding whether his troops should advance or retreat

Figure 1 shows the preferred decision-making situation. Here, our baseline judgment capability is stronger than the judgment demands of the situation. This allows our judgment to thrive—to seek out and render for us acceptable decisions and solutions. Here, we have a *judgment surplus.*

Hopefully, no matter the judgmental demands placed on us, our evaluative judgment is capable of rendering a solution. Unfortunately, this is not always the case. Even if our basic judgments are strong and well developed, any or all of the three judgment assassins can render our judgments weak and ineffective, particularly when we are faced with extreme judgment demands.

Figure 2 depicts the undesirable scenario in which the judgment assassins—stress, frustration, and clutter—negatively impact our judgment capabilities. The effectiveness of our judgment is thus reduced

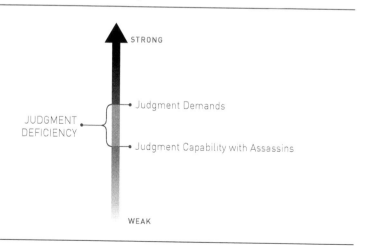

Judgment Deficiency—*Over Your Head*

Figure 2: Judgment Deficiency

to below the level required to find solutions, make good decisions, and solve problems. In this situation we have a *judgment deficiency*. Put simply, we find ourselves *in over our head.*

So now let's learn the particulars of the judgment assassins: how to recognize them, why they undermine our judgment, and, most important, how to defeat them.

TRUTH #4: STRESS

Our data reveals unequivocally what most people already know:
Stress is the biggest detriment to the use of good judgment. If left unchecked,
stress can rear up and obliterate even the strongest judgment. By a wide
margin, we make our worst decisions when under stress.

Our experiences with stress are complicated and specific to us. For
some people, the internal conversation on how to effectively deal with
stress is going to last their entire lifetime. With all this in mind, here are
some excellent tools to help understand and deal with this interminable
judgment assassin.

The definition of *stress* resides under a huge umbrella. Many people
consider stress as a large, one-size-fits-all concept—any event or idea
or person that upsets them is considered the source of their stress. And
many use the term *stress* as a catchall phrase to identify any type of mental or emotional strain in their lives, from anxiety to danger to frustration
and beyond.

A more sophisticated approach to understanding and alleviating
stress, and the one that we are going to use in this book, lies in the concept that there are distinct categories of stress with distinct sets of both
causes and remedies. Moreover, your personal and professional success
depends on you being able to differentiate between these categories of
stress and then being able to mitigate that stress. To do so, you must

move beyond any general concept of stress toward identifying the specific category that you might experience.

An individual may be affected by a single form of stress, or a combination of varying degrees of some or all forms of stress, or by no stress at all. Therefore, the best remedy for you differs depending on which category creates the greatest negative impact for you. The mistake of defining *stress* as a generalized concept, or interchangeably with *dread* or *anxiety*, can cause a mistake in selecting the correct remedy. This will never allow you to reduce your actual stress level. If you deal only with the generic *idea* of stress and getting your so-called stress under control, you are misdirecting your energies.

Any, none, or all of the categories of stress could be your undoing. Moreover, you have a *coping threshold* for each category of stress that is unique and individual to you. Knowing which category of stress is your personal weak point will help you shore up your coping skills and reduce the negative impact on your professional success.

To most effectively and efficiently cope with your actual area of stress, you must do the following:

1. Understand exactly which category or categories are most problematic to you.

2. Focus your energies on increasing your coping skills in that area(s), to diminish the detrimental effect that stress has on your success.

Should you be in a situation where it is not possible to eliminate the source of stress (a very likely scenario, given the nature of many jobs), you have no choice but to increase your ability to cope with that stress.

Throughout the course of our work with evaluative judgment over several decades, we have identified four primary categories of stress that continually strike at the heart of evaluative judgment, good decision-making, and success:

- **Stressor #1:** *Problem-Solving Energy*
- **Stressor #2:** *Known Workplace Stress*
- **Stressor #3:** *Self-Criticism*
- **Stressor #4:** *Known Personal Stress*

Now let's consider each of these critical categories of stress in detail.

Stressor #1: Problem-Solving Energy

You experience vague feelings of dread and generalized anxiety: Something bad is going to happen. You don't know exactly how or where or when it will occur, but you cannot shake this feeling. It affects your problem-solving energy level and commitment.

The strength of your *problem-solving energy* is highly predictive of workplace success. In many of our best/worst performer studies, problem-solving energy has been the component of the value structure that is the most statistically correlated to high performance and success. Often it is even more significant than problem-solving *ability*. Therefore, pay close attention to your problem-solving energy. It is very important.

Problem-solving energy is related to stress, and is a primary factor in your ability to deal effectively with uncertain and somewhat vague situations. It fluctuates up and down depending on your ability to manage *anxiety-type stress* (also called *background stress*).

Anxiety-type stress is created in the workplace, or within the world at large, when there are unclear circumstances and somewhat vague issues causing problems and requiring attention. Compared with clear, precise, identifiable stressors, these vague stressors are often difficult to articulate or identify as a culprit behind this type of stress. Often there is no single stressful event to identify.

Anxiety-type stress is accompanied by a feeling of being drained—of having too much to do and not enough time to do it. My clients who suffer from a lack of problem-solving energy often tell me they are not sure why, but they feel overwhelmed at work and constantly anxious.

Anxiety and uncertainty cloud our judgment and may render decision-making and problem-solving ineffective. Countering and contending with uncertainty requires a great deal of personal energy— energy that could be used to solve problems if it were not being diminished by stress. As anxiety-type stress *increases*, the ability to handle difficult situations *decreases*. Thus, this area of your value structure determines how stress will affect your ability to deal effectively with difficult or unclear situations.

Whereas this area of the value structure had only a moderate impact until recently, over the past decade this particular stressor has gained in intensity on average within the population, more so than any other type of stress. This form of stress is now the dominant negative influence in the lives of many people, and is the fastest-growing *negative* area of the value structure within the population.

Consider that in daily life and work, most of us are called upon to resolve problems. Some people like to refer to these problems as "challenges," "issues," or even "opportunities," but they are still *problems*. For many, problems are common, part of the everyday routine. They are made even more difficult by the presence of difficult people.

Usually (and fortunately), we have available to us a variety of resources to help mitigate our professional problems: technology, money, cooperative teams, outside consultants, personal fortitude, creativity and innovative ideas, or even a calming tone of voice. However, just because we *have* resources available to us does not mean that we will necessarily *use* these resources.

To apply our resources to the solution of problems, we must first be able to *recognize*, *organize*, and *mobilize* our resources—and that requires *energy*. Effort and exertion, or *energy*, are required to recognize our resources and put them to use in solving what are often our most demanding problems. Energy helps us

- Continue advancing forward, even in the face of adversity
- Stay motivated
- Foster innovation, creativity, imagination, inspiration, and perseverance
- Solve problems
- Keep committed
- Resist the temptation to quit

The personal energy required to recognize, organize, and mobilize problem-solving resources can be physical, mental, emotional, or spiritual—or some combination of these. An abundance of problem-solving energy has an enormous impact on your abilities and success. Conversely, a *lack of energy* has

- a dramatically negative impact on ingenuity, inspiration, and creative thinking;
- a dramatically negative impact on our overall decision-making and problem-solving—and ultimately on our success; and
- a dramatically negative impact on our general resourcefulness— our ability to handle difficult situations and difficult people.

It is far more common—and far more to our detriment—that we lack the *personal energy* to recognize, organize, and mobilize our resources, than that we have an actual lack of resources. Often people and organizations have a plethora of problem-solving resources, yet due to an overall *lack of energy*, these resources remain dormant, unrecognized, and/or unutilized.

And thus the problems remain unresolved.

Background stress can be overwhelming if left to gnaw and fester. The great majority of people who are unable to handle the issues and circumstances of their lives are not suffering from clinical psychological dysfunction, but from their inability to cope with this stress. These individuals give up and quit, even with easy access to the necessary resources to persevere and solve their dilemma. If instead they can mitigate the stress that they feel is clouding their lives, they can "get their lives back."

When feelings of anxiety arise in a person, they can be powerful and destructive, even though they might be difficult to explain or understand. If a person lacks the ability to manage his or her background stress, these feelings can drain the lifeblood right out of a formerly energetic, creative, motivated, and passionate decision-maker and problem-solver.

Remember, it is not always easy to put your finger on exactly *why* you feel this type of anxiety, but when you experience it and are incapable of managing it, it zaps your energy—and with it, your ability to muster the energy necessary to solve problems.

Please note: *Energetic* is different from *extroverted*. You may be quite restrained, reticent, and introverted—and yet still have a surplus of problem-solving energy and verve.

Strong

Should you have appropriate levels of problem-solving energy, you are well suited for demanding environments that involve intense and stressful problems or people.

You have the ability, judgment, and *energy* to recognize, organize, and mobilize any resources at your disposal—which helps you deal with difficult situations. Furthermore, if this is a well-developed area of your value structure, you also possess a high level of problem-solving *patience*.

Others will notice the energy you exude. Colleagues instinctively know that you always bring a high level of energy and determination to the table to help find a needed solution. If the members of your team or group within your workplace are unable to muster the required vigor or effort needed to resolve an exceedingly difficult situation, you become their go-to person.

Consequently, your energy to do more than solve immediate problems can grow and feed on itself in a very positive way. People who have developed this area of their value structure have an excess of energy that enables them to handle complex situations and "difficult" people. We therefore sometimes refer to our corporate clients who own this problem-solving energy as having "customer service" energy.

If your value structure is developed in this area, it brings with it a high level of energy for workplace activities—something that will assist you in solving both immediate and critical dilemmas. Should you find yourself in a difficult, unusual, or even emergency situation, a high level of problem-solving energy inspires a burst of innovation, imagination, resourcefulness, and perseverance. It also helps you to recognize the resources that are available to take care of the dilemma. Moreover, you have the energy to keep your anxiety under restraint even in the direst of circumstances, so that you can keep maneuvering toward a solution.

Unfortunately, high levels of problem-solving energy are becoming rarer among the population. There are entire companies and businesses that have only a few employees who have developed this quality in surplus.

Maintain your personal problem-solving energy in all that you do. It can be one of your biggest allies as you seek success.

Very Strong

If you are fortunate enough to have extremely high levels of energy and be able to maintain this area of your value structure, you possess a surplus of problem-solving energy and creativity, and a wonderful knack of coping with complicated situations and difficult people.

You are energetic, innovative, and creative. (Remember this has nothing to do with whether you are introverted or extroverted, but rather your problem-solving energy level.) You do not merely solve problems and predicaments; you solve them with vitality and vigor. Typically, you direct your excess of problem-solving energy toward outside-the-box problem-solving. If you are this kind of person, you know it—and those around you know it as well. When they have to undertake difficult people and difficult situations, they rely on *your* energy.

Work hard to develop and maintain this unique level of problem-solving energy, for it is highly predictive of professional success.

Be aware that your gift for coping with difficult people may leave you frustrated when working with someone who lacks problem-solving energy—someone who tends to give up quickly when facing adversity or who lacks resourcefulness. Your judgment could suffer when you are working with "drained" individuals or a team with an energy deficit, so be on the alert for this type of frustration within yourself. Being conscious of this possibility can help you avoid it.

Weak

Many of us occasionally lack problem-solving energy and at times feel overwhelmed with work. It is important, however, to distinguish between the occasional—and perfectly normal—feeling of being pushed to the limit at work with a particularly difficult task, project, customer, or problem, and continuous, day after day, week after week, unceasing exhaustion and fatigue, and an accompanying lack of energy. We all feel tired sometimes, but if we still are able to maintain problem-solving energy, we can find even difficult tasks exhilarating and perform them well. But if you find yourself consistently, repeatedly, and utterly lethargic and drained of problem-solving energy, then you should seriously consider finding ways to reduce background stress.

If this area of your value structure is weak, your problem-solving energy is being diminished or compromised. This depletion of energy is related to your inability to manage vague anxiety-type stress—a deficiency that tends to cripple any problem-solving resources you have on hand.

Be honest with yourself about whether you are lacking in this area. Recognize who you are, not who you would like to be. If you have a shortage of problem-solving energy, acknowledge it, consciously think about it, and decide to do something about it. Do not operate in denial, for eventually you will pay the price in ineffective decision-making and problem-solving.

If you often feel anxious, overwhelmed, and stressed, there is a good chance that you have difficulty identifying the exact origin of your stress or naming the specific stressor. Your stress is likely an overall feeling of anxiety; you are overwhelmed, run down, worn out, or mentally exhausted. Despite being (or perhaps because it is) tough to pinpoint or articulate with precision, background stress is a very powerful form of stress. If left unchecked, it can greatly diminish your performance and success.

Should you succumb to this form of stress, it might be caused by having more responsibilities than you can handle, and thus a feeling that you have *too much on your plate*. If you have too much to do, or too many "top" priorities, you become frustrated and lose touch with your personal vitality—and your energy declines even more. You feel that nothing is being done as well as it could be or should be. A self-defeating process is now under way.

With weakness in this area of your value structure, you may feel as though you are spinning plates: You are exerting all your energy just to keep the plates up in the air and prevent them from falling on the ground, and you have no energy left to move forward and get ahead.

The work environment can be partially to blame for a lack of problem-solving energy. When we, through our consulting business, examine the aggregate levels of departments, divisions, or various sub-groups within corporations and find overall weakness in this area (as we commonly do), we know that there is probably a problem within the structure of the organization.

Of course, an inefficient work environment also might be partially or even entirely *your* fault. Perhaps you are not being as efficient as you can be with your work duties or the time you allot to them.

Most people—even those who do not work particularly hard—understand the *notion* of working hard, of doing whatever it takes to get the job done. It is an essential characteristic of the value structure that any successful person must possess. In other words, doing whatever it takes is not going above and beyond what is required; it is merely doing what you need to do to be successful.

Getting the job done is what successful individuals and organizations expect. A surplus of problem-solving energy helps ensure that you do what you need to do instead of just giving up, whether you're rendering business decisions, studying for an exam, or balancing a budget. In most work environments, giving up is unacceptable.

Be that as it may, even the most motivated and energetic individuals can be overwhelmed and subjugated by difficult events and circumstances. If your work environment is inefficient and chaotic, lends itself to poor communication, and is constantly filled with uncertainty—and you do not participate in personally restorative activities to counter those effects—it is very possible that anxiety and stress will become a hindrance to your success.

You likely experience workdays that are mostly uneventful, absent of crises or calamities. On these days, with the proper training and skills, you do not need to exert a high level of problem-solving energy. The issues before you are routine and predictable, so even with a minimum of problem-solving energy, tackling them can be straightforward and even pleasurable. However, when things go wrong (and occasionally things *go horribly wrong*), you are going to need every speck of problem-solving energy you can muster for the appropriate, expeditious resolution of the problem. In these situations, a lack of problem-solving energy is problematic.

So how can you muster the necessary and beneficial problem-solving energy to handle both emergency-type situations and routine work environments that, for a host of reasons, may be sapping your strength?

Success Tip #1: Restructure your workload.

If you find that circumstances are overwhelming you within your workplace, and you're unable to deal effectively with difficult situations, then the solution often lies in some "professional restructuring." Improving efficiencies related to your time and duties can reduce your level of stress and thereby increase your problem-solving energy. To more efficiently accomplish your work and get your stress under control you could, for example, moderate your number of direct reports or subordinates; delegate some tasks or duties; or alter your routine or workflow.

You may not be in a position to reduce your tasks, delegate responsibilities, or alter your corporate structure. If you are, however—and if managing difficult situations and background stress is not your strong suit—such restructuring is especially important.

Success Tip #2: Recharge your batteries.

Use the "three Rs"—rest, relaxation, and restorative activities—to reduce anxiety-driven stress.

Just like a car battery, you too can be recharged. In your case, this can happen most easily through activities that you personally enjoy and that have nothing to do with work: reading, playing golf, camping, going for a walk, eating out, or bowling, for example.

Devote some effort to identifying the best leisure interests *for you*. What constitutes a restorative activity is deeply personal and represents a form of self-knowledge. As early as 1400 B.C., ancient Greek philosophers advanced the idea to *know thyself*. Those very words were carved on the doorpost to the entrance of the Oracle at Delphi, where people would go to seek advice about the future.

Before we can consider future agendas and then achieve those agendas, we have to know who we are as individuals. We have to know our capabilities and limitations. A powerful route to such self-knowledge is knowledge of the disciplines and activities that lead us to restoration and renewal.

Fortunately, nowadays the process of identifying your personal restorative activities does not require a philosophical journey to the ends of the earth to chitchat with a soothsayer. Many of us return to the office with a new attitude after just setting aside a restful and relaxing weekend. We come back Monday morning rejuvenated, with a higher mental energy level that we can use to tackle any difficult situations awaiting us at work.

So find an activity that you enjoy outside of work, and engage in it when you can. Our data suggests that for most people, engaging in enjoyable activities for about three hours per week will suffice. You may wish to participate more often, if you are willing and able.

Success Tip #3: Open the lines of communication.

Workplace anxiety is often caused by situations where a lack of communication prevails. In fact, the number one need expressed by line workers in organizations is *better communication*.

When solutions seem to hide in the shadows, it can demoralize everyone at work. One of the best cures for reducing workplace-driven anxiety is to improve communication, clarity of expression, openness, and articulation, on both the individual and corporate levels. Open and honest conversation—*whether the news is good or bad*—helps reduce background stress by dispelling fears, relieving concerns, and minimizing the apprehension of the unknown. The goal should be to talk frankly with colleagues about issues, without feeling intimidated or responding defensively.

. . .

If your problem-solving energy is in short supply, try to restructure your workload, engage in the three Rs, and keep the lines of communication open at work. Additionally, an Internet search for *stress* reveals thousands of documents, books, articles, and courses devoted to stress and its harmful effects, and what to do about it.

A lack of problem-solving energy is problematic and not always easy to repair. But you can raise your problem-solving energy level, and lower your anxiety or background stress, with effort and diligence. Take a deep breath and start now.

Stressor #2: Known Workplace Stress

Unlike *problem-solving energy*, which involves the effects of background, vague, hard-to-identify, anxiety-type stressors, *known workplace stress* has to do with the effects of obvious, easy-to-pinpoint stressors within your professional and work environment. These recognizable stressors include events, people, or ideas that place difficulty directly and noticeably on you.

There are many potential examples, depending on your workplace or other environment: layoffs, a hostile company takeover, a new boss, bankruptcy, an inability to meet sales goals, costly government regulations, and so forth. Whatever your occupation or field of endeavor, the specific topic(s) of these kinds of stressors are usually easy to identify. For some people, the list of such stressors seems endless:

- ▸ *My boss is a pain.*

- ▸ *My coworkers are incompetent, so I have to do everything myself to get it done right.*

- ▸ *I have to testify in court next month about a former employer.*

- ▸ *I don't have the right training to properly use the new machine in my workplace.*

- ▸ *I lack the budget that is necessary to meet my objective or goal.*

On the positive side, people generally are much better at dealing with these obvious stressors than with vague background stress.

The *effects* of the known stressors—and not the quantity or extent of stress experienced—are much more of a determining factor in human performance, success, and overall accomplishment. When people can identify the stressor—when they can reasonably observe it, point to it, and talk about it—they are better able to cope with it and do something about it, and thus reduce its detrimental effects.

Some people become upset and unnerved at even the slightest difficulty. They fall apart at the proverbial hangnail. They make mountains out of molehills, and are unable to muddle through the tiniest and most insignificant inconvenience. They overreact to minor stressors—being a few minutes late, for example, even if the schedule is not time critical. They always have an obstacle, complication, or person to blame, or an excuse or crisis to create.

On the other hand, there are people who confront genuine obstacles, huge complications, and extreme difficulties within their workplace, and yet conduct themselves with poise and composure, maintaining a level head and always working toward the resolution of their problems without much complaint. There is no hardship, no matter how severe or unyielding, that they do not overcome or manage.

The difference between these two kinds of people is quite simple: It lies in their coping skills—their ability to cope with adversity. The latter is able to cope; the former is not.

Many have found encouragement and solace in the poem "Serenity Prayer," written in the late 1930s by theologian Reinhold Niebuhr:

> God, give us grace to accept with serenity
> the things that cannot be changed,
> courage to change the things
> which should be changed,
> and the wisdom to distinguish
> the one from the other.

The word *wisdom*, as used in this poem, is another word for *judgment*. Thus it is your judgment that helps you recognize the difference between those things you can change and those things you cannot.

In other words, the poem advises devising a plan to change the things you can in order to alleviate your stressors, and additionally to learn to accept (or cope with) the things you cannot change. So although your coping skills may be pushed to their limits, if you maintain a positive and hopeful attitude, you will find the strength to cope with any hardship or stress you might face.

The importance of coping with known stressors is something you may not immediately realize because of your chosen field or profession. For example, the work stressors in the world of aviation sometimes are acute: an engine fire, structural icing, weather below minimums, bird strike (two engines flaming out over the Hudson!), combat. Conversely, many misfortunes or stressors in other professions are less immediate: a production mistake, a new set of objectives to meet, a coworker quitting. Nevertheless, any organization or business is capable of experiencing adversity and hardship, and the obvious stress felt by employees is every bit as intense and profound.

The particular industry that people work in is irrelevant. When plopped down in the middle of any emergency in any field, decision-makers have no choice: They must be able to cope. They must continue to use their best judgment toward the resolution of the problem—period.

A few lucky people actually have a low volume of stress because they experience hardly any problems. They live carefree both at the office and outside of it. Nothing keeps them up tossing and turning at night. Every day is a holiday. But most of us do not have lives like that—we actually *do* have problems and stress in our lives. Moreover, life sometimes seems like one problem after another.

However, remember: It is not the *amount* of stress that matters most—it is the *effects* of stress that are most predictive of our performance and success. So the development of our coping skills, which help reduce the effects of workplace stress, becomes vitally important to our success.

Strong

Many individuals who score well in this area encounter overwhelmingly stressful situations within their work environment. This is a function not necessarily of the *amount* of stress that impacts their professional success, but of *how they deal with* their stress. In fact, many of those who have completed our judgment assessment are shocked at how strongly they scored in this area, particularly if they confront many stressors of great magnitude at work. There is no mistake, though: Their scores in this area are strong because they are able to keep their stress under control despite tremendous known stressors.

Remember, keeping stress under control indicates not *the absence of* stress, but rather *an ability to cope with* stress. The presence of multiple high-stress events in your life does not suggest that you lack coping skills.

Be thankful if you are one of those people who deal effectively with obvious stressors, for you have developed phenomenal coping skills that help you manage stress. This ability to cope in the face of adversity is a key ingredient in the recipe for performing to your highest potential and achieving high levels of success.

A well-developed value structure in this area manifests not only in excellent coping skills, but in a reduction of the negative effects of any work-related stress in your life. A powerful, dynamic, upbeat attitude operates within you as you deal with your workplace realities. Even if you experience negativity or adversity during your day, your value structure provides for you the necessary ability to cope with these and keep stress at bay. Confronting this judgment assassin helps clear the way for you to use your fundamental judgmental abilities to their highest potential—which leads directly to better decision-making and success.

Moreover, there are practically no negative consequences to having highly developed coping skills. There is no real downside. The only miniscule potential pitfall for those with exceptionally well-developed coping skills is that such an optimistic attitude can lead to naïveté on occasion, which can mean you are sometimes duped. You may give too much benefit of the doubt, and your view of the world might be slightly Pollyannaish. Even so, there is really no such thing as too much of a positive attitude.

Other than that, on our judgment assessment, the strongest score here is exactly what we like to see, as it reveals

- ▸ outstanding coping skills,

- ▸ a robust ability to mitigate stress, and thus,

- ▸ a reduction in the negative effects of stress.

When you greatly reduce the effects of stress, you are able to use your best judgment and put forth your best decision-making and problem-solving abilities. Be thankful should you have a well-developed value structure and an ability to cope—and make sure to maintain that positive attitude!

Weak

Those who are weak in this area of their value structure lack the ability to cope with known stress—which leaves them with detrimental effects that are a heavy burden to bear. Stress is one of the biggest hindrances to the use of good judgment, and impairs the ability to perform to the highest potential.

If you lack well-developed coping skills, then sooner or later a known stressor in your workplace is going to have an exceedingly negative impact on you (if it has not already). When you lack sufficient coping skills, you are very susceptible to obvious stressors. The result is inadequate value clarity and impaired judgment, resulting in poor choices.

You can improve how you handle known or apparent workplace stressors through the development of stronger coping skills. Unlike the vague, elusive background stress at the root of low problem-solving energy (discussed on page 215), insufficient coping skills are associated with easy-to-identify—and often immediately apparent—stressors.

You must develop coping skills to manage known workplace stress. Dedicate yourself to gaining supremacy over it. If you do not, the effects of the stress will undermine your judgment, your capacity to make your best decisions, and your ability to remain in control of challenging and nerve-racking predicaments.

Success Tip #1: Pinpoint the stress.

Identify the kind of stress that is affecting your performance. Known workplace stressors, unlike background stress, are specific issues or problems that are easily discernible. The first step in reducing this kind of stress is to identify what is causing it. While this might seem obvious, many do not focus attention squarely on what is causing them stress.

This should not be a difficult exercise. The sources of your stress should be rather obvious, whether they are immediate and acute (say, a life-threatening accident or an equipment malfunction) or prolonged and chronic (such as layoffs, a new boss, a difficult coworker, or bankruptcy proceedings).

Success Tip #2: Make a plan.

Develop a plan to quell and conquer the identified workplace stress in your life. As you actualize this plan, you should have two primary objectives:

1. Attack and/or eliminate the stressor.

2. Improve your coping skills.

The particulars of your plan depend on your specific circumstances. They might vary from something as simple as merely increasing your awareness of stress, to a long, drawn-out multiyear set of specific goals and criteria (for example, furthering your education or learning to meditate).

Let's consider your plan in a little more detail so it becomes practical to implement.

The first objective—*to attack and/or eliminate your specific work-related stressors*—is the most straightforward component to reducing the effects of work-side stress. Typically, either you can do something about work-side stressors, or you cannot. Preferably, you eliminate the stressors altogether, but if that option is unavailable, you should strive to at least reduce their impact on you.

If the source of your stress is, for example, an overbearing boss or coworker, then an open, honest, respectful conversation might resolve the issue. Or if you are stressed because of antiquated equipment that hinders your performance, then present a plan to your supervisor to upgrade with new equipment, or implement a new and more efficient workflow.

Consider various options and solutions to your current work environment that might help alleviate the stressors in your workplace. Be creative; the possibilities are limited only by your imagination. Spend whatever time, effort, and energy it takes. You might even conclude that the best course of action for you is to eliminate the stressor with a change of environments—a switch to a new job or career. Whatever you decide, if you hit upon a solution that is doable—do it!

The second and most important objective in the reduction of workside stress is *to improve your coping skills.* Coping skills put those persistent, deep-rooted stressors into a proper context and perspective, diminishing their negative impact.

I have had hundreds of conversations with individuals who score poorly in this area and feel beaten down by high levels of stress. While the specific circumstances around each stressor vary, the common thread to a successful resolution, without exception, involves not only a robust attempt at mitigating the stressors, but also improving the ability to cope with stress. So if there is a circumstance that you truly *cannot* change, you must reconcile your predicament so that you reach a degree of satisfaction and contentment with it. Otherwise, your stress will increase to destructive levels.

Do not interpret this as an excuse to accept the unacceptable, or to portray yourself as a victim if you are not one, but there might be circumstances that we do not desire or prefer, yet we are unable to change. If you are in such a negative circumstance, use your coping skills to provide you with as much serenity and composure as possible, and the ability to continue to use your good judgment.

As you strive to improve your coping skills, think back to a particularly difficult work-related problem that caused you undue tension and strain, but that you solved effectively and efficiently. As you reflect, ask yourself where you believe your coping skills came from. The answer to that question reveals the *source* of your coping skills—a knowledge that might allow you to take command of, and employ, your coping skills more effectively in the future.

Success Tip #3: Develop a positive attitude.

For most people, the primary source of their coping skills is a positive, optimistic attitude put forth every single day. This might sound simplistic, but that doesn't mean maintaining a positive outlook is easy to do. Even so, it is well worth the effort. The success of any plan to reduce the effects of stress depends to the highest degree on an ability to maintain a positive attitude.

A positive attitude is an immensely important component of your value structure. It is a value, a judgment, and a choice. Each of us—including you—decides whether or not to adopt the habit of optimism. And our data tells us repeatedly and unequivocally that those who inhabit a positive outlook are much better equipped to cope with adversity and stress. It is the very best coping skill of all.

As each day passes, outside stressors and problems come and go endlessly. As you resolve one problem, another pops up, and you must be able to cope with it as well. A positive attitude provides hope even when you are faced with multiple problems and ongoing adversity. If you engage a crisis or problem with positivity on your side, you resolve dilemmas and impasses quicker, more consistently, and more thoroughly.

Take the development of a positive attitude very, very seriously, because it is one of your primary coping mechanisms. Whether or not you maintain a positive attitude is your choice—one of the most important choices you will ever make. You will need it more times than you think in the work world.

Although it is not something we are able to hold in our hands, a positive attitude positively exists. A positive attitude is

- Tangible, palpable, noticeable, and *real*
- Much more than plastering on a smiling face

- Sincere and genuine

- Habitual when you allow it to feed on its own energy

Sometimes, though, we better understand something by what it is not. A positive attitude is not

- Pretentious or shallow

- Dishonest, deceptive, or deceitful

- Falsehearted

Some people resist having a positive attitude, adopting a negative one instead as a way of getting back at or competing with someone whose behavior they do not like. But their negative attitude is passive-aggressive behavior—a reaction that tends to do little or no good in the end. If you find yourself in this situation, consider that you might be giving someone else too much control over your emotions and behaviors. You, not someone else, should be in charge of your emotions and attitude. If you allow someone else to influence you in this way, then the other person gains control over you.

If you consider this discourse on attitude and coping skills to be overly "touchy-feely"—and I know from experience that some people do—examine the benefits in a more objective manner. Remember that the data reveals, without equivocation, that judgment is one of the principal factors in high performance and success. The data also reveals, through millions of data points, that the inability to cope with stress is one of the biggest detriments to the use of good judgment—and that a positive attitude improves coping skills, which mitigates the negative effects of stress.

Therefore, if high performance and success are two of your ultimate goals, you owe it to yourself to maintain a positive attitude. It enhances your coping skills; lowers your stress; and improves your judgment, decision-making, and problem-solving. Thus, a positive approach improves your performance in everything that you do.

Success Tip #4: Get outside help.

Finally, search the Internet, talk to a close friend, or seek counseling to find other ways to improve your ability to cope and reduce the effects of work-related stress. There are entire industries and resources built around the idea of reducing known work stressors. If you learn to reduce your stress, *everything* you ever do will be better.

. . .

As a final thought on coping skills and the effects of stress on your judgment, ask yourself these two questions:

1. *What are the stressors in my life, and can I reduce or eliminate them?*

2. *Am I honestly doing everything I can to have and to maintain a positive attitude?*

Advancing a positive attitude is often easier to talk about than to truly put forth in real-life situations. However, the time, energy, and effort spent toward maintaining a positive outlook is well worth it. There undeniably is no better choice: You become better able to cope with the rigors of stress if you maintain a positive attitude.

Stressor #3: Self-Criticism

Another form of stress is *self-criticism*—what we call *self-induced stress*. Being overly self-critical involves replaying past failures and personal flaws over and over in your mind without resolution. It doesn't really matter whether these feelings are justified. Nor does it matter whether other people affirm or deny your sensitivities. What matters here is the effect on you and your decisions—it's very real, and sometimes very profound. The level of self-induced stress is determined by the degree to which a person tends to be personally accepting—or personally critical.

Self-induced stress arises when we are harder on ourselves or more perfectionistic than necessary. High levels of self-criticism are associated with high levels of personal stress, which undermines evaluative judgment, which undermines success.

This is the area of the value structure where many people suffer from their worst, most negative judgment. They tend to be overly perfectionistic and more self-critical than necessary—which increases personal stress and hinders their success. Ironically, it is quite common for individuals to have very strong judgment and yet possess debilitating levels of self-criticism.

High levels of self-criticism interfere with, and eventually weaken, performance in the workplace. Extreme self-criticism is a useless distraction: It causes individuals to spend undue time second-guessing themselves, rather than utilizing their evaluative judgment to render good decisions. Furthermore, it damages relationships with those colleagues who have difficulty relating to someone who is overly self-critical.

Unfortunately, this area of the value structure is difficult to improve upon. Self-criticism can become deeply ingrained in a person's sense of self. Within our corporate work over the years, we have encountered many individuals who are overly self-critical. In conversation, they quickly acknowledge their high degree of self-criticism. Then, incredibly, they often confess that they do not wish to improve it, for they believe their perfectionism to be the main driver of their success!

However, our database of hundreds of thousands of profiles reveals no correlation whatsoever between being self-accepting and failing to achieve success, or between being self-critical and finding success in a professional environment. It is a bogus argument. Our data repeatedly tells us that being *self-accepting* is more effective for high-level performance and for personal and professional satisfaction. To be motivated solely by accomplishments and the notion of *perfect* outcomes, and to let this be the determining factor of your degree of self-acceptance, is foolish. On the contrary, a degree of self-acceptance undergirds work-related judgments and therefore helps *support* professional accomplishments and success.

A person's level of self-criticism is often primarily influenced by the amount of criticism a person has experienced throughout their lifetime.

If parents, teachers, siblings, coaches, or mentors have been overly critical of someone as a child or young adult—even if such criticisms were genuinely meant to be constructive—the result is often the creation of a self-critical value structure and thus a high level of self-induced stress that stays with that person as he or she ages.

A variety of large-scale studies by well-known leadership organizations consistently reveals that at least six compliments need to be offered to offset one criticism. However, the reality is that relatively few of us live and work in such an environment of constant flattery. Many people exist in a world that is almost the opposite—that is, a world with a six-to-one ratio of criticisms to compliments!

In fact, many of us are raised in an environment where few, if any, words of praise are spoken when desired outcomes occur, and where criticism is offered when outcomes are less than perfect. Moreover, it is a common practice to hold the belief that the expected norm is for the events of life and work to go as planned and for outcomes to be successful. This sometimes leads to the belief that, therefore, compliments and praise should be reserved only for those situations where outcomes are *well above* the norm—in other words, why offer praise when events unfold as expected?

Self-induced stress is intergenerational in effect, with its influence passed from one generation to the next. Self-accepting parents who raise children in environments of praise and affirmation tend to instill that outlook in their children. These individuals tend to be driven by the positive, or by a desire to achieve. Conversely, self-critical, perfectionistic parents tend to instill their tendencies in their offspring, including the tendency to be driven by the negative, or by a desire not to fail.

There can be good reason, of course, to want to avoid making mistakes: In some professions, a particular mistake can be catastrophic or even deadly. One incorrect dose can kill the patient. One bad pitch can lose the game. One horrific business decision can bankrupt the company. Still, no one makes fewer mistakes by being excessively self-critical or by beating themselves up every time they err.

It is important to find a balance between using self-criticism as appropriate constructive criticism to improve performance, and using self-criticism inappropriately as destructive stress, which detracts from performance. Do not allow your mistakes to become the primary measure of yourself. Too much self-induced stress leads to distraction, which only leads to *more* mistakes.

Take a cold, hard, objective look at the level of your self-criticism—and if you are weak in this area, acknowledge it and work as hard as you can to improve it.

Strong

Congratulations! If you are appropriately self-accepting, you are one of a small percentage (approximately ten percent) of the population.

If you are developed in this area of your value structure, a strong score indicates an appropriate level of self-acceptance; the capability for self-affirmation; and the ability to be comfortable with, and accept without undue personal criticism, your flaws and mistakes. You will be generally content with who you are—or, as the saying goes, "comfortable in your own skin."

If you are self-accepting, it is likely you were raised in an environment that was not overly critical but instead filled with praise and acceptance. If you were not raised in such an environment, you have beaten the odds in managing to overcome and reject the criticisms that negatively influence the personal values and behaviors of so many others.

Individuals who are self-accepting may very well loathe making mistakes as much as or even more than self-critical individuals do. Yet they remain better able to contextualize and learn from their mistakes, and to appropriately incorporate the ramifications into their future judgments and decisions. Thus they avoid the destructive behavior that comes from the self-induced stress arising from high levels of personal criticism. When others ask, "Doesn't that bother you?" their answer is, "Of course it does!" The difference is that they are able to maintain perspective about themselves and their abilities. That perspective separates them from those whose overly harsh self-criticism fills them with self-induced stress.

Now, it can be difficult for self-accepting individuals to comprehend just how fantastic it is to possess this strength. Because it is a part of their value structure, it comes to them naturally and without effort, and they probably take it for granted. So if deep down inside you understand that you are genuinely self-accepting, and if you are able to identify intuitively with those values, celebrate that and all that it means, and do your best not to allow yourself to become self-critical.

Occasionally, frustration develops between a self-accepting individual and an overly self-critical individual. A self-accepting individual may be able to neither understand nor tolerate someone with high levels of self-criticism and self-induced stress, and so may develop a negative posture with that person. Should this frustration develop, however, the outcomes are generally less destructive than when frustration is experienced in other areas of the value structure. The reality is that due to their open and accepting nature, self-accepting individuals most often develop a positive, helpful, and affirming relationship with those who tend to be more self-critical.

Moderate

Moderate development in this area of the value structure is marked by a tendency to use self-criticism as a form of motivation. This is *very* common, occurring in approximately sixty-five percent of the population.

Being in the moderate range does not imply that you were raised in an environment that was less than loving and nurturing. It merely indicates that you use a degree of self-criticism as a form of motivation.

Moderate self-criticism is rarely a hindrance to personal or professional success. However, be careful not to let moderate self-criticism turn extreme.

Weak

As self-criticism moves beyond moderate to detrimental levels, it reaches such a degree as to become visibly noticeable to others. Depending on individual circumstances, self-criticism may begin to negatively affect someone's work environment and thus the potential for long-term success.

Slightly over twenty-five percent of the population lacks development in this area of the value structure, and the majority of people experience their very weakest judgment here.

If you lack self-acceptance, your tendency is to be much too hard on yourself: You are a perfectionist and self-critical to the extreme. You experience high levels of self-induced stress because of the excessive pressure you put on yourself, and you tend to fixate on things that do not go perfectly.

Weakness in this area of the value structure is indicated by the following:

- ▸ Lack of self-acceptance

- ▸ Proclivity to overemphasize negative events in your mind

- ▸ Predisposition to exert energy on things that did not have an ideal outcome or go exactly as planned

In other words, you focus on the *one* thing you did wrong, and disregard the *nine* things you did right.

Extreme weakness here is likely to flow over into a critical approach to others. You are prone to manifest passive-aggressive tendencies, which may alienate those around you. The negativity associated with high levels of self-criticism proves distasteful for many, including teammates, colleagues, and superiors.

As mentioned on page 235, it is likely that if you have a high level of self-criticism, it has been exacerbated by an exposure to disproportionate amounts of criticism as compared to compliments. This may come from work experiences, school experiences, parental upbringing, and so forth.

But you're in luck! There are effective ways to combat high levels of self-criticism.

Success Tip #1: Don't overreact.

Take mistakes seriously—but do not make too much out of it. In most instances, being aware that you are more self-critical than you should be—and that your self-criticism tends to make you more negative when you consider others and their actions—can help you avoid overly critical interactions with yourself and other people. This awareness assists you in anticipating and controlling your negative responses before they occur.

Success Tip #2: Learn to lighten up.

Self-critical people may think that they never do anything well enough, and believe they are responsible for fixing everything. Learn to enjoy the good things, and not dwell on the bad. The reality is that you are your own worst critic. Be wary so that your self-criticism is not self-destructive.

Success Tip #3: Accept your limitations.

Whatever our occupation, it's important that we learn from our mistakes and keep trying. Nevertheless, if you are prone to persistent, habitual, recurring mistakes and have not seen much improvement over time, there is the possibility that your chosen profession is not for you. Think about whether you should, and could, change your type of work.

But remember that we are all human, and we are not perfect. Thus we really should strive to be accepting of ourselves. If that sounds like a bit of esoteric pop psychology, then incorporate the purely data-driven point of view: We have millions of statistically valid data points backing up the fact that there is a greater likelihood for improved performance and continued long-term success if an individual is more self-accepting and less self-critical.

Success Tip #4: Consider the source.

If you realize that you are highly self-critical as a result of being excessively exposed to criticism for extended periods of your life, objectively consider the sources of that criticism.

Often, criticism comes from well-meaning and generous people who do not fully consider the implications of what they say or do; from ignorant people who do not know any better; or—in some cases—from weak or mean-spirited people who intentionally try to put others down. Strong people understand that they do not advance themselves by routinely criticizing others, whereas small-minded people often try to build themselves up by tearing others down. Unfortunately, this is a common practice and a primary cause behind future self-criticism.

An objective consideration of the source of your self-critical nature is a good first step for placing the criticism in context. This process of examination and discovery can prove extremely helpful in determining whether you should take the criticism to heart—or disregard it.

Remember, however, that what is working against you here is your stress driven by your self-criticism, and not stress arising from other people's criticism of you. It is up to you to decide whether you are going to take ownership of the criticism you receive from others and use it to your benefit—or whether it makes more sense to reject and repudiate it.

If you decide the criticism is valid, legitimate, and constructive in nature, you can use it to genuinely help you improve yourself, and therefore it becomes worthy of your sincere consideration.

If the criticism is not valid, purely negative in nature, and nothing more than a cruel attempt to belittle you, you should reject it entirely.

After a lifetime of self-criticism, this may be difficult to do, but nonetheless it is a very worthwhile effort.

Success Tip #5: Avoid the perfectionism trap.

Do not descend into the pitfall of perfectionism. Using *perfect* as the only standard of judgment is frustrating and counterproductive. The idea that if something is not perfect, then it is bad makes for a difficult benchmark.

Choose to learn from any mistakes rather than using them as a foundation to beat yourself up. Allow yourself satisfaction and gratification for those things that you perform well, although perhaps not perfectly. Understand that there is a tremendous difference between the genuine satisfaction of a job well done and the sensation of stress that arises because something was not quite perfect. The belief that something could have been performed just a teeny-tiny bit better or quicker is a never-ending cycle of self-criticism.

Success Tip #6: Choose your own outlook.

Adopt the understanding that none of us can change the past, but we can influence the future.

No matter the reason, whether it's the transference of outside criticisms or your own unique value tendencies, high levels of self-criticism indicate that you've adopted a self-critical value structure. That is a *choice* you made at some point in the past.

Accepting the criticisms that others may have placed on you is also a *choice*. Yes, it is worthwhile to determine the reasons—or people—behind your self-critical stance, but eventually you must move beyond blame. You must draw the proverbial line in the sand and do something about your self-induced stress. Your future self could be not only a more self-accepting individual, but also a less stressed and, as our data unambiguously reveals, more successful individual.

. . .

While changing what we believe about ourselves sounds simple enough, change in this area is difficult. Yet if we are self-accepting, we are more likely to be successful and happy, and to perform at higher levels. Is that not what you want for yourself?

A colossal industry has arisen to assist those who lack self-acceptance. Books, therapists, television shows, seminars, educational courses, college degrees, coaches, counselors, and hypnotists delve into the psyche of those who are overly self-critical, and they offer a plethora of solutions. If you recognize that you are overly self-critical, avail yourself of these. They will help you achieve your success.

Stressor #4: Known Personal Stress

Our personal life, our opinion and view of ourselves, and our personal relationships should be a source of refuge and shelter, the proverbial anchor in the storm. If they are not, then our personal value structure can easily become a source of stress.

This area of the value structure determines the effects of personal stress that is produced by personal circumstances, including specific issues and people that you can identify and describe, regardless of whether or not you actually have the power to change them. Known personal stressors are easy to pinpoint: Conflict with a family member, the death or illness of a loved one, a tight financial situation, drug use, arguments with someone close to you, health issues, moving to a new home, divorce, or a pregnancy are all classic examples. Rather than the *amount* of this type of personal stress, however, the *effect* of that personal stress is the true determining factor in overall contentment, quality of life, and professional performance and success.

As with known *work* stressors (see page 225), most people are better than they realize at dealing with known *personal* stressors. The advantage comes from our ability to cope better with known, obvious stressors as opposed to vague, hidden stressors. By a wide margin, the number one personal stressor is *financial adversity*, and it often can bleed over into adjoining areas, causing additional stress. For example, financial problems can wreak havoc in a spousal relationship.

Your personal coping skills determine the degree to which you are able to manage obvious personal stressors and your capability in dealing with adversity in personal matters. If you are able to mitigate the known stressor, you might be able to reduce your stress levels rather quickly.

Our known stressors, both personal and work-related, are two areas of our value structure that fluctuate the most. They vary based on a combination of coping skills and the degree and intensity of stress being experienced. In particular, our known *personal* stressors tend to fluctuate with higher intensity and within a shorter time span than known *work* stressors.

Because of its proclivity for fluctuation, personal stress tends to be slightly less statistically predictive of workplace success than the other areas of stress. However, it's clear that failing to attend to high levels of personal stress will negatively influence your judgment and performance at work—and thus your success—in the long run.

Personal stress, when not controlled, eventually affects the workplace. At that point, you have not only the personal stress adding undue hardship and dragging you down, but the added difficulty of trying simultaneously to maintain high levels of performance at work. Some people are adept at putting on their game face as they leave home, and they perform outstanding work temporarily. However, the overwhelming majority of people who experience long-term debilitating personal stress eventually succumb to that stress—and then it bleeds over into their work life, often causing work performance to suffer, perhaps in very destructive and public ways. In fact, our data shows that personal stress flowing into the workplace negatively affects work performance just as often as stress that originates at work.

There is an interesting concession here, though: Some people do thrive on a *small* (key word is *small*) dose of work stress, though one must be careful not to confuse the difference between positive (excitement) and negative (stress). Take into account the manifest difference between exciting, challenging, profound, significant work and purely stressful work. *Stress* implies negative adversity—with which you must be able to cope. High-level, high-energy, profoundly important work may have an associated stressful component, too—or it may not. Nevertheless, a bit of chaos or conflict, impending deadlines, or a high workload that includes a *small* dose of actual stress does get the juices flowing for some people—possibly surgeons, soldiers, athletes, and so forth. It may add to the stimulation, exhilaration, and sense of accomplishment of such work.

However, in no circumstances is stress arising from personal matters beneficial. Someone's personal life might be exciting—full of adventure, passion, high energy, and an endless stream of enthusiastic capers and escapades—but this is distinctly different from the obvious personal stress that arises from true adversity, which requires an ability to cope.

Also, as with known workplace stress, some people encounter only a minor amount of personal stress in their lives—and yet experience an extreme negative impact as a result. Conversely, other people are able to cope well with an enormous burden of personal stressors. The difference between these kinds of people is not in the *amount* of stress they experience, but in their *ability to cope* with stress. So this area of the value structure specifically determines the ability to put forth and maintain a positive approach, mindset, and attitude in the presence of personal stress, and does not necessarily reflect the amount or quantity of stressors in someone's life.

If you know you are experiencing the negative effects of personal stress, take it seriously. Most people possess at least some tools for coping that improve their ability to mitigate stress. Therefore, feeling the effects of a personal stressor is an indication that your stress level is outstripping your defense mechanisms and overwhelming your coping skills.

Through our corporate work, we have run large-scale studies to examine the ramifications of stress within several different kinds of workforces. The data confirms what we already intuitively know: that as stress—one of the biggest detriments to judgment—is lowered, judgment and decision-making, and the overall mood, effectiveness, and efficiency of the workforce, improves. A reduction in personal and professional stress helps remove a significant barrier to achievement, so that workers in occupations across the board are able to use their best judgment and make their best decisions.

Strong

Strong judgment in this area provides well-developed coping skills that can help you resolve personal issues. Personal "anchors"—perhaps a spouse or other family member, your faith, good friends, or a combination thereof—can help keep you grounded and centered, and help guide you through personal difficulty. Maintaining a positive attitude in the face of hardship, and an unwavering commitment to deal straightforwardly and frankly with personal adversity, helps lower personal stress levels tremendously.

Remember, an ability to cope with personal stress does not mean that your life is *without* personal stress; it means that you have an ability to *handle* stress. Personal coping skills will help you keep private stress at bay, which helps lessen its negative effects on your judgment and decision-making, both at home and at work. When excessively stressful events *do* occur in your life, coping skills may weaken and you may experience correspondingly higher levels of stress. Yet you can take comfort in the fact that you are likely to retain at least a modicum of coping skills, allowing you to still deal with those events somewhat effectively.

It is likely that one of your coping skills is the sustainment of a consistently positive attitude. Always strive to maintain that positive attitude, and also consciously and tenaciously guard your coping skills, because they help keep stress at manageable levels.

A side benefit of a strong ability to cope with personal stressors is the enhanced potential for improvement in any weak areas of your personal life. For example, if you have low self-esteem, but your ability to cope with personal stress is strong, then any efforts to improve your self-esteem are more likely to succeed because you are not encumbered with the distraction of personal stress.

Weak

Should you lack development in this area of your value structure, it is likely that at some point you will suffer adverse effects resulting from personal stress.

For those who have not learned to cope, debilitating effects of stress can result from (for example) a divorce in the family, the death of a close family member or spouse, mental or physical abuse, addiction, or personal bankruptcy. If not dealt with in a straightforward and honest fashion, extreme levels of stress can degrade your ability to use your good judgment. Stress that is locked up inside or left unchecked can eventually cause harm to both your personal and professional life, and can undermine or ruin your chances for workplace success.

It is very rare for an individual to be able to maintain high levels of professional performance over the course of extended periods of extreme personal stress. So what can be done to mitigate the oft-debilitating and adverse effects of profound personal stress?

Success Tip #1: Acknowledge the situation.

A simple acknowledgment of your specific personal stress is a great first step. Talking about the stressor can trigger an immediate reduction in your stress level. To bring further resolution, appropriately share your dilemma—whether openly or confidentially, as your case may require—with a close friend, family member, priest, or counselor. Some people prefer to seek out a support group.

Success Tip #2: Take the long view.

Recognize that the complete resolution of your personal stress may require a long-term plan—and patience. Decide that this is all right, taking on a *So be it!* attitude. Then become committed to working through your stress in whatever way seems likely to be effective for you.

Long-range planning is a systemic endeavor, so make sure your systemic judgment (review the information starting on page 111) is an active component of your decision-making process.

Success Tip #3: Stay positive.

Throughout your entire stressful ordeal, maintain a positive attitude. It is the all-time best coping skill. (For an in-depth review of how to adopt and maintain a positive attitude, read pages 232–233.)

Without a positive attitude, you may lose hope. Without hope, in the presence of dilemma and adversity, you may be left with only despair, which will

- ▸ raise your level of stress,
- ▸ diminish your judgment,
- ▸ compound your problems, and
- ▸ hurt your chances for success.

In the presence of despair resides the judgment-ruining manifestation of stress—the number one detriment to the use of your good judgment.

. . .

You owe it to yourself and to everyone in your life not to be distracted and overwhelmed with stress.

Of all the areas of my corporate work, I believe the best, most worthwhile, and most positive is helping individuals mitigate the crushing burden of personal stress. Take an honest, objective look at yourself. If you know you are experiencing the negative impact of personal stress, do something about it *now*. Refer to the two-pronged approach that we discussed earlier (see the discussion about known workplace stress, on pages 255–234):

1. Attack and eliminate the stressor(s).

2. Improve your coping skills.

I talk often with individuals who have lived for many years with the detrimental effects of personal stress. Some people do it for so long that they become numb to the existence of their stress, and no longer do anything to try to make it go away. Well, there are few greater joys than reducing the effects of personal stress. The benefits of doing so will flow into every nook and cranny of your life.

The Power of Positivity

A client told me about the recent deaths that had occurred in his family, one after the other: his daughter in an automobile accident, his spouse to cancer, and both of his elderly parents. After hearing about the tragedy he has just experienced, I was surprised to learn that this person scored remarkably well in personal stress area of our judgment assessment.

In fact, he had the best score possible.

During our subsequent conversations, I continually felt as if *he* were counseling *me*. His positive attitude was stronger than any I have ever seen. Truth be told, today I am better equipped to handle adversity as a result of experiencing his positive outlook firsthand. And that's saying something, because I had extremely strong coping skills before we had ever met.

This man, through his faith, his remaining family, his ability to maintain the long-term view, and above all else, his consistently

Continued

strong, resolutely positive attitude, was able to not only persevere, but also regain happiness in his life.

Imagine the coping skills required to keep from becoming completely distraught and broken down in the face of such personal hardship as he experienced. Yet his hope never turned into despair. He maintained an optimistic approach within his value structure, and it led to his continued success.

This, my friend, is the true power of a positive attitude.

TRUTH #5: FRUSTRATION

Frustration—the second of our three judgment assassins—is one of the biggest detriments to the use of good judgment. No matter how incredibly strong our decision-making abilities may be, if frustration gets in the way, we may stumble and start making poor decisions that go against our better judgment. Frustration is a very serious issue—for anyone:

- Frustration can ruin professional and personal *environments*.
- Frustration can ruin professional and personal *relationships*.

Frustration arises from a clash within the value structure. It typically manifests when people are collaborating with individuals whose value structures differ from theirs. If this conflict between value structures and the subsequent frustration are left unchecked, it can easily and quickly undermine good judgment.

Many of us have made a poor decision against our better judgment because of our frustration over the situation, issue, or person in question. Often in these situations, we know that we know better, but our good judgment is overpowered by our frustration. Furthermore, any bad decision that we make can compound the already high level of frustration being experienced.

In an effort to mitigate situations such as these, let's delve into what is most likely to fuel our frustration and hinder our judgment, problem-solving, and ultimately our success:

- **Frustration Fuel #1:** *People Who See It Differently*
- **Frustration Fuel #2:** *Very Strong or Exceptional Judgment*
- **Frustration Fuel #3:** *Job "Fit"*

Frustration Fuel #1: People Who See It Differently

Why don't you see it the way I see it?

How many times have we felt that if we only explained our point of view, the other person would see it our way? Unfortunately, this is not typically the case. If we direct our explanations at someone whose value structure differs from ours, there is a good chance that person will still see it differently and be unable to comprehend our valuations.

People who see things similarly have similar value structures, and those who see it differently have differing value structures. The potential for frustration to develop and erupt often depends on the area of disagreement in play. Some areas tend to spark high levels of frustration, while others tend to provoke nothing more than an eye roll or a shoulder shrug.

Moreover, even though you and others have similar beliefs or opinions, there are some people with whom you just do not mesh. Perhaps there are conflicts within the value structures that come about due to differing strengths in particular areas. For example, someone who is a very good decision-maker may feel frustration when dealing with someone who is a poor decision-maker—even if they both tend to like most of the same things. Furthermore, any significant disparity in judgment strength among work colleagues, clients, and even customers suggests the potential for frustration between individuals in that area of judgment. For example, if one person is very tolerant (as discussed in the section on intrinsic judgment, starting on page 47), and his or her colleague is intolerant, it can lead to enormous conflict and frustration.

Bear in mind, too, that differences in the value structure are more than just a differing of opinion. Our value structures are at the core of who we are as unique individuals. Our ideas based on our value structure are natural to us, because they *are* us. We often take for granted our value structure—and therefore our notions of performance, conduct, and behavior—and so we often assume that others view the world as we do. It is sometimes hard to even comprehend the judgments and decisions, even small and insignificant ones, of someone with a starkly different value structure. The arguments that result can be endless, often leaving no room for compromise.

For example, someone with highly developed extrinsic judgment, who by his or her very nature is dependable (as discussed starting on page 79), likely cannot understand the choices and actions of someone with weak extrinsic judgment—that is, an undependable person. And this will be true no matter how hard they try to get along.

At the other end of the spectrum, anyone with moderate or weak areas of judgment needs to be on the lookout for expressions of frustration from people who show very strong judgment most of the time. In this case, you might be the victim of frustration that is expressed *toward* you and your decisions.

Frustration Fuel #2: Very Strong or Exceptional Judgment

As I have mentioned, our work with evaluative judgment includes the detailed examination of hundreds of thousands of judgment assessments, thousands of interviews, and over one hundred best/worst performer studies. Our clients range from small partnerships to multibillion-dollar corporations.

We have found those areas of the value structure that lead to success and those that lead to failure. In addition, we've zeroed in on the highly developed upper echelons and studied the effects of having extremely well-developed judgment. We refer to this highly developed judgment as *exceptional judgment*. *Exceptional,* as used here, refers to judgment that is stronger than average by a full standard deviation, based on multiple best/worst performer studies. Exceptional judgment is the *very strong* segment of *strong* judgment.

Exceptional judgment represents an area of judgment in which superior strength positions the user decidedly beyond the average person in capability. Exceptional judgments are a marvelous precursor of success, and affect the bearer personally on a consistent basis. Those with exceptional work-side judgment are predictably strong in their work performance and positive engagement in the external world. Their judgments provide for them the ability to render effective decisions and solve problems in a broad range of situations. Finding appropriate solutions is natural, instinctive, and intuitive. They "get" what many others don't—and they get it much quicker than most.

Exceptional judgments sometimes can seem downright otherworldly to someone who does not possess them. Yet, as is often the case, sometimes too much of a good thing fosters an environment predisposed to negative consequences. When judgment becomes highly developed, there is the *potential*—although not necessarily the *likelihood*—for negative behaviors, actions, and performance to develop. And there is no hiding this area of extremely strong judgment!

Let's first make a comparison to someone who is very tall: Such a person cannot change that fact, nor can he or she hide it from anyone else. Moreover, tall people can use their height to their advantage, or not. They can use it in positive ways or negative ways, but they cannot deny their height. Such is the case with exceptional judgment.

In fact, you can also compare exceptional judgment to the proverbial bull in the china shop: You, the bull, are lucky to be strong and fit—but if you are not careful, you might break some china. Therefore, while exceptional judgment brings many positives with it, you should also be wary lest some negatives manifest themselves into any exceptional areas of your value structure.

And the most common negative expression of people who have exceptional judgment is conflict—expressed in the form of *frustration*. It might be related to a problem, a situation, an event, or an opportunity, but most often the frustration arises due to another person or a group of people. Why?

Individuals with exceptional judgment have a natural desire to move beyond observation and assessment, and to actually tackle and solve problems within their areas of very strong judgment. This desire arises because they tend to quickly conceptualize their predicament, and they understand when it is time to bring it to resolution.

These two features—desire and aptitude—stand in stark contrast to the abilities of those who are not so quick, competent, or strong in their judgment and who tend to be moderate or poor decision-makers. These individuals may take notice of consistently strong decision-makers, but they are often left wondering how those people do what they do!

The distance between the two groups sometimes seems insurmountable. Imagine that you are in the middle of a dilemma, predicament, opportunity, or crisis, and the solution to it is far away, perched on the top of a distant mountain peak. If you have *very* strong evaluative judgment, it does not matter that the solution is far away on that distant mountain: You are able to see it clearly. You have *value clarity*. Your value clarity helps the solution just "appear" to you. Value clarity facilitates good judgment, helping you quickly formulate good decisions and take appropriate actions.

However, if you have only moderate or weak judgment ability, you have *value fog*. You experience difficulty seeing through the haze and the murk of the decision-making process. Your value fog renders you slow to locate the faraway solution—if you find it at all—and therefore you struggle to resolve issues and problems, and are quite likely to make poor, slow, or haphazard decisions.

The upshot: Individuals with exceptional judgment are apt to instantly and easily recognize with clarity a viable solution, whereas those with weak judgment seem stuck in a decision-making fog. Thus they often wonder why others do not see the solution, something that comes so naturally and effortlessly to them. They come to feel exasperated and annoyed—*frustrated*—that the resolution of the problem is right there in front of everyone for them to see, yet others still have questions or doubts about the course of action to take.

Furthermore, if someone else presents a solution that is different from the one offered by the person with exceptional judgment, it too causes conflict and frustration.

Frustration Fuel #3: Job Fit

Does another person or task at work irritate you?

Another issue with people who have exceptionally strong judgment is that this strength has the potential to negatively influence their job fit. You see, exceptional judgment indicates high judgmental ability. Individuals with very strong judgment overall tend to need a "big" job. So if the judgmental demands of a particular job are few, it is possible that the job is not stimulating enough for those with high judgmental abilities—and job boredom may set in.

If their job is not judgmentally stimulating, then it becomes even more important that such people thoroughly *enjoy* what they do. However, there's a catch-22 here: Often, whether or not they enjoy their job is directly related to the degree of judgmental demands from the job. As such, a large disparity between an individual's judgment *capacity* and the judgment *demands* of his or her job quite frequently causes an issue with job fit. As a result, it is common for individuals with exceptional judgment to get promoted beyond an entry-level position rather quickly—or otherwise to quit their position due to job boredom and frustration.

This concept of *job fit* applies in similar fashion to whether a person "fits" well with other people (Frustration Fuel #1).

So how do we avoid fueling the flames of frustration?

Success Tip #1: Be aware of frustration.

Always remain conscious of the potential for frustration to rear its ugly head. Awareness of this pitfall is the very best way to avoid frustration and conflict. Also, make a conscious attempt to keep your frustration under control when you find yourself involved with others who exhibit either less or more strength of judgment.

When dealing with frustration, an ounce of prevention is worth a pound of cure. So first examine closely those areas where you suspect your judgments are near the extremes, either *very strong* or *very weak*. These are the areas where you are most susceptible to frustration.

Success Tip #2: Determine the origins of your frustration.

If you find it difficult to keep frustrations from flaring up, make a great effort to determine their origins.

Temporarily forget the specifics of the task or person involved, and examine your frustration in terms of your value structure and evaluative judgment. Very often, this points directly to the source of your frustration, which quickly provides for you a solution.

For example, if you believe that you tend to be intrinsically dominant and you are dealing with someone who is extrinsically dominant, then no doubt therein resides your frustration. A simple understanding of one's exceptional abilities is often a great step forward in alleviating common conflicts, frustrations, and difficulties in work relationships, work environment, self-improvement, and overall success.

Success Tip #3: Do some soul searching.

Should you experience recurring frustrations, and yet be unable to identify how or why, consider whether you have the right fit in your current job. Furthermore, if after much soul searching you are unable to articulate the exact reason for your frustration, maybe you're even in the wrong profession. Or if your source of frustration can be described as *many things at many times with many people, all day long, from the moment you step into work until the moment you leave,* maybe it's time to look for something else.

Then again, maybe it's just time for you to get over yourself.

Success Tip #4: Use your powers for good.

If you know you have exceptional judgment, remember to use it always as a force for good.

There is no hiding extremely strong judgmental ability, just as someone who is very tall can neither change that fact nor hide it from anyone else. As previously mentioned, tall people can use their height to their advantage or not—and furthermore, they can use it in positive ways or negative ways: to hurt (by physically threatening someone who is smaller) or to help (by assisting a shorter person who struggles to reach a can of food on a high shelf). Similarly, a person with strong intrinsic judgment, for example, cannot just shut off this ability in an attempt to relate to others—and also can choose to use it in ways that are helpful or harmful to the self and to others.

Remember, most people do not have exceptional judgment. If you suspect that you do have one or more areas of exceptional judgment, use your strong judgment to help people, not undermine them. Do not unwittingly slide into condescending or mean-spirited behavior toward others when you feel frustration. Instead, learn how to recognize frustration, cope with it, and squash it in advance if possible. Do not let the negative behavior of frustration cloud and ruin your excellent judgment.

Success Tip #5: Maintain a positive attitude.

Frustration develops out of stress, and remember that the all-time best possible way to cope with frustration is to maintain a positive attitude every single day. This is not always easy to do, but it starts with a choice that anyone can make. (For a thorough reminder of how and why to initiate, and hold on to, that positive attitude, see pages 232–233—or even reread the entire chapter on stress.)

A simple way to start having a positive attitude *right now* is by celebrating any exceptional judgment areas you may have. Having exceptional judgment provides you with fantastic innate benefits. Be excited and grateful, and do not fear your strong judgment. True, there are possible pitfalls—but exceptional judgment also can serve as an enormous strength for you, greatly facilitating your success.

TRUTH #6: CLUTTER

On the surface, you might think that clutter is not that big a deal— nothing more than a pile of stuff in the corner, a minor distraction. Well, you would be wrong. Too much clutter is a *very big deal*. In fact, clutter is one of the big three risks to the use of good judgment, and therefore an assassin threatening your success.

Webster's Dictionary defines the noun form of *clutter* as "a large amount of things that are not arranged in a neat or orderly way: a crowded or disordered collection of things." Its definition for *clutter* as a transitive verb is "to fill or cover with scattered or disordered things that impede movement or reduce effectiveness."

Our data reveals without equivocation that there is a direct connection between being able to maintain and hold concentration, and being able to use good judgment. This is especially true when you are operating in the midst of interruptions, commotion, confusion . . . and *clutter*.

Simply put, clutter distracts us. When we are distracted, we lose our focus and concentration. A loss of focus and concentration greatly impedes evaluative judgment. As such, any conversation about the harmful effects of clutter should center on a conversation about focus and concentration.

The level of focus necessary for a person to be successful varies from job to job and from environment to environment. Some endeavors, such as a surgery, mountain climbing, aviating, and high-rise window-washing, are so demanding in the need to maintain focus that a momentary lapse in concentration is liable to cause dangerous and life-threatening consequences.

Other activities—such as cooking, bicycle riding, or driving—might, on the surface, be considered less demanding, yet they also require a high level of focus and concentration. Although these activities are routine and commonplace, they must be performed competently and safely. After all, a distracted driver is a dangerous driver, as we've learned from the relatively new phenomenon of texting while driving, which has caused an increase in the automobile accident rate and led many locales to outlaw texting while driving.

Moreover, many jobs and roles require an ability to ignore the clutter of extraneous distractions while appreciating the business at hand and also incorporating unexpected information that crops up. Vocations in the fields of medicine, sports, law enforcement, homemaking, and coaching require this diligence and discrimination. Individuals in these jobs require strong focus in order to distinguish between that which is important and that which is not.

Does poor judgment cause distractions, or do distractions cause poor judgment? Does someone text and drive because they have poor judgment, or does their poor judgment result from the distraction of texting while driving? This philosophical conversation interests some, but it doesn't matter within the context of this conversation. The bottom line is that if we reduce the clutter in our lives, we use better judgment, make better decisions—and are more apt to find our success.

There is another philosophical conversation that revolves around the clutter foisted upon us by others versus clutter that we foist upon ourselves: Does clutter arrive from outside circumstances, or are we the ones responsible for bringing clutter into our lives? For our purposes, the answer doesn't really matter. Simply remember our prime directive with regard to clutter negatively impacting our evaluative judgment: *Reduce clutter, improve judgment.*

Clutter Style #1: Strong Focus

If this area of your value structure is strong, you have an ability to remain focused on tasks even in the presence of clutter and distractions; a talent for blocking outside influences; and a resiliency that allows you to maintain unbroken concentration.

You have a seemingly natural ability to do the following

- Determine whether a situation demands a broad or a narrow focus.

- Know *when* and *where* to direct your attention.

- Sustain any necessary intensity of concentration for long periods of time.

You also have a talent for moving back and forth between varying tasks, and for not allowing vital tasks, responsibilities, or actions to fall by the wayside.

Someone with this level of development who is working in an office environment could concurrently answer the phone, fax documents, respond to email, and maintain a schedule and appointments. Each of these tasks is a separate, stand-alone task, but strong focus and concentration will keep them all on the individual's personal radar screen and within his or her attention span.

If this describes you, your "clutter filter" allows you to maintain your attention on the appropriate components of your current environment while you also exclude extraneous information, data, and disruptions. Your strong focus and discriminatory ability help you avoid the pitfall of being distracted by irrelevant diversions. This strength is a tremendous aid to your success, as within most endeavors and work environments there are many items competing for your time and attention.

Of course, some jobs and activities do not require a person to maintain a strong focus. Unlike the busy daytime office worker, a third-shift receptionist's duties might comprise a series of short, easy-to-complete tasks requiring little focus. However, for many occupations and activities, an ability to maintain focus is highly desirable.

Clutter Style #2: Very Strong Focus

There is a potential downside to having a very strong focus: Because of your intense concentration on tasks and projects, you have an occasional tendency to shut out coworkers and other people. This may lead to other separate, potentially negative issues.

For instance, you may be labeled as someone who does not listen or does not care. Of course, you might *not* care about a particular subject or conversation, but do not let your very strong focus give a false impression merely because at the time you are zeroed in on something else. With your well-developed focus, you are quite capable of acknowledging the subject or conversation, and then getting back to the more important task.

Clutter Style #3: Moderate Focus

With only moderate development in this area of the value structure, you are somewhat susceptible to distractions and to breaks in your concentration. In order to avoid being distracted, and to make your best possible decisions, you require the peace and quiet of isolation even more than others with more developed focus.

Clutter Style #4: Weak Focus

Those who lack development in this area have difficulty sustaining their focus and concentration. In essence, they show an overall lack of adeptness at managing their attention. They are easily distracted, and occupations that require a high degree of focus and concentration will prove problematic for them until they improve their abilities in this area.

If this describes you, this component of your value structure alone does not indicate that you are absent-minded, scatterbrained, frivolous, or unreliable. However, it does indicate that you should employ techniques to develop and enhance your focus and concentration.

Some people consider their strength in this area of judgment to be an indicator of the amount of workplace privacy needed to do an optimal job. This simple idea of providing extra space has been effective for our corporate clients in helping improve the effectiveness of employees who are moderate to weak in this area of judgment.

Here are some suggestions on how to go about reducing distractions and improving your discriminatory ability.

Success Tip #1: Seek solitude.

Seek a bit of quiet and solitude, if at all possible, when making important decisions. Striving for more isolation, insulation, and privacy can help you avoid being distracted from the task(s) at hand. One practical way to do this is to change your immediate and proximate physical environment to enhance your focusing abilities when dealing with problems and challenges.

Sometimes just having a door—and using it to ensure privacy—can be of great benefit to you at work. Do not let a colleague's expectations of your open-door policy negatively affect your own need for privacy and silence. Moreover, redirecting traffic away from your office (if you have one) or moving your desk to a quieter location can help too.

Open-door policies are intended to foster communication and collaboration, but don't take it too far with the actual removal of office doors. The idea of one big, friendly, open office space without walls and packed with many desks and smiling faces is trendy in certain circles, but it can wreak havoc on an individual's ability to maintain focus, and thereby it can negatively impact judgment.

In fact, the actual removal of walls and doors may produce the opposite of the intended metaphorical benefit. If pressed for a definition, company management would likely define a *wall* as an impediment to communication between colleagues or departments. Similarly, a *door* would be considered an obstacle between superiors and subordinates. Industries that rely on creativity, brainstorming, inspiration, imagination, problem-solving, and innovation would have a natural aversion to anything that would be considered slowing down or hindering the positive qualities that would propel the company to greater success. However, to take away the literal walls and doors may only generate confusion, exhaustion, lack of concentration, and irritation among the very people who are relied upon to produce results.

If there are loud ringing phones in an area, ask that the volume be turned down. If your computer or phone is set to alert you every time you receive an email, disable the notification. Turn off the radio, if you have one, when making important work decisions.

If at all possible, situate yourself away from the water fountain, break room, elevator, and other high-traffic areas. Such positioning will immediately improve your efficiency, effectiveness, and (most likely) job satisfaction.

If you work in an environment other than an office, brainstorm some similarly effective yet simple techniques for your personal situation. In some occupations, reducing distractions may be all but impossible. If this is the case with your job—especially with noisy, distracting environments such as a manufacturing assembly line, or the emergency room of a busy hospital—you need to put forth a double effort to maintain focus and concentration.

If you know that you are vulnerable to distractions, start by admitting it, and utilize these simple techniques to reduce them.

Success Tip #2: Practice focusing.

When you're not at work, devote extra time and energy toward improving your focus. Developing this skill is easy to do, and the practice will transfer over and prove a boon to you at work. Here's how

- *Pick a subject and concentrate on it.* Notice how long you can stay focused before you are distracted.

- *Practice several times a day.* Chances are, improving your concentration requires only a few minutes of your time.

If you do as directed, you will begin to learn the art of focus and concentration. Devote regular practice to this skill; it can be somewhat perishable, and you want to be at peak performance when you use it to handle the demands of your job or role.

Success Tip #3: Make snappy decisions a habit.

Of course you must avoid ill-thought-out or knee-jerk reactionary decisions, but if you are pressed for a solution, straightforwardly proceed through the decision-making process (see page 190) and resolve the issue as soon as you can. By making your decisions before getting distracted, you develop the habit of avoiding distractions.

A habit of making succinct, to-the-point decisions can contribute to quick and immediate improvements in your ability to maintain focus.

Success Tip #4: Reduce mental clutter.

As important as it is to seek out quieter environments, it is even more important to reduce the amount of clutter in your life. Not only does clutter fill the actual spaces of our lives; it also fills our minds. When we carry clutter in our head, we expend too much mental energy in managing it. Clutter distracts. So a reduction in clutter, both mental and physical, can be magnificent for our focus and immediately improve our judgment.

Think about how good it feels when you clean off your desk, streamline your computer files, or organize the garage. The same is true when you check off items permanently from your mental to-do list. Reducing mental clutter frees up some space in your mind, allowing your focus—and thus your judgment and decision-making—to improve immediately. This is true no matter the level of a person's focus, but it is especially important for those who know from experience that they are susceptible to distractions.

Success Tip #5: Reduce clutter in your personal life.

Allocate more attention and effort to reducing the amount of clutter in your personal life. If you are weak in this area of your value structure, you are easily overwhelmed by the distraction such personal clutter creates. Clutter undermines your ability to see the big picture as it relates to your personal life, and it impedes your ability to live in an organized way. It therefore hinders your ability to reach your goals and achieve your dreams.

Do not confuse the *chaos* of clutter with *excitement*. They are not the same thing, although some people may experience them in a similar way. Chaos is negative interference, whereas excitement is a positive and exhilarating motivation.

Some individuals are much more susceptible than others to the negative impact of clutter. Therefore, do not gauge the amount of clutter in your life by the amount present in someone else's life. Each individual has a unique *clutter threshold*; when you cross yours, you'll find that too much "stuff" is impeding your judgment. So if you find yourself regularly distracted, you may be approaching or on the other side of your personal clutter threshold. That means it's time to work on reducing the physical clutter in your home, your car, and your yard. Don't forget to clean out any figurative clutter in your personal life and relationships.

Do it *now*—and reap the rewards of a less chaotic and tumultuous life. You will improve the chances of achieving your goals and dreams.

Success Tip #6: Refine your professional focus.

Reflect on the needs of your occupation, and determine what your work requires in its focus level. If you believe the attention demands of your job are greater than your concentration abilities, you'll need to work toward improving your focus at work.

Depending on how often you find yourself distracted, you may wish to engage outside assistance to further your capabilities. Search the Internet for books, courses, organizations, and ideas that might help you improve your focus, reduce clutter, and live a more organized, goal-oriented life. Many organizations, consulting firms, and professionals are devoted explicitly to the improvement of focus and concentration, developing organizational abilities, and reducing clutter.

YOUR JUDGMENT
COUP DE GRÂCE

Common sense tells us—and our large body of data reveals—that individuals who have and use well-developed evaluative judgment are much more likely to reach their success. Of course, the meaning of success is highly personal and varies tremendously from person to person and from group to group. But whatever your definition of success—be it money, fame, fortune, better grades, a promotion at work, a healthier lifestyle, more friends, fewer friends, quiet solitude, a simple life, stress-free days, a sexy wife, a rich husband, a rich wife, a sexy husband, living alone in a hut, *whatever*—you are much more likely to achieve that success if you have and use strong evaluative judgment as you render your decisions and choices.

With that in mind, here are a few final suggestions. Consider them *the coup de grâce of your decision-making arsenal.* They work, no matter what your individual "value package" looks like—whether your judgment scores are strong or weak, whether there is parity or dissimilarity among your global indicators, whether you have strong coping skills or none whatsoever, and whatever your unique value lens to the world.

Based on current averages and trends within the population, I have weighted these suggestions toward systemic evaluative judgment. Remember, by a wide margin, most people show their weakest judgmental development within the systemic. It is common for individuals to have strong, well-developed intrinsic and extrinsic judgments, yet poor systemic judgment. Regardless, these final suggestions will aid your problem-solving even if you are blessed with well-developed intrinsic, extrinsic, *and* systemic judgment.

It won't be possible to use every suggestion in every situation, but incorporate them as time and circumstances dictate. Pick out the ones that work best for you. Add them as you can to your judgment arsenal.

Slow Down the Decision-Making Process

Very few decisions, even in most emergencies, need to be made *right now*.

You are much more likely to take advantage of your evaluative judgment when you deliberate rather than react. You are more likely to include an I (intrinsic), an E (extrinsic), and an S (systemic) component in any decision by merely adding a few more seconds to your problem-solving process. The point here is not to *delay* your decisions, but to *avoid reacting* when you don't need to react.

Sure, there are moments when there is no time to ponder—for example, when an eighteen-wheeler is about to T-bone your car. (Hint: Slam on the brakes, *now*.) But those situations are few. So even when your boss is screaming for an answer, take a momentary pause and review with your mind what is best to do I-, E-, and S-wise. It can make a huge difference in the quality of your choices.

Those who learn the art of deliberation, even when they employ just a quick reflection, tend to be much better decision-makers—and much more successful overall.

Anyone at any time can make a good decision. However, good, *quality* outcomes of complicated situations that are based on knee-jerk reactionary decisions (pages 170–177) are just as likely due to good luck as to evaluative judgment. And you don't want to place your success in the fickle hands of good luck.

Compartmentalize Before Events

Compartmentalization is a mental process that helps reduce the negative impact of the three judgment assassins: stress, frustration, and clutter. It is such an important mental process that I chose to devote an entire section to it here rather than mention it briefly within the judgment assassin sections.

As a fighter pilot in the U.S. Navy, I compartmentalized before every flight, no exception. As I stepped onto the tarmac, I placed all my stress, frustration, and clutter into a cubbyhole in my mind. I set it there and locked it in place until the postflight was complete. If one of those issues escaped from my mental cubbyhole and began its dirty work of distracting and negatively influencing, I consciously locked it away again. Only after the flight was over did I deal with the issues that would've been capable of negatively impacting my evaluative judgment during the flight.

The need for compartmentalization is not limited to endeavors and occupations as demanding as flying supersonic fighters from aboard an aircraft carrier. Athletes, executives, supervisors, actors, physicians, salespeople, homemakers, students, electricians, janitors, mechanics—*anyone* who needs to perform to a high standard—should compartmentalize. At times, we all have clutter, frustrations, and stress that will undermine our ability to perform at our best and will hinder our success if we don't compartmentalize before our tasks or problem-solving missions.

Suppose that you would like to ask your supervisor for a raise, and also suppose that talking to your boss is usually an unpleasant and unproductive experience. Furthermore, your boss has appeared markedly stressed lately because of pressures brought about by your boss's boss.

You know that one way for you to convince your boss to increase your pay is to demonstrate outstanding performance day after day. Well, your best performance is facilitated through your best judgment, and your best judgment is that which is free from clutter, frustration, and stress. Therefore, if you want a pay raise, you should compartmentalize before your shift so that your best judgment can shine through. Your goal is to perform task completion, teamwork, brainstorming, and so forth, all at their highest level.

Compartmentalizing will reduce the negative influence of the frustration and stress you feel toward your boss, and will allow you to do better work during your shift. Only when your shift is over should you devise a raise-asking strategy with which to approach your boss. Indeed, there might be free moments during work to devise your strategy. The point is, do not allow the judgment assassins of clutter, frustration, and stress to undermine your judgment.

Whatever it is you are about to do, perform at your peak. At all times, have your best evaluative judgment available to you. Compartmentalizing diminishes the impact of the three assassins on your success.

Compartmentalization is *not* intended as a form of procrastination. When your flight, sales presentation, exam, surgery, sporting event, workday, or whatever is over, the issues will be there, waiting for you. At that time, *and only at that time*, should you deal with them.

Create a *habit* of compartmentalization. It might be a quiet moment before your shift starts. Maybe you'll compartmentalize on the drive, commute, or walk to work. Or maybe you'll compartmentalize during your morning shower or breakfast. Whatever works for you and your schedule, work in the necessary time for compartmentalization. Make it part of your routine.

After you practice doing this for a little while, you will be amazed at how well you can substantially reduce the negative impact of the judgment assassins.

Consider Implications and Consequences

Successful people never just operate on cruise control. They prepare for the unexpected. You too can do this by asking big-picture, long-range, systemic questions. Ask them no matter what you're doing, how long you've been doing it, whom you're with, or how safe and secure your upcoming course of action seems.

Play the "what if" game. Conjure up extraordinary circumstances. How would you handle them? Ask yourself these questions repeatedly, and make them part of your routine as you tackle demanding scenarios:

- *Why are we doing this?*
- *What is the point? What are we* really *trying to accomplish?*
- *More important,* why *are we trying to accomplish it?*
- *Is it worth it?*
- *What could go wrong if we make this decision?*
- *What are the potential consequences?*
- *What will this decision look like in the future (ten minutes, ten hours, ten days, ten years down the line)?*

Fulfilling a checklist like this is a particularly satisfying exercise for those with an extrinsic-dominant value structure (which is *very* common), who prefer to be doing something, *anything*, even if it is not necessarily a fruitful exercise. Some people just feel better when they do something like, for example, ask questions. So some highly E-dominant individuals routinely *ask*, but unfortunately do not bother to *answer*, such systemic questions. I have seen this trait in a host of executives working at the highest levels of their organizations. Don't short-circuit the benefit of this worthwhile systemic exercise: You have not given due consideration to implications and consequences until you *answer* the questions—and then use the answers to help drive your decisions and actions.

Consider Best-Case/Worst-Case Scenarios

The contemplation and vetting of best-case/worst-case outcomes, while it does require intrinsic and extrinsic judgments, is primarily a systemic exercise.

Come up with what you consider to be the most positive and best outcome, and weigh it against what you consider to be the most negative and worst outcome. Then, using your best evaluative judgment, estimate the odds of each actually occurring.

Use those odds to impact the course of action you choose to undertake.

Of course, for each judgment scenario there often are a multitude of options and circumstances to choose from, with the most plausible outcome usually falling somewhere between best and worst. And sometimes "best" is not so great and "worst" is not so bad. Furthermore, there are situations where the worst I, E, or S outcome is not worth the risk. Conversely, there are times where the potential I, E, or S upside overshadows any downside.

By practicing best-case/worst-case scenarios, you develop systemic sensibilities that develop your ability to say with confidence, "Hold on a second," or "Maybe there is a better way," or "I'm really uncomfortable with this," or "I've thought it over and let's do it."

Play Devil's Advocate

This is a very simple judgmental exercise, so don't just give it lip service. Use your best evaluative judgment to talk yourself out of whatever it is you're about to do. If you find that talking yourself out of it is rather easy to do, maybe your evaluative judgment is suggesting that you *not* do it.

Just make sure you don't *pretend* to play devil's advocate after the fact as an excuse to justify a poor decision. During some coaching sessions, individuals who have made poor choices justify them by claiming they were playing devil's advocate, when in actuality they were deceiving themselves. Often their high intrinsic or extrinsic dominance fostered a false devil's advocate application: "Hey, I tried to talk myself out of it, but I couldn't!"

Don't play that game.

Proposition a *genuine* counter-position. If you are unable to justify that counter-position using your strongest evaluative judgment, then you take greater confidence and comfort in knowing that you are making a wise decision.

Question Assumptions

Consider that ideas are safe, and questioning is safe—granted that we voice our questions while including the intrinsic components of courtesy and respect, to avoid intrinsic conflict (unless that conflict is what we seek).

Then again, there are times when our job is not to *question*, but to *do*. The U.S. Marine on high alert guarding the post might not have the luxury to question assumptions. However, at most times, for most of us, we can.

To question an assumption is to focus our evaluative judgment squarely on what we have believed, up to this point, to be both real and unquestionable. So, if we do *not* question, we are turning off our evaluative judgment. This is a very bad habit to develop—and unfortunately, a pervasive one.

From the entry-level unskilled laborer to the chief executive officer, judgment profiles are often skewed, overly dominant in certain areas and entirely lacking in other areas. These skewed profiles foster a propensity to zero in on developed areas of judgment, while making assumptions in less developed areas—a risky proposition at best.

The next time you hear the words, *I just assumed*, you just heard someone admit to turning off their evaluative judgment and leaving their fate in the hands of serendipity. Don't be that person.

Ignore the Intrinsic and Extrinsic (maybe[5])

Most of us have either strong intrinsic or strong extrinsic judgment (or we know others who do). It is quite common to be able to relate to others, or to know someone who can relate to others. And a strong work ethic is not a foreign concept to most of us, whether we actually have that

---

5   There is a *very tiny* percentage of the population that does need to tone down their consideration of implications and consequences as they render decisions. However, since this applies to less than five percent of people, in all likelihood it does not apply to you as you go about the business of making decisions.

drive ourselves or not. However, many people have gone the entirety of their lives experiencing little value placed on systemic judgment by either themselves or others.

Therefore, to keep your decision-making from being clouded by intrinsic and extrinsic considerations, temporarily ignore them as you step through the decision-making process. Briefly put on your systemic-thinking cap and consider nothing else but the big-picture realities of your situation. Don't worry; you won't lose the human factor or your work ethic. But by temporarily ignoring these, you will learn to elevate and develop your strategic thinking—the consideration and application of ideas.

CONCLUSION

Our journey began with the tragic account of a pilot and her ten-year-old son who were killed when their plane crashed in bad weather shortly after takeoff from Augusta, Maine. This was just one of many tragic accidents from which to choose. Yet I chose this one, and for two particular reasons.

First, I have a corporate client in Maine, and I had flown my private plane into the very same airport just a few days after her tragedy. The awful weather she experienced had cleared out, but the ground was still covered in ice and snow, and I was able to gain a sense of what she encountered.

Second, she was a meticulous, experienced pilot . . . who *knew better*.

Given nothing more than the basics of her accident, you might conclude that she was some spoiled, clueless, impatient, egotistical fool without a lick of common sense, living large off of Daddy's money while traipsing around the country in her multimillion-dollar jet. Should you have drawn that conclusion, however, you would be utterly, unequivocally, and indisputably *wrong*.

Her name was Jeanette Symons, and she was in fact a highly educated, highly motivated, highly trained, extremely smart, extremely capable, self-made entrepreneur of the highest caliber. You might say she was one of the most famous people you've never heard of.

Jeanette graduated from UCLA with a BS in systems engineering.

She was a world-class athlete, earning a scholarship in gymnastics, lettering in the sport in 1980, and almost making the U.S. Olympic team. A back injury forced her to quit gymnastics, so she took up the sport of diving, earning a scholarship there just as she had in gymnastics.

Upon graduation from college, she moved to Georgia and worked for Hayes Microcomputer, a modem manufacturer. A few years later, in 1988, Jeanette and three others decided to venture out and start a company of their own. She thought they might be able to do it better. Their fledgling company, located in California, was Ascend Communications, and she would serve as its chief technical officer and executive vice president.

Within a few years, Ascend *transformed the Internet* with the hardware that Jeanette designed and manufactured. If you ever used dial-up to connect to the web in the 1990s—complete with that familiar chirpy, hissing, squealing connection tone—then you used a product Jeanette developed. It has been said that Jeanette Symons may not have invented the Internet, but she certainly built it.

Ten years later, Jeanette and her cofounders sold their fledgling start-up company for *$24 billion*.

Not one to rest on her laurels, three months later Jeanette cofounded her second Internet telecommunications company, Zhone Technologies. During that time she finalized her adoption of two children from one of the former Soviet republics, Kazakhstan.

In 2003, Beth Schultz, an author for *Network World*, wrote an article titled "The Epitome of Power." Schultz asked top-tier industry experts whom they would like on their fictional telecommunications "dream team":

> Executive power starts with personal integrity. Who has it? That's one question I posed to a group of venture capitalists and executive recruiters recently when I asked them to help me build an ultimate network industry "Dream Team."
>
> I required this executive power team to include a CEO along

with leaders for an imaginary start-up's financial, marketing and technology departments. No holds barred, I told them—yank 'em out of retirement, steal 'em from competitors, rob other companies of their business acumen, market savvy, technical expertise—who would they want on the executive management rosters?

"You want someone who is smart, highly pragmatic, who has great leadership skills, is high energy and hard-working, with a demonstrated history of ability to deliver products. You need someone who knows the limits and who, from an integrity standpoint, is not afraid to speak the truth," says Susan Moore, a general partner with Onset Ventures.[6]

Of course you can guess that Jeanette Symons was the first choice as vice president of engineering for this telecommunications industry dream team.

In 2005, Jeanette left Zhone Technologies. Using her own money she founded Industrious Kid, a company that provided a safe and secure Internet experience with age-appropriate content for children ages eight to fourteen. The inspiration for Industrious Kid was her own two children.

Wanting her children to experience the joys of an outdoor lifestyle, Jeanette moved to the friendly community of Steamboat Springs, Colorado. Flying her private jet, she commuted back and forth to her California company.

As her achievements grew, Jeanette received countless innovation and technology awards, and regularly delivered keynote speeches at universities, conventions, and major technology events. She sat on numerous boards, particularly those that served to enhance education opportunities for underprivileged children. The National Center for Women & Information Technology (NCWIT) would later name the very prestigious annual Symons Innovator Award in her memory.

---

6 B. Schultz, "The Epitome of Power," *Network World* (December 22, 2003), http://www.
networkworld.com/article/2329221/wireless/the-epitome-of-power.html.

As friends and colleagues learned of Jeanette's tragic death, there was an outpouring of love and admiration. Press releases, blogs, and online forums expressed shock and sympathy.

Ed Gubbins, editor of the blog Telephony Online, received the following message from Mory Ejabat, Jeanette's longtime friend and business partner:

> We all share in the shock and sadness over the tragic loss of our friend and colleague Jeanette and her young son. Jeanette was a devoted mother, a committed and dedicated business partner, and a caring friend. She will be deeply missed. Our thoughts and sympathies are with her family.
>
> Jeanette's vision was formative in launching Zhone, and her influence is at the core of our company's foundation. She was an important mentor to many at Zhone, and her drive, assuredness, and intellect were an inspiration to us all. Jeanette lived life abundantly and never did anything halfway. The contributions she made both socially and to the field of telecommunications will endure indefinitely. We celebrate a brilliant life and grieve that she wasn't with us longer.[7]

"She was fearless in her professional and personal pursuits. She had a passion for creating technologies that brought people together," said Tim Donovan, vice president of marketing and cofounder of Industrious Kid.[8]

Jonathan Lambert of Workhabit wrote:

> I knew Jeanette personally, and she was a whip smart, hardworking, driven individual who represented the kind of "just do

---

7   E. Gubbins (ed.), "Remembering Jeanette Symons," Telephony Online (blog), February 4, 2008, https://business.highbeam.com/437286/article-1G1-174226770/ zhone-ascend-cofounder-jeanette-symons-dies.

8   M. Hogarth, "East Bay IT Veteran Jeanette Symons Dies in Plane Crash," *San Francisco Business Times* (February 11, 2008), http://www.bizjournals.com/eastbay/stories/2008/02/11/ story12.html.

it" entrepreneurship that's made the [Silicon Valley] an amazing place to work.

The first time I met Jeanette Symons was at an airport, where she had flown in to conduct meetings and interviews with Peter Atkins and myself. I liked her almost immediately. She was self-assured, honest, [and] incredibly straightforward to work with, and [she] conducted herself like someone who knew how to get things done.

Jeanette has a long history of innovation, including being one of the founders of Ascend Communications, and has a lot of friends in the Bay Area—friends that are grieving her loss tonight.[9]

Brian Del Vecchio, who worked closely with Jeanette during the early days at Ascend, arguably said it best:

And Jeanette Symons was the brilliant, uncompromising, ass-kicking engineer and executive who told us all what to do and showed us how to do it. In my twenty-five-year career in the networking and Internet industry, I have never met her equal, man or woman.

Jeanette's depth of knowledge about telecommunications technology, hardware design, and software engineering was stunning, and matched by something none of the cardboard standups in Streitfeld's opening paragraph had: a mental blueprint of how the whole system worked, from the chirpy song of analog modem negotiation to the politics of transit routing among top-tier ISPs. I watched her argue with Marty Schoffstall, founder of PSINet, and laugh over wine with Mike O'Dell, founder of UUNET. I never saw Jeanette intimidated by anyone. There were times

---

9   J. Lambert, "Remembering Jeanette Symons," *Workhabit* (blog), February 2, 2008, http://www.workhabit.com/blog/remembering-jeanette-symons.

when she was the only woman in the room, but just as often she was the smartest, most powerful personality in the room.

And damn, I miss her.[10]

In my quest to learn about Jeanette Symons, I dug deep. I communicated directly with her family, close friends, and associates. I read through hundreds of articles written about Jeanette. All because I wanted to know:

Was there some hidden dangerous pattern to her behavior, some flaw known only to her close inner circle?

As is often the case when this type of tragedy strikes, individuals come forward, sometimes anonymously, with personal stories of how they were not surprised, and telling tales of how poor judgment and foolish risk-taking were the norm for this individual.

That was simply *not* the case with Jeanette Symons.

Not once was there any indication that she was a dangerous pilot; that she engaged in risky behavior personally or professionally; or that she had a pattern of poor judgment. In fact—just the opposite. After her death, large numbers of people came forward to offer overwhelming praise and to laud her piloting skills and her demeanor.

Don Heineman, a flight instructor at Steamboat Springs Airport, spoke well of her: "I think she was an excellent pilot and a very sharp lady. To me, she was very impressive. She was just a peach of a lady. I'm going to miss her."[11]

Bob Maddox, another Steamboat Springs pilot, said, "She was a qualified, rated, and highly experienced pilot."[12]

Tim Donovan, her business partner, also spoke very favorably of her as both a friend and a pilot:

10 B. Del Vecchio, "Jeanette Symons Built the Internet," *Flawless Ruby* (blog), June 3, 2012, http://hybernaut.github.io/blog/2012/06/03/jeanette-symons-built-the-internet/.

11 M. Lawrence, "Steamboat Woman, Son Killed in Jet Crash," *Steamboat Today*, February 2, 2008, http://www.steamboattoday.com/news/2008/feb/02/jet_crash/.

12 Ibid.

She was a dear friend and mentor. She was incredibly successful in her professional and personal life. She was a very good pilot, very well practiced and meticulous. We've all flown with her over the years, many times.[13]

She's been flying for over twenty years. She's a top-notch pilot.[14]

She'd never take risks. She wouldn't have left if she didn't think she could take off safely.[15]

Others described Jeanette as a super person, a great engineer, a highly skilled professional, and a visionary.

Many spoke of her devotion to her family, noting she was a "hands-on mother, very active in the lives of her children."

The list of accolades went *on and on and on and on and on*. Listen to her own words:

The worst part is people recognizing me. I get recognized a lot more often than I'd like. At work that's fine, that's what I do. But when I'm not at work, I want to be low key.[16]

She talked about her flying:

People go, "Oh, so you just love to fly." And I've got to say, I do. It's one of the most just relaxing things there are. But what it really is—and people make fun of me—is if you go into my airplane, it looks a lot more like a minivan, stacked with stickers and snacks and books and activities and such in the back. The beauty of flying a plane is that it gives me and my family incredible

13 E. Allday, "Bay Area Exec and Son Perish in Plane Crash," *San Francisco Chronicle*, February 3, 2008, http://www.sfgate.com/bayarea/article/Bay-Area-exec-and-son-perish-in-plane-crash-3229910.php.

14 F. X. Quinn, "Mother, Son Believed Killed in Maine Plane Crash," *U-T San Diego*, February 2, 2008, http://legacy.utsandiego.com/news/state/20080202-0829-planecrash.html.

15 "Flights Were Grounded Before Fatal Plane Crash," *Sun Journal*, February 6, 2008, A2.

16 J. Guynn, "Chief Technical Officer Co-pilots Latest Telecom Sector Start-up." *The Free Lance-Star*, June 4, 2000, E8.

freedom. So I can be in any city in the country in a meeting on Friday morning and home playing with my kids Friday night.[17]

In an interview with *Steamboat Today*:

Nothing beats flying at night in the winter. It's a blanket of stars with the Milky Way over you. It's like nothing you've ever seen.[18]

In an interview for *Girl Geeks*:

I think the best business advice I ever received was probably to *listen*. Sounds stupid, but as we grow a company, it is really easy to begin to believe that you know best . . . The most important thing to remember is that all sorts of people and other companies know more about what they do than you do . . . Gotta listen to everyone . . .[19]

Are those the words of an impulsive, clueless, incompetent, egotistical fool? *No way. No how. No chance.*

I've read hundreds of quotes from and about Jeanette Symons. I've communicated directly with many who knew her firsthand, personally and professionally.

I met and spoke in person with Dennis Hayes, founder and CEO of Hayes Microcomputer, where Jeanette had her first job out of college. I introduced myself and told him that I was writing a book and that my research had led me to a woman named Jeanette Symons.

Before I could utter another word he said, "Oh yes, I remember Jeanette. She was absolutely brilliant, one of the most capable people I ever met. She was an out-of-the-box thinker."

---

17 "An Interview with Jeanette Symons, Founder and CEO, Industrious Kid," by L. Sanders, L. Nelson, and L. Kennedy, National Center for Women & Information Technology, October 19, 2007, http://www.ncwit.org/audio/interview-jeanette-symons.

18 Lawrence, 2008.

19 "J. Symons, CTO, Ascend Communications," Girl Geeks, http://www.girlgeeks.org/chat/symons.shtml.

Keep in mind that at the time of our conversation, Jeanette had not worked for him for almost thirty years. Her impression on Hayes was profound. He called her a genius and said that he never saw anyone who could solve a problem like Jeanette. He recalled that when she zeroed in on an issue, she was relentless with it until it was solved.

To a person, all agree that she was smart, intelligent, hardworking, and grounded, with extraordinary ideas and dreams and goals—an incredible lady with great judgment. She had her detractors, as most people do, but even her detractors did not question her judgment.

So why am I going into such detail about Jeanette Symons and her bad decision? To make a point—a point that might very well be the most important lesson to take away from this entire book. And that point is:

If we are not careful and vigilant and protective of our judgment, any of us are capable of a bad decision.

Sure, not all of our decisions are a matter of life or death—but sometimes they are, and you never know when the next decision might be.

So what happened to Jeanette that caused her to make that fateful decision to launch into terrible weather with an ice-covered airplane? The answer lies, as it does so often in our lives, within the value structure.

As it turns out, Jeanette crashed on her young daughter's birthday. Could it be that Jeanette was so intrinsically dominant, and so desperately wanted to see and celebrate with her daughter who was back home, that it overwhelmed all other considerations and so she launched?

Or . . . could it be that Jeanette was so extrinsically dominant that, by golly, she was going to launch for no reason other than she had filed her flight plan and scheduled her launch for that day?

Or . . . could it be that Jeanette's systemic judgment was so weak that she lacked a personal radar and sense of danger?

Well, I don't think the reason was any of those. After learning about Jeanette, I believe that her value structure was strong in all areas . . .

- ▸ **Intrinsic:** Jeanette connected and related well to others. She talked about the heartbreak she felt when the ups and downs of the business cycle sometimes forced her company to lay off employees. Early in her career, she thought the best part of her job was building products in a lab. But later on, she felt the best part was helping her customers solve their problems; she enjoyed that personal connection. Clearly, this shows well-developed intrinsic judgment.

- **Extrinsic:** Jeanette's drive and ambition were beyond question. Her employees, in good humor, once gifted her with a bat and a whip because she was so driven to produce. No one ever questioned her work ethic, or her drive to turn out the next great problem-solving product. I believe Jeanette's extrinsic judgment was strong, probably throughout her entire life.

- **Systemic:** Jeanette was considered a visionary, someone who consistently saw and understood the big picture, the long-range view. She was consistently praised for knowing where the industry was headed, long before others had any inkling. She knew her limitations, and she understood what could and could not be done. No doubt she had a strong systemic component to her decisions, particularly later in her career.

Clearly, Jeanette's intrinsic, extrinsic, and systemic sensibilities all influenced her decisions and choices.

No, Jeanette's decision to launch in terrible weather with an ice-covered plane was not rooted in a general weakness within her basic value structure. I think the cause of her tragedy was that she failed to recognize the tremendous impact of one or more of the three judgment assassins (clutter, frustration, stress) on her decision-making that day.

I have learned that during her fateful trip, Jeanette was under a great deal of personal stress. Recall our conversations about stress (starting on page 213): its many forms and the many ways it can negatively influence our evaluative judgment.

Also recall that it is not the *amount* of stress, but more importantly the *effects* of stress that determine its influence on our evaluative judgment.

In other words, our ability to *cope with* stress is a bigger determination of the impact of stress than the actual number of stressors we encounter. And the truth is, some people are just better at coping than others.

Yes, we can improve on our coping skills—but at any given time, if the stressors we experience are more potent than our ability to cope with them, they can outstrip our coping mechanisms and render our judgment ineffectual.

Now pause for a moment, *and think back across the timeline of your life*, to various difficult experiences and circumstances when you felt an enormous burden of stress. If there were particular periods when you felt exceptionally overwhelmed with stress, remember how difficult it was then for you to make your best, most sound decisions. In fact, these were likely the times when you made your worst decisions. The reason for your difficulty is clear-cut and straightforward: *Your evaluative judgment was being undermined.*

When we learn of tragedies such as Jeanette's, we may want (or even feel the need) to dissect every detail of her life that caused her stress, to figure out just what it was that clouded her judgment. That can be a noteworthy exercise. We may feel that if we can understand exactly what caused her stress, we can avoid that situation from happening in our life. For her family and friends, they will forever be asking themselves why.

However, there are as many different stressors as there are different people: divorce, bankruptcy, not meeting sales goals, losing our job, drug abuse, issues with family members, death, trauma, public embarrassment, sitting in traffic, even waiting in line—the list of situations that might cause stress is endless. Each of us, as we go through life, will likely encounter issues and situations that test every last one of our coping skills. And what may seem petty to one person can be overwhelming to another.

The lesson here is not to focus excessively on the specific causes of Jeanette's stress, but to understand that her stress overwhelmed her ability to cope, and obliterated her otherwise strong judgment.

And if we are not vigilant, it can happen to us too.

There is no doubt that Jeanette wanted to launch. Her trip was over, and she wanted to return home; nothing wrong with that. That is what we do at the end of a trip—we return home. Unfortunately, there was one big issue standing in the way: the weather. On this evening, the weather was such that it required Jeanette to bring forth her best judgment, and unfortunately her best judgment was clouded with stress.

Our *ability to assign appropriate value* manifests into our *evaluative judgment*, which is the primary driver of our decisions, informing us *what to do* and, just as important, *what not to do*. But no matter how strong and well developed our ability to assign proper value is, it can be undermined by three things: stress, frustration, and clutter. On that night in February 2008, I believe that Jeanette's stress overwhelmed her otherwise strong judgment and good sense to the point that her momentarily weakened judgment "allowed" her to launch with an ice-covered airplane, in terrible weather, which ultimately lead to her death and the death of her child.

Shortly after Jeanette's accident, as I stood in the snow at the very same Augusta, Maine, airport, trying to picture in my mind those last minutes of Jeanette's life, I was consumed by the eternal impact of her decision. I felt a sort of regret that I was not there the night she launched. Being an experienced pilot myself (military, airlines, general aviation), and being rather assertive in my value structure, I am firm in my belief that had I been there that day, I would have convinced Jeanette to delay her flight. Even though she was someone I had never met, I would have gone up to her, politely confronted her, and convinced her otherwise.

Making go/no-go decisions was something I had studied, and experienced, my entire adult life. A large part of my job as a U.S. Navy fighter pilot was devoted to contingency planning . . . in excruciating detail. I had been trained to consider mission objectives, combat load, Probability of Kill (Pk), aircraft gripes/maintenance issues, flight lead, fuel assets, enemy threat, and yes, *weather*—and countless more parameters—to not only to determine whether to launch, but whether to continue the entire mission.

I remember during one particular night-combat launch aboard the aircraft carrier USS *Saratoga*, I was strapped into my F/A-18 on the flight deck behind the island (what we call the *six-pack area*). The F/A-18's engines were turning, but my jet was broken. Several built-in-tests (BITs) had failed. My jet had many problems, serious problems.

I anxiously called the senior chief to my aid. He plugged in his communications, and amid the darkness and noise and commotion and chaos, the process began.

The nose of my jet was swung open, and panels on both sides of the fuselage were raised. We knew exactly what was required for launch, and it seemed the entire maintenance team, all expertly trained sailors, were scurrying about my jet.

As I waited, I recall watching other jets launching, their light show displaying before us as they tapped afterburner down the catapult. That particular mission included about forty aircraft. A jet was being launched off the front of the aircraft carrier roughly every thirty seconds, so we knew we had no more than about twenty minutes to solve the problem.

The air boss knew of my dilemma, and as the last plane besides mine launched, he was ready to shut me down. With only seconds to spare, the maintenance technicians finished their troubleshooting, the panels and aircraft nose were swung shut, and my jet was buttoned up. I told the boss I would run my checks on the way to the catapult.

As I lined up for the catapult, the final BITs completed and my jet was given the thumbs up. I was given permission to launch. However, even with my jet hooked to the catapult, engines turning, fuel tanks full, and bombs loaded—*ready* to launch and *wanting* to launch—I would have shut down if those tests had failed. I would have made my decision (*no-go*) and let my squadron mates carry on without me that night, no matter how much I had wanted to join them in the skies.

It is likely that most of you who have flown commercially have had your flight either delayed or cancelled due to weather. As a commercial airline pilot, I have been in the cockpit of an aircraft where, if specific types of de-icing or anti-icing were not available, we would not launch due to weather. Period. End of discussion.

As a civilian recreational pilot, my father *twice* decided to delay overnight a return flight home due to weather, while another plane at the same airport at the same time decided to launch. Those other pilots crashed and died due to the very same weather my father chose to avoid.

Over the course of my flying career, these types of experiences have provided me with a keen insight into the go/no-go decision.

Furthermore, unlike Jeanette Symons on the night of her tragic flight, I was not under the destructive influence of the three judgment assassins, and would have easily seen the folly of her choice. Jeanette did not have a lifetime of experience with the go/no-go decision, and was therefore less well-versed in this area of decision-making. But most important, her judgment was likely clouded with stress.

If I had been able to describe to Jeanette the situation right before her eyes, the situation that I believe her stress did not allow her to see, and if I had been able to persuade her to straightforwardly contemplate what she was about to do, her strong judgment would have risen above the effects of the stress, and she would have agreed that yes, flying on that night was a bad idea.

I would have said:

Ma'am, your plane is covered in ice, and it is getting worse. The commercial commuters have even called it quits for the night. With all this freezing rain coming down, there is a good chance that even the de-icing of your plane will miss an ice-covered patch. The taxiways and runways are completely covered in snow and ice.

On top of that, it is now nighttime, making flight in these conditions even more difficult. Whatever your reasons for wanting to leave now, they are not worth it.

Ma'am, please pause for just one moment and contemplate what you are about to do, and the risks you are about to take.

Her systemic judgment would have taken hold and beat back any sense of urgency, and she would have delayed until the following morning, when she could have left in better weather and with an ice-free airplane.

But unfortunately, she did not have commercial aviation guidelines at hand; squadron mates with whom to confer; or a lifetime of go/no-go experiences on which to rely. She only had herself, and her judgment was being undermined by stress.

There is a tendency among many people to believe *it won't happen to me* or *I know better.* Be careful with those tendencies. The world is littered with damaged or bankrupt companies, lost jobs or careers, ruined relationships and divorces, missed opportunities, undue stress, ill will, broken dreams, delayed or squandered success, or simply lives less well lived, all because of that erroneous assumption: *It won't happen to me.*

Consider this: Are you smarter than Jeanette? Are you more motivated than Jeanette? Are you more experienced than Jeanette? Are you more hardworking than Jeanette? Are you more accomplished than Jeanette? Are you more of a visionary than Jeanette? Chances are, no, you're not.

But even if you are every bit as accomplished and successful and visionary as Jeanette was, you too are not entirely immune to a lapse in judgment, and even a momentary lapse can sometimes lead to severe, permanent, and heartbreaking consequences.

To fully reach and maintain your success, you must devote time and energy to the care and development of your judgment. The protection of your judgment must be constant, dedicated, and vigilant. You must learn to recognize the assassins to your judgment—and fight tooth and nail to defeat them.

The lesson of Jeanette Symons is not a game of one-upmanship, of comparing our judgment with hers. Her death illustrates the very real and crucial need to have and use good judgment *at all times*, no matter our level of skill, talent, or intellect. Until the very moment of her fateful departure in her ice-covered plane, no one who knew her would have ever imagined she was capable of such a poor decision. However, on that night, she was. This incredibly intellectual, competent, and quite brilliant entrepreneur and mother made such a perplexing, catastrophic error in judgment that it resulted in her death and that of her son.

Her tragic lesson is an opportunity for us to learn. Understanding her tragedy can help us gain insight in order to further develop our own value structure. After all, she was motivated, smart, and well trained, with incredibly strong judgment overall. And until that very night, she was one of the most successful people in the world.

So, in our own quest for success, as we go about the business of making decisions and solving problems, we can and *must* keep close at hand the six undeniable truths that lead to success.

THE THREE GLOBAL JUDGMENTS

1. **Intrinsic** (tolerance and compassion)

2. **Extrinsic** (trainability and work ethic)

3. **Systemic** (understanding and using strategies)

THE THREE JUDGMENT ASSASSINS

1. **Stress**

2. **Frustration**

3. **Clutter**

Include the first three in your evaluative judgment. Avoid the last three at all costs. It's that simple.

Of course, even though it's really just that simple, there will be times when the six truths can be difficult to incorporate, particularly during periods when one or more of the judgment assassins are exceedingly intense—something I personally believe was the case that fateful night with Jeanette Symons.

Nevertheless, if we abide by these six truths regularly and faithfully, not only will they help us make use of our best available judgment, but over the long haul they will help us *improve* our judgment. And in order to fully achieve and maintain our success, we must wrap our skills, knowledge, training, and intellect in the protective warm blanket of this good judgment.

As you strive to achieve your success, keep this book handy and refer to it often. Always remember that your evaluative judgment is not arbitrary. It is defined and expressed by a structure—*your* unique value structure, which manifests into *your* decisions, *your* behavior, and ultimately *your* success. Mold your value structure into the value structure of success.

Make good judgment a *habit*, part of your everyday life—in every waking hour, in everything you say, in everything you do, everywhere you go, with everyone you meet, in every decision you make, in every situation whether big or small, for the rest of your life, from this moment forward, *starting right now*.

With good judgment, you will find that your success is more intense and long-lasting, and that your life is richer, fuller, and downright more fun.

I wish you all the best, with all of your most sought-after dreams and goals. And now, with kindest regards, I welcome you to . . . your judgment journey.

ABOUT THE AUTHOR

 **CDR Barry W. Hull, USNR (Retired), founder** and partner of the consulting firms Athena Assessment Inc. and Pilot Judgment Inc., thinks it's a bit braggadocious to say he is one of the world's foremost experts in decision-making and evaluative judgment. But he is, and many of his enthusiastic clients will gladly tell you so. His life experiences and education as a retail business owner, consultant, combat decorated F/A-18 Hornet pilot, and airline pilot, and his study and in-depth analysis of evaluation, give him an expertise and understanding of judgment and decision-making equaled by very few.

His consultancies have worked with more than 350 companies—improving judgment, developing leaders, and enhancing the hiring process. Analyzing and interpreting the judgment data from his company's judgment assessment has enriched a wide range of clients, including healthcare, retail, manufacturing, construction, legal, financial, automotive, education, law enforcement, military, technology, athletics, and more. His opinions and insights into judgment are valued at the highest corporate levels. He lectures on behalf of the Federal Aviation Administration as an expert in evaluative judgment as it relates to safety.

Military combat operations, including flying into Baghdad on the first night of Desert Storm, brought him local and national media attention and a mention in more than one book about the subject. He has appeared numerous times on the major and cable television networks and has been a military analyst for Fox News, featured on *60 Minutes II*, the History and Discovery channels, as well as a variety of newspapers, radio stations, and other media outlets.

He considers it his privilege to have helped so many as they progress along their judgment journey. In fact, the repeated suggestion from many of his Athena and Pilot Judgment clients—having helped them to better understand their judgment and to find their success—prompted him to write this book.

Made in the USA
Lexington, KY
16 March 2018